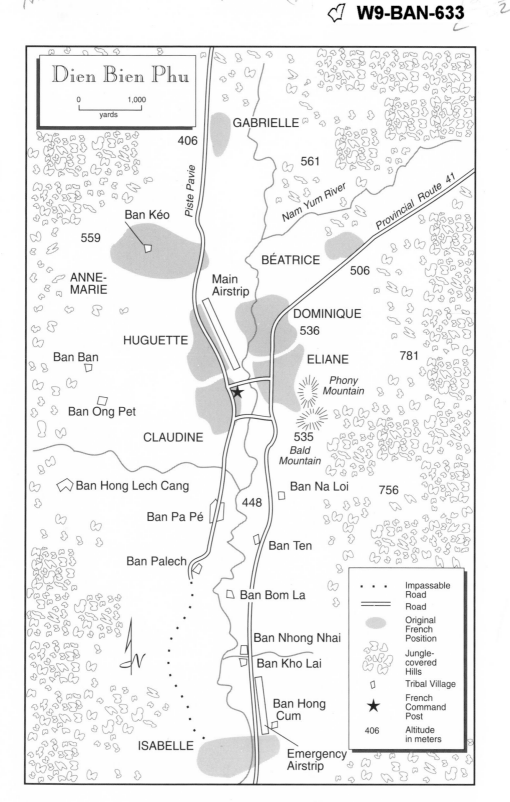

NAM

1ˢᵗ Ed (19

W9-BAN-633

Dien Bien Phu

0   1,000
yards

GABRIELLE

406

561

Piste Pavie

Nam Yum River

Provincial Route 41

Ban Kéo

559

ANNE-
MARIE

BÉATRICE

506

Main
Airstrip

DOMINIQUE

536

HUGUETTE

ELIANE

781

Ban Ban

Phony
Mountain

Ban Ong Pet

CLAUDINE

535
Bald
Mountain

Ban Hong Lech Cang

Ban Na Loi

756

448

Ban Pa Pé

Ban Ten

Ban Palech

Ban Bom La

Ban Nhong Nhai

N

Ban Kho Lai

Ban Hong
Cum

ISABELLE

Emergency
Airstrip

· · · Impassable
        Road

——— Road

        Original
        French
        Position

        Jungle-
        covered
        Hills

        Tribal Village

★   French
        Command
        Post

406   Altitude
        in meters

Dien Bien Phu

Also by Howard R. Simpson

Tiger in the Barbed Wire (1992)

Cogan's Case (1992)

A Very Large Consulate (1988)

A Gathering of Gunmen (1987)

Junior Year Abroad (1986)

The Jumpmaster (1984)

The Obelisk Conspiracy (1975)

Rendezvous off Newport (1973)

The Three-Day Alliance (1971)

Assignment for a Mercenary (1965)

To a Silent Valley (1961)

Dien Bien Phu

The Epic Battle America Forgot

Howard R. Simpson

BRASSEY'S INC.
Washington • London

Brassey's Inc.

Editorial Offices	Order Department
Brassey's Inc.	Brassey's Book Orders
8000 Westpark Drive	c/o Macmillan Publishing Co.
First Floor	100 Front Street, Box 500
McLean, Virginia 22102	Riverside, New Jersey 08075

Brassey's books are available at special discounts for bulk purchases for
sales promotions, premiums, fund-raising, or educational use through the
Special Sales Director, Macmillan Publishing Company, 866 Third Avenue,
New York, New York 10022.

Library of Congress Cataloging-in-Publication Data
Simpson, Howard R., 1925–
  Dien Bien Phu: the epic battle America forgot / by Howard R. Simpson.
    p.   cm.
  Includes index.
  ISBN 0-02-881047-3
  1. Dien Bien Phu (Vietnam), Battle of, 1954. I. Title.
DS553.3.D5S56 1994
959.704'1—dc20   93-14420
                                                                        CIP

10 9 8 7 6 5 4 3 2 1

Printed in the United States of America

TO THE DEAD

An AUSA Book

The Association of the United States Army (AUSA) was founded in 1950 as a not-for-profit organization dedicated to education concerning the role of the U.S. Army, to provision of material for military professional development, and to the promotion of proper recognition and appreciation of the profession of arms. Its constituencies include those who serve in the army today, including Army National Guard, Army Reserve, and army civilians, and the retirees and veterans who have served in the past, as well as all their families. A large number of public-minded citizens and business leaders are also an important constituency. The Association seeks to educate the public, elected and appointed officials, and leaders of the defense industry on crucial issues involving the adequacy of our national defense, particularly those issues affecting land warfare.

In 1988 AUSA established within its existing organization a new entity known as the Institute of Land Warfare. Its purpose is to extend the educational work of AUSA by sponsoring scholarly publications, including books, monographs, and essays on key defense issues, as well as workshops and symposia. Among the volumes chosen for designation as "An AUSA Institute of Land Warfare Book" are both new texts and reprints of titles of enduring value that are no longer in print. Topics include history, policy issues, strategy, and tactics. Publication as an AUSA Book does not indicate that the Association of the United States Army and the publisher agree with everything in the book, but does suggest that the AUSA and the publisher believe this book will stimulate the thinking of AUSA members and others concerned about important issues.

Contents

Foreword

The battle of Dien Bien Phu, in which the Communist-led Vietminh forces crushed elements of the French colonial army in Indochina, ranks with Agincourt, Waterloo, and Gettysburg as one of the great military engagements of history. It spelled the end of France's crumbling empire in Asia, and while nobody foresaw the possibility then, it eventually opened the way for America's commitment to the region over the years that followed. So it was a decisive episode that indirectly set in motion a process that was to have profound and pervasive consequences for the United States. To this day, the tragic Vietnam experience haunts Americans as they contemplate the nation's global priorities.

No American is better qualified to tell the tale of Dien Bien Phu and its significance than Howard R. Simpson. Not only did he visit the battlefield at the time, but as a member of the U.S. diplomatic mission in Indochina during that period, he also witnessed the tangle of events that led to the encounter. However, recognizing that even his firsthand observations were not enough, he has returned to France and Vietnam to research the story further through interviews and documents that have since become available. In addition to all this is his skill as a narrator. The result is a book that is credible as well as readable—and will undoubtedly remain a classic on the subject.

As Simpson makes clear, France did not lose at Dien Bien Phu itself. The struggle against the Vietminh had been dragging on for eight years, and the French people were sick of the inconclusive effort, which had poisoned their society and divided their weak government. The French commander, Gen. Henri-Eugène Navarre, was miscast. A cold, solitary figure convinced of his superior talents, he spurned intelligence accounts that did not fit his prejudices and, as a French War College study subsequently reported, operated on the basis of his "preconceived" ideas. He refused to credit his opponent, Gen. Vo Nguyen Giap, with the ability to amass the firepower necessary to pound the exposed French garrison—which is precisely what Giap did.

Giap had been preparing for the showdown for months. Like lines of ants, Vietminh troops trudged by bicycle and on foot through jungles to the site, laden with everything from weapons and ammunition to huge stocks of rice, which had to be carried into the remote, impoverished area. With almost superhuman zeal they pushed their howitzers up the mountain slopes to heights overlooking the French, who had foolishly deployed themselves in a broad valley on the theory that they had to protect the route into nearby Laos. "It was difficult, *n'est-ce pas*, very difficult," Giap told me as he reflected on the battle during an interview in Hanoi in March 1990. "Only motivated soldiers could have performed such a feat."

Both the French and the Vietminh were racing against a deadline. An international gathering at Geneva, which had begun earlier, was scheduled to take up the Indochina issue on May 7, and everyone knew, as the chief U.S. delegate, Gen. Walter Bedell Smith, remarked, "You don't win at the conference table what you've lost on the battlefield."

Despite the moving clock, Giap was cautious. Rejecting the counsel of his Chinese advisers, who had urged him to stage a frontal assault, he ordered his men to tunnel their way toward the French positions. They dug for eight weeks until finally, on the afternoon of March 13, Giap gave the signal. Raked by the Vietminh's big guns and attacked on the ground, the first French objective collapsed instantly, and another fell the next day. Not long before, Col. Charles Piroth, the one-armed French artillery chief, had pledged to Navarre that he could easily silence the enemy cannon. But now he was humiliated. At dawn on March 15, he pulled the safety pin out of a grenade with his teeth and blew himself to bits. He had said the previous night, "I am completely dishonored."

France probably might have fought on had not the French citizenry clamored for peace. It is often forgotten that after their triumph, the Vietnamese Communists could have laid claim to all of Vietnam had not the Soviet Union and China, for reasons of their own, leaned on them to concede to a partition pending elections. When, with the approval of the Dwight D. Eisenhower administration, the South Vietnamese regime reneged on the elections, neither Moscow nor Peking objected—an indication that both hoped to improve their relations with the West.

But Hanoi did not give up hope of unifying Vietnam under its control. Thus a new war began to gather momentum—and it ultimately engulfed the United States.

There was no equivalent of Dien Bien Phu during the American war, though President Lyndon B. Johnson, Gen. William Westmoreland, and others mistakenly perceived a repetition of the battle at Khe Sanh early in 1968. But this battle was a diversion by Giap, aimed at luring U.S. forces away from the coastal cities so that he could launch the Tet offensive. He knew that the Americans and the French were different and that he lacked the muscle to challenge America's overwhelming might in a single confrontation.

But Giap did pursue a strategy not unlike the one that he had carried on against the French. He waged a war of attrition, confident that he would gradually wear down America's will to continue. His main concern was victory, not casualties. "How long would you have gone on fighting against the United States?" I asked him during our talk in Hanoi. He replied without hesitation: "Another twenty years, maybe a hundred years, as long as it took to win, regardless of cost."

Thus, America, like France, was up against a foe that considered its cause to be sacred—and was ready to make horrendous sacrifices to attain that goal. Neither learned that lesson until it was too late.

STANLEY KARNOW

Acknowledgments

My thanks to all those who assisted me in this project. The list includes Gen. Gerard Delbauffe, Le Contrôleur Général des Armées and chief of information, French Armed Forces; Col. Paul Gaujac, director of the French Army Ground Forces Historical Service; Gen. René de Biré, president of L'Amicale des Anciens Combattants de Dien Bien Phu; the archives staff of the Foreign Legion Museum at Aubagne; Col. Bui Tin, former editor of the Vietnamese army journal *Nhan Dan* and veteran of Dien Bien Phu; and Gen. Tran Cong Man, former commander of Vietminh sapper units, now an official of the Vietnam Journalist's Association, Hanoi.

Thanks also to Col. Déodat Puy-Montbrun and former Caporal Chef Robert Blondeau for their help in clarifying the role of the GCMA (Groupement de Commandos Mixtes Aéroportés, "Composite Airborne Commando Group") and broadening my contacts; former Adj. Luong Van Ou of the GCMA and T'ai partisans; Chinese historian and war correspondent Qian Jiang, who shared his knowledge of the Chinese Military Advisory Group in North Vietnam; Col. Jean Lucciani, formerly of the First Foreign Legion Parachute Battalion; Caporal Chef Claude Sibille, formerly of the First Chasseurs Parachute Regiment; Col. Maurice Blanchet of the Transport Group "Béarn," who piloted the last medevac flight into Dien Bien Phu; and all the survivors who took the time to complete my questionnaire on the battle. Special thanks for the assistance of two old friends and Dien Bien Phu veterans, Pierre Schoendoerffer, novelist, film director, and member of the Académie française, and Daniel Camus, photographer and *grand reporter*.

I am also grateful to my daughter Maggie, who, with assistance from her sister Kate, spent considerable time delving into the Indochina records in the National Archives for declassified telegrams and other material on official U.S. attitudes toward the Navarre Plan and America's role at Dien Bien Phu.

Finally, I wish to thank the editors of *Military Review*, the publication of the U.S. Army Command and General Staff College, for allowing me to excerpt portions of my article on Dien Bien Phu previously published in that magazine.

A number of books helped me recall events, dates, and individuals involved in the battle and the special atmosphere of North Vietnam during the early 1950s. These include Erwan Bergot, *Les 170 Jours de Dien Bien Phu* (Paris: Presses de la Cité, 1979); Gen. Marcel Bigeard, *Pour une parcelle de gloire* (Paris: Plon, 1975); Gen. Tran Do, *Stories of Dien Bien Phu* (Hanoi: Foreign Languages Publishing House, 1963); Bernard B. Fall, *Hell in a Very Small Place: The Siege of Dien Bien Phu* (Philadelphia: J. B. Lippincott, 1967); Gen. Vo Nguyen Giap, *Dien Bien Phu* (Hanoi: Éditions en langues étrangères, 1964); Dr. Paul Grauwin, *J'étais medécin à Dien Bien Phu* (Paris: Éditions France-Empire, 1992); Stanley Karnow, *Vietnam: A History* (New York: Viking, 1983); Peter Macdonald, *Giap: Les deux guerres d'Indochine* (Paris: Perrin, 1992); Gen. Henri Navarre, *Agonie de l'Indochine 1953–1954* (Paris: Plon, 1956); Douglas Porch, *The French Foreign Legion: A Complete History of the Famous Fighting Force* (New York: HarperCollins, 1991); Jules Roy, *La Bataille de Dien Bien Phu* (Paris: Juilliard, 1963); and Pierre Schoendoerffer, *Dien Bien Phu: De la bataille au film* (Paris: Lincoln-Fixot, 1992).

Introduction

The Indochina War (1946–1954) was a long and bloody struggle pitting a battle-tested French colonial army against the determined Vietminh, a Communist "people's army" dedicated to the liberation of Vietnam from French rule. The deciding battle of that war was fought during the spring of 1954 in and around Dien Bien Phu, a small mountain village in the T'ai tribal territory of northwest Vietnam.

Dien Bien Phu was not a massive engagement in conventional terms, but it was a decisive military contest and a microcosm of the international political-military clashes to emerge in the wake of World War II. It was also a grim theater of courage and misjudgment, tenacity and failure. Monumental blunders on a high level had doomed the garrison long before the final assault. Unforeseen tactical errors, veiled by the fog of battle, contributed to the ultimate defeat. This unique military engagement changed the face of Southeast Asia and served as a prelude to the costly battles that U.S. forces would later fight in the jungles and paddies of South Vietnam.

I first saw Dien Bien Phu in late November of 1953, arriving in the valley aboard one of the first French air force C-47 "Dakota" transport planes to land on the newly repaired airstrip after its seizure in an airborne operation on November 20. Three French parachute battalions had secured the village and the strip despite strong resistance from a reinforced Vietminh garrison. I had been covering the Indochina conflict since February 1952 as a U.S. Information Agency (USIA) war correspondent and already knew some of the officers and men at Dien Bien Phu from previous operations in North Vietnam and Laos. During my stay at Dien Bien Phu, I observed the establishment of strongpoints and the arrival of reinforcements, visited the fortified positions of various battalions, picked up what information I could from senior officers at the command post (CP), and accompanied Maj. Marcel Bigeard's elite Sixth Colonial Parachute Battalion on a thirteen-mile patrol probing for Vietminh units in the surrounding hills.

By mid-December Gen. Vo Nguyen Giap's forces were already closing in on the the ill-fated fortress, and it was impossible to venture far from the valley without costly contact with Vietminh regulars. Prior to my departure from Dien Bien Phu, a Foreign Legion officer, frowning toward the mist-covered heights dominating the defenses, volunteered that "this time" the Viet were coming in strength. "It will be a real *baroud* [fight]," he told me. His prediction proved only too true. I was on home leave in San Francisco on May 7, 1954, when Dien Bien Phu fell after a fifty-seven-day siege. Those of us who knew the situation had seen the writing on the wall for some time. Regardless, it was still difficult to appreciate the scope of the Communist victory.

The Geneva Accords of July 1954 had ended the war and the French were preparing to leave Indochina when I returned to Saigon. A number of friends captured at Dien Bien Phu had been released by the Vietminh. Others had died on the long death marches or in the prison camps. The survivors revealed the truths of the battle and the hell of their captivity.

I left Vietnam in 1955, was reassigned to Saigon in 1964 as an adviser to the prime minister, and visited the country again briefly in 1971 on official business. My return to Vietnam in 1991 as a journalist allowed me to conduct a long interview with General Giap and discuss the Indochina War and Dien Bien Phu with Vietminh veterans. More recently, I was given access to declassified documents on Dien Bien Phu in the French army's archives at the Château de Vincennes. Foreign Legion headquarters in Aubagne permitted me to photocopy personal accounts of the battle penned by Legionnaires following their return from captivity.

Most rewarding were the interviews with the survivors of Dien Bien Phu. Despite the years that have passed, the battle remains etched in the memories of the participants. Some of those I sought had died in the interim or were inaccessible. However, thanks to a number of personal contacts, I was able to meet with a cross section of those who had endured the siege. Others cooperated by completing a questionnaire to explain their part in the battle.

In the spring of 1992, I was lunching with Col. Bui Tin on the terrace of the Café Select in Montparnasse. The colonel, a Vietminh veteran of Dien Bien Phu who had also fought the Americans and become an editor of the Vietnamese army journal *Nhan Dan*, had left Vietnam in 1990 after deciding that "Marxism-Leninism was finished." He was writing a book and making ends meet in Paris by baking cakes for a restaurant. As we sipped our aperitifs and watched the passersby, the colonel reflected on old battles. "Dien Bien Phu," he told me, "was the perfect rehearsal for our war with the Americans. All the commanders of our corps and divisions during the U.S. war had served at Dien Bien Phu."

If Dien Bien Phu had taught the Vietminh—the precursors of the North Vietnamese army (NVA) and the Vietcong (VC)—some valuable lessons, the same could not be said for American military planners. The United States had supported the French effort with massive infusions of arms, equipment, and funds in an attempt to prevent the Communist domination of Southeast Asia. American diplomats and military officers had been observing the Indochina War at first hand, and the U.S. Military Assistance Advisory Group (MAAG) had been participating indirectly as noncombat advisers. As the Battle of Dien Bien Phu developed, U.S. officers visited the mountain fortress as observers, and high-ranking American commanders from Hawaii and Tokyo arrived in Saigon and Hanoi to discuss possible direct U.S. intervention in support of the French. Following the French defeat, and despite the fact that the United States itself was soon to become directly involved in Vietnam, American planners and strategists largely ignored the French experience. The French had lost. We, with our overwhelming technological power, were going to win. Our gung ho spirit and can-do philosophy obscured the lessons of history.

In January of 1968, 40,000 North Vietnamese regulars surrounded the 6,000-man U.S. Marine Corps garrison at Khe Sanh. This series of strongpoints in the hills near the Laotian border and just below the demilitarized zone separating North and South Vietnam bore an unsettling resemblance to Dien Bien Phu. The two-and-a-half-month siege of the American base at Khe Sanh raised the specter of the French defeat, gnawed at President Lyndon Johnson, and posed troubling questions about U.S. commander Gen. William Westmoreland's conduct of the war. In the end, U.S. artillery, massive B-52 strikes, and marine doggedness broke the siege. Close to 500 American marines died at Khe Sanh, and NVA deaths were estimated at approximately 10,000 men. General Giap's forces had been badly battered, and American military information officers were claiming victory, but the fact remains that the situation at Khe Sanh had often been touch-and-go. During the siege, and for a brief time thereafter, there was renewed interest in Dien Bien Phu and the Indochina War. But this interest faded as our own war of attrition ground on.

What were the valuable lessons relative to our own Vietnam experience that we chose to ignore? I have listed some of those I consider the most important.

Underestimation of nonconventional units or a guerrilla enemy by regular forces is a cardinal military sin. Western military commanders seem particularly prone to repeating this costly error. Conventional training, tradition, and a reliance on technology have often combined to produce a false sense of security and a dangerous tendency to denigrate the enemy's capabilities.

xx   INTRODUCTION

The French High Command and many staff officers in various regional headquarters refused to admit the true worth of Gen. Vo Nguyen Giap's regular divisions, his regional forces, and his omnipresent hamlet and village militias. The Vietminh enemy was measured and judged by European standards and superficially found wanting. Only field commanders, battalion- and company-grade officers, and soldiers who had experienced years of combat in Indochina expressed a constant, if grudging, respect for the Vietminh. Their warnings of continual improvement in the enemy's performance failed to impress the desk-bound planners poring over their maps in the air-conditioned offices of Saigon and Hanoi.

Dien Bien Phu was an example of how a military dreamworld can triumph over reality with tragic results. The Vietminh artillery capability was said to be limited. The French High Command doubted whether General Giap could move what guns he did have through the jungle. If he did, it was reasoned, they would be smashed by French counterbattery fire and air attack before they could do any damage. But Giap's artillery was far from limited; he did move his guns through the jungle, and the counterbattery fire and air attacks failed miserably. Further underestimations were applied to the enemy's supply capabilities, his physical stamina, the tenacity of his troops, and the strategic and tactical expertise of the Vietminh general staff. The same attitude toward the NVA and the VC and the same differences of opinion between planners and combat commanders were often replayed in the late 1960s and early 1970s. But this time the headquarters' air conditioning was more efficient, and the uniforms were American.

An overdependence on air support and supply can lead to disaster during a guerrilla-type campaign in difficult terrain or adverse weather conditions. Despite warnings from their own air force generals, the French High Command proceeded to install a major fortress in an isolated mountain region that would have to be supplied and reinforced by air over long distances. Once enemy artillery had neutralized the airstrip, all supplies and reinforcements had to be delivered by parachute and under heavy antiaircraft fire. The Vietminh had a constant ally in the weather. The typhoonlike storms, heavy rains, and impenetrable fogs of North Vietnam annulled and disrupted French supply drops and air strikes. The jungled mountains screened General Giap's divisions and artillery emplacements from observation aircraft and fighter-bombers. The promises of French air power never produced the expected results. This fact, in turn, had a negative psychological effect on ground troops who had learned to depend on effective air support in the flat, more open expanses of the Tonkin Delta region. Target identification was difficult in the mountains, and a pilot's split-second decision as to whether a village was friendly, enemy-occupied, or hostile could lead to tragedy. Such mistakes had a direct bearing on the loyalty of the mountain tribes upon whom the French depended for irregular forces and intelligence information. The planned air interdiction of the Vietminh supply routes to their divisions at Dien Bien Phu was unsuccessful not only because of the weather but also because of a multiple trail system and the Vietminh's excellent camouflage, trail discipline, and rapid road repairs.

It is true that the French air capability in Indochina was limited in comparison to the massive deployment of U.S. aircraft during the Vietnam War. But once again, despite the tonnage of bombs and ordnance expended, the hoped-for results were short of the target. In addition, the "collateral damage"—a sanitized military phrase meaning dead and mutilated civilians—was enormous. In a war that was being won or lost in the hamlets and villages of South Vietnam, where the loyalty and cooperation of the peasants was essential to success, the heavy bombing and the free-fire zones alienated the population and increased support for the VC. Despite our over-whelming superiority in the air, the Ho Chi Minh Trail(s), modeled on the Vietminh routes to Dien Bien Phu, continued to funnel NVA regulars, arms, supplies, and even tanks into South Vietnam throughout the war.

The Gulf War showed what aircraft can do operating over open desert terrain in comparatively good weather with a negligible threat of attack from enemy aircraft. But such successes should not blind us to the realities. More recently, as America moved closer to military involvement in Bosnia, the U.S. Air Force chief of staff, General Merrill McPeak, told the Senate that air strikes on Serbian positions would be effective and virtually risk-free. Considering that the weather conditions over the forests and mountains of Bosnia are variable at best and the terrain is ideal for guerrilla operations, such optimism appeared excessive. Once again, we were demonstrating our tendency to place too much faith in technology and ignore the past. In the future, U.S. service colleges should consider war-gaming an exercise in which air support is limited or nonexistent. The results of such a scenario, if not conclusive, should be interesting.

The battle was a clear demonstration of the flexibility of a guerrilla foe and his ability to change procedures to fit a specific tactical situation. Many of the French headquarters officers responsible for the planning of Dien Bien Phu still saw the Vietminh as basically a guerrilla force, a "peasant" army. It was difficult for them to imagine well-organized and well-equipped enemy divisions that would stand and fight in a set-piece battle. However, once this fact was realized, Giap's divisions were viewed as regulars in the classic mold with their own specific tasks and limitations. But General Giap saw his "people's war" as a combination of mutually supporting, inter-changeable guerrilla and classic actions in which regulars, region-als, and militia operated individually or collectively to achieve a common goal. During an interview in Ho Chi Minh City in 1991, he told me that "people's war" not only meant guerrilla operations but rather covered everything from a small-unit action to that of a whole army. He objected to my verbal attempt to separate regular divisions from guerrilla forces and said, "Combatants who fight well as guer-rillas adapt to changes when introduced into regular units."

The same flexibility indicated in the quotation was demonstrated early in the Dien Bien Phu siege when Giap canceled a major assault. His artillery and infantry were in place and his troops psy-chologically prepared for a major effort when they received orders to pull back. The former schoolteacher, now a tactician, had consid-ered the casualties that he had already suffered in frontal attacks, the strength of the reinforced French garrison, and the extent of the new fortifications before deciding that the risk was too great. Instead, he called for thousands of shovels, and the Vietminh began the relentless digging that would spin a spiderweb of approach trenches leading to the outer perimeter of the French strongpoints. "The situation had changed," Giap explained.

Beware the attrition of a hostile environment. It has been said that the jungle is neutral. In reality, it is more neutral to some than to others. The rough mountain jungles surrounding Dien Bien Phu were hard on both the Vietminh and the French forces. But the young men of Giap's divisions were already survivors. Even the city dwellers in their ranks had endured the endemic diseases, hard-ships, and occasional malnutrition common in an austere North Vietnam. Despite this fact, the Vietminh were plagued by tropical diseases, including jungle fevers and the ravages of malaria. But their debilitations could not compare with those of the Europeans serving in the French Expeditionary Corps. Troops called on to march through the jungle suffered from sunstroke, heat exhaustion, and general lethargy. Dysentery and malaria were common, and small cuts, if untreated, could become septic and serious in a short time. The overland column sent from Laos in December 1953 to prove that the fortress could still be reached on foot arrived at their rendezvous point near Dien Bien Phu emaciated, ill, and exhausted.

The crayoned arrows charting a unit's progression on a headquar-ters map overlay failed to reveal the difficulties faced in the field. Fatigue, illness, water shortages, high mountains and deep valleys, impenetrable jungle, uncharted torrents, inaccurate supply drops, and intermittent but deadly ambushes combined to form a veritable purgatory for the men on the ground. Some experienced field com-manders understood the limitations of their troops in the tropical environment. To the extent possible, they avoided overextension despite the admonitions of the general staff. The "sweeps" through difficult terrain often moved at a snail's pace, and care was taken to keep advancing units within range of supporting artillery. Such limitations restricted effectiveness and blunted the cutting edge of offensive operations. Only certain elite units that maintained a high level of physical condition, traveled light, and moved fast could hope to match the enemy in the jungle.

American air mobility and particularly the helicopter made a major difference in the Vietnam War. Quick evacuation of the wounded by "dust-off" pickup saved many lives, workhorse choppers shifted artillery from one position to another, and the infantry were delivered to landing zones near their objectives. Even the North Vietnamese were impressed with the airlift capability of the U.S. forces. General Giap still shakes his head in astonishment when he recalls that "even water" was supplied by choppers. But for those grunts who inevitably had to slog through the thick jungle or the mud of the delta, the environment remained a silent enemy filled with the same hazards that had confronted the French.

Too much Western influence can be fatal to a "national" army in the third world, exerting negative psychological pressures that weaken morale, degrade battlefield performance, and cause rifts in alliances. In a more distant epoch, the French Expeditionary Corps of the 1950s might have been an efficient, professional fighting machine. But by 1953 it was fast becoming an anachronism. As one of the last existing colonial armies, it was showing the strains and cracks caused by new directions in the postwar world. The winds of political change were already buffeting the sources of its recruitment, and the old paternalism that had held its famous regiments together was becoming outdated. The normally dependable North African and West African troops who had fought for France in World War II were still performing well in Indochina, depending on the quality of their French officers and the veteran noncommissioned officers of their own races. But the seemingly never-ending war in a far-off land and exposure to Vietminh propaganda were taking their toll. Leaflets, loudspeaker appeals to isolated posts, and word-of-mouth campaigns in the dingy bars near military camps often posed the questions: "What are you doing here? Why did you come here to die? Why do you fight us when you should be liberating your own country?" Many colonial troopers had begun to ponder the answers, particularly when rumors of unrest and opposition to continued French rule at home reached Indochina.

Although colonial armies are now a thing of the past, their legacy lingers on. The Army of the Republic of Vietnam (ARVN) was never able to shed its origins as a European-trained colonial force. When

U.S. advisers took over the role of the French, the tinge of colonialism remained, providing a continuing theme for VC propagandists, who never failed to refer to the ARVN as a "puppet" army. Today, as the world's superpower, the United States faces unsought responsibilities and involvement in international brushfire wars and limited-intensity conflicts. Much of the success of our attempts to establish anything resembling a new world order will depend on our sensitivity to those with whom we work to bring it about. To us, "colonialism" is a historical label. To many in the third world, it remains a valid negative symbol.

The effectiveness and morale of a military force is directly linked to the support of the government and people of the nation involved. The fierce and prolonged resistance of the outnumbered, outgunned, and abandoned French garrison at Dien Bien Phu was a phenomenon. Obviously, these were professional soldiers with their own codes of tradition and sacrifice. They knew that they were fighting a war that was unpopular at home. That fact reinforced their solidarity and created a desire to produce victories that would justify their effort in Indochina. But the wheel of history was turning, and they were in its path. France was already seeking a political solution to the war when they were committed to battle, and government support for the war effort was faltering. In addition, any chance of the rumored intervention by their American ally was to sputter out like a damp fuse. The combatants of Dien Bien Phu were in a uniquely catastrophic military situation.

On the other hand, the Vietminh assault troops knew that their whole nation was mobilized behind them in a "people's war" for independence. To us, the stultified words of their Communist dialectic and propaganda ring hollow. For them, the slogans identified the goals for which they fought. The Vietminh infantryman who returned again and again to the attack at Dien Bien Phu was hardly a student of Marxism, but, encouraged by the political cadres, he was seeking something that he had never had and was willing to die for it.

The same pattern, with variations, repeated itself during the Johnson years. The VC, with North Vietnamese support, were just as determined as their Vietminh predecessors to pursue their objectives. Our draftee troops, unsure of the war's purpose and lacking public support at home, fought surprisingly well. But, for many, the prime objective was to live through their tour of duty. The frustrations of their lonely war led to narcotics use, racial friction, and a vacuum of morale that produced the practice of "fragging."

It may be hard to imagine a repetition of Dien Bien Phu today, but the warning is there, nevertheless. Any modern army engaged in overseas combat in which the individual soldier—particularly a conscript—has doubts about the purpose of his commitment is fighting at a disadvantage. This disadvantage is compounded if the enemy, rightly or wrongly, has a firm belief in his cause. It can become even more pronounced in the face of heavy losses, meager rations, and prolonged hardship.

Writing about a battle can be a humbling experience, particularly since I was actually on the ground at the beginning of the campaign, and many of the officers and men involved were friends or acquaintances. As an official war correspondent, I had the option of coming and going when I chose. This fact leaves me with a slight feeling of guilt, a lingering sense of voyeurism that will always separate me from those who had to remain and endure the fifty-seven-day siege. That said, I am grateful for the opportunity of having known these men and sharing, if not their burden, at least some of their experiences.

1

"Go! Go! Go!"

"If only it had rained that day!"
    Major Marcel Bigeard, Commander,
    Sixth Colonial Parachute Battalion

An early morning mist blanketed the Hanoi region on November 20, 1953. The first brightening in the eastern sky revealed the concentration of French air force C-47s parked in rows on the tarmac of the Bach-Mai military airfield. Trucks and jeeps moved between the aircraft, depositing troops, delivering messages, and unloading heavy weapons. The bang of tailgates, the grinding of gears, the shuffle of booted feet, and the occasional shouted order faded quickly, deflected by the silver fuselages. Files of helmeted, combat-ready parachutists were boarding the C-47s, moving awkwardly, like deep-sea divers, under the weight of their parachutes, arms, and equipment. The same scene was being repeated at Gia-Lam, Hanoi's civilian airport.

The parachutists, preparing to take part in the largest airborne operation of the Indochina War, were the cream of the French Expeditionary Corps. The spearhead units, the Sixth Colonial Parachute Battalion of Maj. Marcel Bigeard and the Second Battalion of the First Regiment of Parachute Chasseurs, commanded by Maj. Jean Bréchignac, were battle-tested units led by career officers with extensive combat experience in Vietnam. The First Colonial Parachute Battalion, under Maj. Jean Souquet, scheduled for the second-wave drop on the same day, had an equally high professional reputation. The headquarters of the First Airborne Battle

1

Group, led by Lieutenant Colonel Fourcade, one of the founders of the Commando d'Indochine, were scheduled to jump with Souquet's battalion, although Fourcade himself had chosen to go in earlier with Bréchignac. Airborne engineers, heavy-weapons companies, and surgical teams would also be included in the operation. These paras—the "firemen" of the Indochina War—were often rushed from one hot spot to another, dropping out of the sky to relieve isolated posts under enemy attack, bolstering infantry units during ground sweeps or mopping-up operations, and carrying out commando raids and intelligence tasks for the French High Command.

The men being boosted up the narrow metal steps of the C-47s and pulled aboard by the aircrews had only a vague idea of what awaited them at the end of their flight. But the operational buildup, the number of aircraft involved, and the last-minute briefings had told them that they were about to participate in what they were trained for—a classic airborne assault.

Loaded twenty-five to a plane into the thin-skinned metallic cocoons of the transports, the paras joked with the aircrews, exchanged tension-relieving banter among themselves, and settled shoulder-to-shoulder onto the narrow bucket seats. Some slumped over their dorsal packs to catch up on lost sleep; some chewed gum; others were silent, alone with their own thoughts. The old hands, knowing how deceptively cold a long, high-altitude flight could be, cajoled the crew chiefs into sharing their small hoard of blankets.

They were a mix of origins and races: street-wise youths from the suburbs of Paris and Lyon; stolid Bretons; rangy Alsatians; tough Corsicans; men from all regions of France, from Artois to Provence and from Poitou to Savoy. Many of the paras were short, taciturn Vietnamese or dark-skinned Cambodians who had chosen to join the colonial units. Now, with the personnel and equipment checks completed, the paras resigned themselves to the waiting common to all armies.

Some 300 kilometers northwest of Hanoi, a lone C-47 completed a long, arcing turn to make another pass over the mountain-ringed Muong Thanh Valley. With typical French élan and a seeming disregard for danger, this aircraft carried a precious cargo of decision makers. Air Force Lt. Gen. Pierre Bodet (deputy commander in chief, Indochina), Brig. Gen. Jean Dechaux (commander of the Northern Tactical Air Group), and Brig. Gen. Jean Gilles (commander of airborne forces, Indochina) were crowded into the fuselage, along with a group of airborne pathfinders and the specialized radio equipment that had transformed the C-47 into a flying CP. The decision that they had to make would depend on the weather. If there was rain over the mountains or if the fog persisted in the valley, Operation "Castor" ("Beaver") would have to be annulled.

The jungle below appeared and disappeared in shifting swaths of gray fog. Jagged limestone mountains capped with thick foliage rose like broken teeth from the jungle canopy, their summits catching the first hint of dawn. The aircraft steadied, twin engines thrumming, as it skirted the sixteen-kilometer-long, nine-kilometer-wide valley. The fog dissipated to reveal the silver band of the Nam Yum River twisting along the valley floor. A scattering of stilted, high-roofed huts far below on the banks of the river marked the T'ai tribal village of Muong Then, or "Heavenly Spirit." On the acetate-covered maps spread before the generals, the village bore the Vietnamese name of Dien Bien Phu, or "Principal Frontier Post."

A brisk north wind was breaking up the clouds and driving the fog from the chasms as the C-47 finished its run and began another slow turn. Other villages appeared, and the observers could see thin spirals of smoke rising from cooking and brush fires. Lieutenant General Bodet drew on his cigarette and glanced at his watch. Although the C-47 had a supplemental fuel supply, it would soon be time for a definitive decision. Brigadier General Gilles, his para beret pulled low on his forehead, kept his one good eye on the landscape. The gruff "Père" Gilles was not a talkative man at the best of times, and he now seemed to be brooding. He knew that 1,500 paras of his first wave were loaded and ready. He also knew from intelligence reports that they could expect firm opposition on the ground.

Two companies of the 920th Battalion of the Vietminh 148th Regiment were known to be based at Dien Bien Phu to protect their command post. In addition, a heavy-weapons company of the 351st "Heavy" Division, armed with 120-millimeter mortars, was reported to have reached the valley. But no one in the command aircraft or at Hanoi headquarters knew that elements of the 920th Battalion had orders to carry out tactical exercises that morning over the ground designated as "Natasha," the drop zone (DZ) assigned to Major Bigeard's battalion.

The first rays of a timid sun suddenly glowed through the clouds. The tall, angular Dechaux joined Bodet and Gilles to examine the terrain. There was little doubt—the fog was burning off, and the sky was clearing. At 0652 the generals sent a coded message to the Hanoi headquarters of Maj. Gen. René Cogny, commander of ground forces, Tonkin: "Fog dissipating at Dien Bien Phu." At 0815 the first C-47s of an armada of sixty-five rolled down the runways of Bach-Mai and Gia-Lam and lifted off, climbing over the Red River and the suburbs of Hanoi to steady on a course to the northwest.

Fortunately for their morale, the paras were unaware that two of the generals in the command aircraft, Gilles and Dechaux, as well as Brig. Gen. René Masson, General Cogny's deputy in Hanoi, had already gone on record as being opposed to Operation "Castor." Terse excerpts from the secret report on a November 17 meeting in Hanoi, chaired by Gen. Henri Navarre, commander in chief, Indochina, emphasized their opposition.

> . . . During this meeting General Navarre asked Generals Masson, Dechaux and Gilles if they had any objections regarding the execution of the airborne operation on Dien Bien Phu, named "Castor."
>
> All were unanimous in advising against the operation and presented tactical and technical objections.
>
> General Dechaux in particular stated that the maintenance of this new airborne base would exert a heavy burden on the potential of his transport aircraft and, as the weather was often different in the [Tonkin] Delta and above the basin of Dien Bien Phu, there would undoubtedly be difficulties in ensuring adequate supplies to the base.
>
> General Navarre nevertheless maintained his decision to carry out operation "Castor" by presenting the [following] arguments:
>
> • Of a strategic order: Protection of Laos
> • Of an economic order: Seizure of rice, particularly in the valley of Dien Bien Phu

Thirteen days earlier, a report prepared for the High Command by Col. Dominique Bastiani, a veteran parachute officer and thoughtful tactician serving as General Cogny's chief of staff, had torn holes in the logic of Operation "Castor." Bastiani had pointed out that Lai Chau, the capital of the T'ai tribal confederation near the Chinese border, was likely to fall to the Vietminh despite the projected occupation of Dien Bien Phu. More important, he had challenged the High Command's reasoning that a French presence at Dien Bien Phu would "block" a Vietminh move on Laos, explaining, "In this country one does not block a direction. That is a European notion with no value here. The Viet passes everywhere, as we've so often seen in the Delta." The colonel had also pointed out that the rice harvest of Dien Bien Phu would supply a (Vietminh) division for a short three months, thus only partially supporting an invasion of Laos, and warned that Dien Bien Phu could become a bottomless pit absorbing French battalions that could be fixed in place by only one Vietminh regiment. He had argued that, faced with a growing threat to the delta, the French High Command was about to immobilize three *groupes mobiles* (roughly equivalent to regimental combat teams) 300 kilometers from Hanoi to meet a hypothetical threat to

Laos. Bastiani had concluded with a warning that the consequences of such a decision could be "very serious." (In his book *Agonie de l'Indochine 1953–1954*, published three years later in Paris, General Navarre would state: "Contrary to what has been said many times, absolutely no unfavorable opinion on the tactical site of Dien Bien Phu was expressed by anyone before the battle.")

Despite these warnings from experienced field commanders, General Navarre's staff in Saigon had gone ahead with the planning for Operation "Castor." Isolated from the realities of the war in their air-conditioned headquarters, they had moved units and arrows over detailed wall maps as if the impassable mountains, swamps, thick jungles, monsoon rains, raging torrents, heavy fogs, and searing heat did not exist.

Although Generals Masson, Dechaux, and Gilles were now carrying out General Navarre's orders despite their misgivings, it was hardly an auspicious atmosphere in which to launch an operation that could well decide the outcome of the war.

General Navarre had arrived in Saigon on May 19, 1953, another general officer in a long line of commanders in chief that had taken responsibility for the French Expeditionary Corps since the start of the Indochina War in late 1946. The fifty-five-year-old Navarre's military career had been intense and varied. A graduate of the French Military Academy of Saint-Cyr, like many of the senior officers serving in Indochina, he had fought as a cavalryman in World War I and France's postwar North African campaigns. During World War II, after supervising a clandestine, anti-German intelligence network in France, he had commanded an armored regiment of the Free French Forces until the German surrender. Following the war, Navarre had occupied a number of staff positions in occupied Germany and had commanded the Fifth French Armored Division. When called to Indochina, he had been serving as chief of staff to Field Marshal Alphonse Juin at NATO headquarters.

Navarre was reputed to have a precise, analytical military mind. He was gray-haired, distinguished in appearance, and always immaculately turned out in a well-cut uniform. He had the cool, effete manner common to many cavalry officers (the traditionally "aristocratic" branch of the French army), which often created an invisible barrier to informal personal contact.

The new commander in chief had come to Indochina under a broad but vague governmental directive to create the military conditions for an "honorable political solution." The term "victory" was significantly absent from the government's vocabulary. Navarre was operating without a real base of support in Paris. Successive governments had fallen, including that led by Prime Minister René Mayer, the official who had given Navarre his Indochina assignment. France was sick of the seemingly endless guerrilla war of attrition that had demolished entire French battalions, required successive waves of reinforcements, inflicted heavy losses on the officer corps, and ruined a number of military careers. The war had taken a less lethal toll among French politicians, but enough damage had been done to stifle any bold initiatives and make most of them wary of taking too direct a role in solving the Indochina "problem."

The Indochina War had changed considerably by the time of Navarre's arrival. Ho Chi Minh's heterogeneous, ragtag force of Vietminh guerrillas that had attacked French units in 1946 though armed only with cast-off rifles and homemade grenades had grown into a disciplined army able to muster regular divisions supported by heavy mortars and artillery. The victory of the Chinese Communists in late 1949 had opened the Chinese border, allowing the Vietminh direct access to Chinese arms, advisers, and training facilities. The Vietminh commander, Gen. Vo Nguyen Giap, a former history teacher who had studied the campaigns of Napoleon and Kutuzov, as well as such Vietnamese military heroes as Tran Hung Dao and Nguyen Hue, had dealt humiliating defeats to the French along the Chinese border at Dongkhe, Caobang, and Lang Son in 1950.

The lassitude and defeatism of the French Expeditionary Corps had been jolted later the same year by the arrival of Marshal Jean de Lattre de Tassigny. The charismatic "Roi Jean" had built a new confidence among his men and dealt some serious defeats to the enemy in early 1951. He had also impressed the Truman administration during a Washington visit to seek more U.S. military aid. The Korean War had erased America's compunctions about helping the French. Indochina was no longer a simple "colonial war." The French were now "fighting the good fight" against Communist expansion in Asia. In 1951 U.S. military assistance had reached the $50 million mark, and de Lattre's lobbying in Washington had helped the figure climb to $60 million in 1952. A fatal cancer had ended de Lattre's reign in Indochina the same year.

Gen. Raoul Salan, the next commander in chief, had been de Lattre's deputy. He was an old Indochina hand, an *ancien d'Indochine*, with long experience in northwest Vietnam, and an expert in the field of intelligence work. By the end of the rainy season in August 1952, Salan had been convinced that General Giap was planning another offensive in the mountains of northwest Vietnam. His fears had proved well founded. In late 1952 Salan had established an air-supplied strongpoint in the valley of Na-San to protect Laos and the T'ai region. He had also seen the mountain-ringed valley as the ideal rendezvous point for French units forced to abandon their border outposts. By fortifying Na-San with its usable airstrip—fifty minutes' flying time from Hanoi—he had hoped to tempt Giap into a trap where his frontal assaults would be smashed by French aircraft and artillery. Salan had chosen the tough, one-eyed parachute officer Jean Gilles, then a colonel, to command Na-San.

Na-San had been a success—up to a point. The air bridge from Hanoi had functioned, the fortifications had been built in record time, a strong presence by the French had reassured their tribal allies, and most of Salan's errant garrisons had been recovered. The Vietminh 308th "Iron" and 312th Divisions had attacked the defenses on November 30 and December 1. On the morning of December 2, a strident bugle call had heralded the Vietminh withdrawal. Over 500 enemy dead had been found in and around the French defensive wire. In Hanoi, the satisfaction over the "victory" at Na-San had obscured the fact that the small garrison at the post of Dien Bien Phu had been evacuated under Vietminh pressure at about the same time that Giap had launched his attacks on Na-San.

The negative aspects of Na-San had not been as tangible as a body count but had been just as real. Although the air supply of the "hedgehog" defense had been satisfactory, its day-to-day operation had revealed weaknesses in air force capability and supply arrangements. The daily milk-run supply flights from Hanoi had drained aircraft and personnel from important duties in the crucial Tonkin Delta. Following the Vietminh withdrawal, it had become obvious that Na-San's worth as an obstacle to Vietminh movements was practically nil. Giap's troops had flowed through the jungle like controlled mercury, choosing their own trails and avoiding or bypassing Na-San.

The Vietminh may have "broken their teeth" on the defenses of Na-San, for which Colonel Gilles had been promoted to the rank of *général de brigade*, but the veteran campaigner had remained unimpressed. For him, the troubling fact that the enemy had taken one of his fortified hill positions in a night attack and held it for twelve hours under artillery fire and napalm attack had called for a reassessment of the value of air-supplied strongpoints.

The commander of Na-San had not been alone in drawing pertinent conclusions from the battle. General Giap had also learned some valuable lessons. Later, in one of his orders of the day, he would state that Na-San had taught him that a fortified camp supplied by air could not be taken without bringing the landing strip under "heavy artillery fire."

Just prior to General Navarre's arrival, Vietminh divisions had made another feint toward Laos, forcing Salan to establish a new defensive airhead on the Plain of Jars, a high plateau in northern Laos, and rush reinforcements to Luang Prabang, the royal capital. After destroying some isolated Franco-Laotian posts, Giap's regular forces had pulled back into northwest Vietnam. Their efforts had not been entirely wasted. The Vietminh had recruited local partisans, established cooperation with the pro-Communist Pathet Lao rebels, and learned valuable lessons in moving and supplying their divisions over great distances. They had also harvested the regional opium crop, a bounty that was to provide ready cash for the purchase of black-market arms and medical supplies in Hong Kong, Bangkok, and Manila.

Relieved at Giap's sudden about-face, General Salan had then prepared to hand over his command to General Navarre. Among the papers and reports left to his successor had been a strong, detailed recommendation that a new "entrenched camp" be established at Dien Bien Phu, a move Salan had described as "essential" to the security of Luang Prabang. General Navarre, a complete neophyte to the Far East, had already been developing the outlines of a tentative military strategy for Indochina. He had decided that he must wrest the initiative from the Vietminh, insist on more reinforcements from France, and develop viable national armies in Vietnam, Laos, and Cambodia to replace French forces in static positions, freeing them for offensive action. Like all his predecessors, he had been concerned with the defense of Laos, the most loyal and anti-Communist of the Associated States of Indochina (Vietnam, Cambodia, and Laos). Laos had also been seen as the likely route for a Vietminh push south along the Mekong River toward South Vietnam and Cambodia. Salan's recommendation on Dien Bien Phu had fit easily into what would soon be known as "the Navarre Plan."

Navarre had launched his plan in his first open letter to the French Expeditionary Corps. "One can only win by attacking," he had declared. This clarion call for offensive action had been received favorably in Washington, where the Eisenhower administration had been measuring the cost of military aid to Indochina against the results and wondering whether any French commander's performance would ever equal that of de Lattre.

On July 17, 1953, three French parachute battalions had been dropped on the Vietminh-occupied border town of Lang Son, a major reception center for Chinese supplies. The paras had withdrawn after destroying a huge stock of arms and ammunition. Lang Son had been a practical example of taking the war to the enemy, hurting him, and not attempting to hold on to useless real estate. The successful operation had been heralded as a perfect example of the Navarre Plan in action. Even the cynics had been temporarily mollified. General Navarre had ordered the evacuation of Na-San in August. The strongpoint had been sitting in stagnant suspension since the Vietminh attacks in November and December of 1952, an empty symbol of power ignored by the enemy. To a commander needing every combat unit and aircraft that he could muster, the move had made practical sense. But it had removed a stanchion of General Salan's recommendation that had projected Na-San and Dien Bien Phu as being mutually supporting bases.

The armada of C-47s continued its route, three by three, rising and falling in the rough thermals high above the green-and-gray checkerboard of the delta paddies. The first mountains of the T'ai region were soon in sight, their abrupt heights forming an irregular, verdant wall cut by deep valleys and crowned by slow-moving clouds. Major Bigeard noted that some of his men were pale and others had become sick. Observing the beauty of the mountains from the aircraft, he reflected how simple life would be if his paras could always remain high above it all. But he had no illusions about what awaited them below. Lieutenant General Bodet had told Bigeard and Bréchignac that they were to pull out toward Laos with minimum losses if things did not go well on the ground. The decision would have to be theirs. Years later, commenting on the result of Operation "Castor," Bigeard was to comment, "If only it had rained that day!"

The thirty-seven-year-old Bigeard was the epitome of what had become known in Indochina as *l'esprit para*. He had the physical presence of a medieval warlord, a tall, lean, hawk-nosed man with a fine disregard for danger and an innate gift for leadership. He had entered the French army as a noncommissioned officer in 1939 and fought in the rearguard action against the invading Germans in 1940. He had been captured and, after several attempts, had escaped from prison camp in 1941. The next year he had rejoined the French army in Africa. In 1944, after parachute training by the British, he had jumped into the department of Ariège, with the temporary rank of battalion commander, to head the local Resistance organization. In Indochina since 1945, Bigeard had profited from his long assignments in the T'ai region to become a specialist in the war of movement and ruse required to survive and win in the jungle. He had also studied the enemy's tactics and adapted some of their methods in perfecting his own. Now, after eight years of continuous combat experience, Major Bigeard, known by his Resistance code name "Bruno," was a living legend. His paras followed him without hesitation into the most difficult situations, always aware that the habitually unarmed "Bruno" would never demand more of them than he did of himself.

Aside from the military exercises under way at a considerable distance from the village, the plain of Dien Bien Phu was a picture of pastoral calm on the morning of November 20. The dirt-topped, neglected airstrip, key to the objectives of Operation "Castor," was overgrown and deliberately holed by the Vietminh. The villagers were going about their tasks in the cool mountain air, working in the paddies, carrying water from the Nam Yum River in cylinders of cut bamboo, and feeding the grunting pigs and scrawny chickens penned under the stilted huts. Old men in black, silver-buttoned jackets and wearing dark berets sat under the trees, smoking their bone pipes. T'ai women in dark, tight-bodiced jackets, long skirts, and loosely furled headdresses had gathered on the riverbank to wash clothes and gossip while their children played nearby. Some villagers had noticed the lone aircraft droning high above. But the "silver bird" was no phenomenon to them. Although rare, such flights were usually distant and harmless manifestations of the war that they had learned to live with over a number of years. To the Vietminh *bo doï*, or infantrymen, maneuvering through the buffalo grass or manhandling their heavy weapons into position on what would soon become DZ "Natasha," the lone, high-flying C-47 had been a momentary distraction. Their officers had taken a more professional interest. Then, reassured that it was not a fighter-bomber, they had dismissed the intrusion as a run-of-the-mill photo reconnaissance mission.

The first C-47s of the armada reached Dien Bien Phu at 1030, thundering from the sparse cloud cover on their drop run. The paras were erect now, helmets secured by tight chin straps. They swayed and fought to keep their footing as the aircraft yawed and bucked. The order came to "hook up." Static lines were snapped in place and tested. Some men checked their stubby MAT-49 submachine guns; others readjusted their heavy burden of extra ammunition and grenades. A chill wind roared through the open cargo door as the jumpmasters moved into place. Each man was alert and waiting. At 1035 the buzz of the jump signal cut through the din of wind and engines.

"Go!" The first para leaped from the cargo door and dropped from sight, his static line flapping in the slipstream. "Go! Go! Go!" The rest of the stick followed, skidding and clattering toward the void: a blast of wind, a plunge, and the gut-wrenching jerk of the chute opening; then a brief reprieve of sudden silence and a swift, downwind drift toward the DZ.

All movement in the valley seemed momentarily frozen. The tribesmen watched in open-mouthed wonder as the endless parade of aircraft spewed the human cargoes. Some of the chutes were already nearing the ground. The Vietminh had been just as astounded, but their discipline and training had cushioned the shock. Strident commands carried over the dry paddies as Giap's regulars rallied to defend their headquarters. Automatic-weapons fire crackled, and bullets whistled skyward, piercing chutes and burning into the flesh and bone of some falling paras. Within minutes most of Dien Bien Phu's inhabitants were fleeing for the hills or neighboring villages, driving their prized water buffalo ahead of them, their belongings suspended from shouldered carrying poles or strapped to shaggy mountain ponies.

At this point the arbitrary, unforgiving law of battle stepped in to demonstrate the fragility of well-laid plans. Major Bréchignac's battalion was being dropped in one pass four kilometers south of the village on DZ "Simone." One of its main objectives was to block any escape attempt by the enemy. Even as Bréchignac thudded onto the DZ, he knew that the speed of the aircraft and the time that it had taken his men to jump had combined to scatter his command over too wide an area.

Bigeard's men were also scattered, but at least most of them were on their DZ or nearby. Here the "fog of battle" had become a thick curtain. In some places the tall elephant grass cut visibility to a few feet. The distant popping of small-arms fire that the paras had heard while drifting to the ground was now an immediate, ripping threat. Bullets clipped the grass and cracked close to their heads. Heavy-mortar rounds exploded in puffs of black smoke. Jagged shards of hot metal scythed the air. Men were firing, falling, and trying to make some sense out of the confusion. Some paras had landed among the enemy. Before they could orient themselves or find their comrades, they were engaged in close-quarter firefights and vicious hand-to-hand combat.

Major Bigeard, working his radio and moving toward the village, was trying to make some sense out of what he would later describe as "a complete mess." Vietminh DKZ-57 recoilless rifles *(sung khong dat)*, heavy mortars, and machine-gun fire had pinned down some of his sections, and the terse casualty reports that he was receiving were not reassuring. Recovering the air-dropped eighty-one-millimeter mortars and their ammunition was proving difficult. The original, concise battle plan was now in tatters. The situation demanded rapid improvisation and aggressive action. Luckily, Bigeard was a master at battlefield improvisation, and his well-trained battalion was an experienced fighting machine.

By 1130, Bigeard had established his CP 250 meters from the village. He had now recuperated four field radios and was working them in tandem. With the help of a Morane spotter plane, he was calling in B-26 strikes on the stubborn defenders, trying to contact Bréchignac or the command group that had dropped with him, and continuing to sort out his companies. He had lost contact with Brigadier General Gilles, who was still circling the valley, but he was maintaining a shaky liaison with Hanoi. By 1330 some of the misplaced mortars had been recovered in time to lay a preassault barrage on the village. Low-flying B-26s roared in to strafe enemy units that had begun withdrawing to the south. The fight for the village was a fierce, hut-to-hut contest against a determined rearguard. When it was over, many of the huts were on fire, the thatched roofs flaming and the dried bamboo of the structures cracking like rifle shots.

Lieutenant Colonel Fourcade, the leader of the First Airborne Battle Group, who had dropped with Bréchignac, had not been able to contain his eagerness for action. Marching to the sound of the guns, he had reached the village as the Sixth Battalion was completing its mopping-up. Bigeard, irritated that Bréchignac had not arrived in time to cut the enemy's retreat route, delivered an acid dressing-down to his friend and superior officer. He told Fourcade that he would have better filled his command function by remaining close to his radios instead of "playing at being a chief of commandos."

Major Souquet's First Colonial Parachute Battalion was dropped on the now-secured "Natasha" DZ at 1500. Bréchignac and his men had appeared to link up with the other battalions. He was furious at not having been able to accomplish his mission. The badly executed drop, the rough terrain that he had had to contend with, and the responsibility of protecting the command group had slowed his advance to a crawl. Bigeard's paras had begun the grim task of gathering their dead and caring for the wounded. Operation "Castor" had cost the French eleven dead and fifty-two wounded. The Vietminh had left 115 dead and four wounded on the field.

By nightfall a defense perimeter had been established, covering the approaches to the now-deserted village. The temperature in the valley had plunged, and an invasive *crachin* rain had begun to fall. The dug-in paras showed no light, contenting themselves with cold rations. The eerie silence was broken only by the sputtering of field radios, murmured commands, and an occasional burst of firing. Patrols moved cautiously through the darkness, alert to any sign of enemy infiltrators or stragglers. The dead were wrapped in parachutes, ready for burial the next day. The most seriously wounded had been evacuated to Lai Chau by helicopter. The huts that were still burning threw a flickering light over a row of mud-smeared Vietminh corpses aligned on the right bank of the Nam Yum River.

The next morning Brigadier General Gilles was flying toward Dien Bien Phu in parachute harness. No longer a spectator, he was to jump with the headquarters of the Second Airborne Battle Group, commanded by Lt. Col. Pierre Charles Langlais, a forty-four-year-old

Breton and a graduate of Saint-Cyr. The wiry, acerbic Langlais had served as a Méhariste (Camel Corps) officer in the Sahara and was known for his quick temper and devotion to his men.

The First Foreign Legion Parachute Battalion, commanded by Maj. Maurice Guiraud, another Saint-Cyr alumnus, was also scheduled for the morning drop. The First BEP (Premier Bataillon Étrangèr de Parachutistes) was a crack unit with an enviable reputation in Indochina. Its ranks contained many Germans who had chosen the hard discipline of the Legion over the uncertainties of life in postwar Germany. Some were veterans of World War II who preferred to practice their military skills as Legionnaires.

The French Foreign Legion, established by King Louis Philippe's Royal Ordinance of 1831, calling for the formation of a "legion composed of foreigners," has traditionally had men of many nationalities and races serving in its ranks. Since its formation, the Legion has fought in all of France's wars and overseas actions, including World Wars I and II, Indochina, Algeria, and Zaire. More recently, Legion units have blocked Libyan attempts to invade Chad, have participated in the Allied flanking attack against Saddam Hussein's forces in the Gulf War, and have served with the UN Peacekeeping Force in Bosnia, Cambodia, and Somalia. This elite corps of French-officered soldiers, who are guaranteed anonymity upon enlistment and French citizenship after five years' service, provided France with a dependable volunteer force during the Indochina War, a force whose casualties were less likely to cause a furor on the home front and attacks on government policy by the public and opposition politicians.

There were also a number of Vietnamese troopers in the First BEP. These local recruits were entitled to wear the Legion's green beret but not the traditional white képi. They considered themselves Legionnaires nevertheless and were proud of the distinction.

Brigadier General Gilles was anxious to join his men on the ground. There was much to do in a very short time. Repair of the airstrip was a top priority. The sooner it was completed, the sooner his paras would be replaced by the air-transported garrison and leave the "chamber-pot" valley. The establishment of a solid defense network was equally important. Gilles knew how rapidly the enemy could move, and he wanted to be ready for them if and when they appeared before his positions.

The general had other preoccupations. Intercepts of Vietminh radio traffic had signaled the Vietminh 316th Division moving toward Lai Chau, seventy kilometers north of Dien Bien Phu. The isolated, picturesque capital of the T'ai Tribal Federation was nestled in a deep valley, on the banks of the Black River, surrounded by high mountains. Aircraft using its small airstrip had to fly through a narrow corridor between the peaks. Even the enemy's automatic rifles could become effective antiaircraft weapons under such conditions.

Prior to Operation "Castor," Gilles had receive two top secret directives. One had outlined the political and administrative actions to be taken at Dien Bien Phu in regard to France's Black T'ai and White T'ai allies. (This nomenclature, including that of the Red T'ai, derived primarily from the color of the blouses worn by the tribal women.) The T'ai Tribal Federation, under its chieftain, Deo Van Long, had remained loyal to France, supplying troops and partisans to fight the Vietminh. The directive had mentioned the "very favorable" attitude of the T'ai to the French, stressed the need for good treatment of the tribesmen, and underlined the prime authority of Deo Van Long in the region. It had also called for the hasty recruitment of more partisan forces and insisted that the T'ai should operate as mobile, autonomous guerrillas, remaining in familiar territory. The second directive, addressed to Gilles personally, informed him that, in the event that Lai Chau was evacuated, he was to take command of all forces in the Northwest Operation Zone, including the T'ai units. Despite its political and symbolic importance, there was general agreement in both Hanoi and Saigon that Lai Chau was indefensible and would have to be abandoned. The majority of the T'ai, who would be elated by the sudden French presence at Dien Bien Phu, remained ignorant of the fate planned for their capital.

The general was also dogged by the problem of troop performance in the difficult terrain of northwest Vietnam. It was all very well for Navarre's staff to talk of offensive sweeps launched from Dien Bien Phu, but the hard fact was that few French units had the stamina and jungle-fighting skills needed for such operations. Gilles had already contributed to a classified report on a previous operation, signed by General Navarre, predicting that French infantry, with the exception of "a few parachute battalions," sent beyond the ten-kilometer range of effective artillery support would be defeated by the Vietminh. Père Gilles had a proprietary confidence in his paras, but there was little doubt that heavy losses, hurried training of replacements in France, and the lack of an adequate breaking-in period prior to combat were affecting the overall efficiency of some para battalions.

Shortly before 0800, as the aircraft steadied for its run, Gilles removed his glass eye and stored it carefully in a pocket of his bulky jump jacket. He could have arranged a helicopter lift into the valley, but the forty-nine-year-old general had chosen to jump with his men.

2

The Vise Tightens

"The entire road got up and moved!"
                    Caporal Chef Robert Blondeau, GCMA

General Gilles hit the ground, doused his chute, stuffed it into its carrying case, and walked toward the village, the case slung over his shoulder. He also put his glass eye in place and discarded his jump helmet for a parachutist's beret. *Le patron* had followed the fight for DZ "Natasha" from the air, but only now would he be able to truly appreciate his new command and get a feel for the terrain. He could see the intensive repair work under way on the airstrip and the paras preparing the first defenses. Gilles knew that they detested such chores. Like all shock troops, they preferred free-ranging operations or sudden coups de main and considered such "mole work" unworthy of their elite status.

He could see the small tricolor flying from a thin tree-trunk pole over the makeshift cemetery where the first dead had been buried. The distant crump of high explosives and palls of gray smoke marked the location of B-26 strikes directed against pockets of Vietminh remaining in the foothills. C-119s were dumping silver cascades of barbed wire over a DZ designated for free-fall cargoes, and companies of the First BEP were still drifting to earth over DZ "Natasha." Gilles was greeted by Lieutenant Colonel Fourcade and presented with an "airborne," a small, collapsible motor scooter of American design. He then put-putted off to the operational CP established under the raised floor of a stilted T'ai hut. Lieutenant Colonel Langlais had been among the jump casualties. Cursing his luck, he would be evacuated to Hanoi the next day with a broken ankle.

15

The sky over Dien Bien Phu had become a flight controller's
nightmare. The supply drops continued as the C-47s that had
launched the First BEP headed back to Hanoi. Until the airstrip was
serviceable, everything would have to arrive by parachute or free-
fall. Iron picket posts for the barbed wire, ammunition, heavy
weapons, electric generators, gasoline stoves, explosives, blankets,
empty sandbags, corrugated roofing, water purifiers, meat and fresh
vegetables, *nuoc mâm* (the fish-sauce staple of the Vietnamese),
wine, beer, and pastis—all tumbled earthward, pushed from the aircraft by sweating "kickers." That afternoon a small bulldozer, needed by the engineers to repair the airstrip, careened into space from
the rear cargo door of a cavernous C-119. It steadied momentarily
under its multiple chutes, yawed, slipped its shrouds, and plummeted earthward in a spectacular free-fall, raising a cloud of dust and
half burying its twisted metal carcass in the ground. A more adequately secured replacement machine was to arrive safely forty-eight
hours later. The chutes of the Eighth "Shock" Colonial Parachute
Battalion of Maj. Pierre Tourret and a heavy-mortar company of
Foreign Legion parachutists blossomed over the valley the same
afternoon.

At noon the next day, after waiting for a sifting rain to lift, the Fifth
Parachute Battalion of the Vietnamese National Army was dropped
on Dien Bien Phu. Commanded by Major Leclerc and with a cadre of
a number of French officers and noncoms, the Bawouan (the rough
Vietnamese pronunciation of BPVN, the abbreviation for Bataillon de
Parachutistes Vietnamiens, the Vietnamese parachute battalion's
French designation) had a mixed reputation. Its Vietnamese troopers—a combination of solid veterans of the colonial infantry, some
former Vietminh, and new recruits—would reflect the inherent con-
tradictions of the French-controlled, non-Communist Vietnamese
government. By nightfall on November 22, 1953, the newly established garrison numbered 4,560 men.

The following day two single-motored, high-winged "Beavers"
landed on the perforated metal stripping laid by the airborne engineers. These solidly built Canadian bush aircraft were ideally suited
for takeoffs and landings on the short, rough airstrips of Indochina.
The first "Beaver" was packed with bicycles. The second delivered
Major General Cogny, commander of Ground Forces, Tonkin, for his
first inspection of Dien Bien Phu.

The forty-nine-year-old Cogny was a tall, impressive artilleryman.
After escaping from a German prison camp in 1941, he had joined
the Resistance. Captured by the Gestapo in 1943 and sent to the
death camps of Buchenwald and Dora, he was liberated in 1945. He
had come to Indochina in 1950 as a member of Marshal de Lattre's
staff and later commanded a division in the Tonkin Delta. This peri-

od of service had convinced him that the delta region, with its dense population, rice production, and proximity to Hanoi, was the key to the war. He had already warned General Navarre of the dangers inherent in shifting units from the delta for action elsewhere. Cogny's attitude toward Operation "Castor" had been ambivalent. Although Colonel Bastiani's strong note objecting to the operation had come out of his headquarters, he had urged the reoccupation of Dien Bien Phu as a "mooring point" for the anti-Vietminh tribal guerrilla units of the region. But the commitment of so many troops to the northwest—particularly the paras that he counted on as a dependable mobile reserve in the delta—was a constant worry. Cogny's flamboyant presence was marked by a bamboo cane and an ever-present cigarette fixed in the corner of his mouth. Cogny and General Navarre, whom Cogny referred to as "the air-conditioned general," were opposites and would never see eye to eye. Ensuing events were destined to produce a feud between them that would continue long after the war.

News of the French assault on Dien Bien Phu soon reached General Giap at his headquarters complex in the mountainous region of Bac Khan, where the limestone hills provided both shelter and cover. This operational center, almost 600 kilometers northeast of Dien Bien Phu, was a beehive of activity as Giap's staff monitored the progression of the 316th Division toward Lai Chau and prepared to launch two other divisions in the direction of Laos. Members of the Vietminh Central Committee, of which Giap was a member, had recently gathered in the mountain redoubt to carry out the directives of Ho Chi Minh and plan strategy for the winter and spring campaigns of 1953–1954. It had been decided to "liberate" Lai Chau and the entire northwest region: launch an offensive into central Laos, keep a substantial portion of regular forces hidden and ready for action, intensify guerrilla attacks in the Tonkin Delta, and begin an offensive in the Central Highlands of South Vietnam to secure "liberated zones" in areas held by the "puppet regime" of Saigon.

Aware that General Navarre would react in some way to his moves on Lai Chau and Laos, Giap had been faced with the problem of troop allotment. He could have directed his main battle force to counter the real threat of a French offensive from the north delta region toward the Vietminh rear. This option would have meant confronting the enemy on flat terrain, where artillery, tanks, and aircraft would provide the French with an obvious advantage. The other alternative had been to choose a more favorable topography where French implantation was relatively weak and the enemy would have to reinforce his strength by drawing on units assigned to the delta. The northwestern territories provided the ideal theater of operations for this second option. There the rough jungle country would reduce the mobility of the enemy, make resupply difficult, and cut the effectiveness of his armor, artillery, and aircraft. The same thick jungle would provide cover for the movement of Giap's divisions while guerrilla attacks were intensified on the enemy's weak spots in the Tonkin Delta. Giap, his staff, and his Chinese advisers had chosen the second option.

Mao Tse-tung had agreed to supply a Chinese Military Advisory Group to North Vietnam in 1950 at the request of Ho Chi Minh. The Chinese Communist leader had warned Ho that the officers he would be sending were of peasant stock, with little formal education. This fact was hardly an obstacle considering the Vietminh need for experienced instructors. General Wei Guoqing, who was from Guangxi Province and was a veteran of the epic "Long March," had crossed the border into North Vietnam on August 12, 1950, with seventy-nine officers and 250 men. This top secret initiative was the beginning of an ambitious program that would send Vietminh regiments to China for training and rearmament, place Chinese advisers in the headquarters of Vietminh regiments and battalions, and provide Chinese specialist troops, such as antiaircraft crews, artillery experts, and engineers, to serve with some Vietminh units.

The scale of the French seizure of Dien Bien Phu convinced Giap that this was the reaction that he had been waiting for. It may have come sooner than expected, and the details remained sketchy, but a six-battalion airdrop constituted a major tactical move. It also posed a number of questions. What were the enemy's intentions? Did he plan to remain in place? Was he going to defend Lai Chau? Would he bring in reinforcements? Was he planning another Na-San at Dien Bien Phu? These questions would remain unanswerable for some time. Nonetheless, considering the threat posed by the French initiative, an urgent decision had to be made. Giap ordered the 316th Division to attack Lai Chau as soon as possible, block the garrison's retreat route south, and intercept any relief column sent from Dien Bien Phu. At the same time three other divisions, the 308th "Iron," the 312th, and the 351st "Heavy," were preparing to move toward Dien Bien Phu. Explaining his reaction to Operation "Castor," General Giap would later write, "For us, the *parachutage* at Dien Bien Phu remained a fundamentally favorable opportunity."

By November 23, Gilles's paras were pushing battalion-strength patrols north and south from Dien Bien Phu. These sorties into hostile territory proved exhausting and hazardous. The paras moved with difficulty through the rough terrain, fording mountain torrents, cutting through heavy tropical growth, examining deserted villages, and sprinting across potentially treacherous stretches of open ground. The jungle guarded its secrets, and the danger of ambush was real. White butterflies fluttered in the shadows, and sinuous leeches slipped into boot tops and beneath clothing in search of warm blood. The perspiring paras were constantly aware of their own vulnerability. Only the sounds of their progress—the clink of equipment, the static of the field radios, and the thud and shuffle of boots—broke the surrounding silence. Morane spotter planes hovered over the patrols like nervous mosquitoes, ready to coordinate B-26 strikes and artillery fire in the event of any enemy action. The light aircraft were reassuring, but the battle-wise paras also knew that they were a dead giveaway of their presence and progression.

Reports from the returning patrols were not good. Bréchignac's battalion had run into stiff enemy resistance not far from Dien Bien Phu along the piste Pavie, the old colonial road linking the strongpoint to Lai Chau. This was the route to be used by the garrison of Lai Chau and the T'ai partisans for Operation "Pollux," the code name for their imminent withdrawal to Dien Bien Phu. The proximity and combativity of Vietminh regulars north of the valley was a clear indication that the enemy, despite the mauling received in Operation "Castor," had not been scared off. By November 25, the 148th Vietminh Regiment and elements of the 316th Division had been identified on the approaches to the surrounding hills. This was serious news, presaging a continual buildup of Giap's forces over the coming months. It was of particular significance to the officers and men of the GCMA (Groupement de Commandos Mixtes Aéroportés, "Composite Airborne Commando Group"; later the GMI—Groupement Mixte d'Intervention, "Composite Intervention Group"). The planning for Operation "Castor" called for these French-led tribal guerrillas—directed by the French Intelligence Service—to use Dien Bien Phu as an operational base and haven. This plan would be impossible if the Vietminh controlled the approaches to the fortified camp.

The GCMA had already proved its worth in the mountainous regions. These Meo, Man, Yao, Lolo, and White, Black, and Red T'ai tribesmen, operating on their own home territory, had become a constant threat to the encroaching Vietminh. Their raids, ambushes, and intelligence gathering had forced Giap to assign several battalions of his best troops in an intense effort to ferret them out. The successful evacuation of Na-San had been accomplished without fighting or losses thanks in large part to the screening action provided by 3,500 Meo tribesmen commanded by a French captain and a few noncommissioned officers. The Meo, whose villages were high in the mountains, had a warrior tradition and made a living from the opium trade. No other assignment in the French army would find a sergeant or corporal commanding a unit of battalion strength.

The GCMA was fighting a unique type of warfare, calling for a special type of soldier. Capt. Déodat Puy-Montbrun was one of them.

Four times wounded, holder of nineteen citations and a *commandeur de la Légion d'honneur* at thirty-six, Puy-Montbrun led his mixed-race commando group on innumerable hazardous operations behind enemy lines. Slipping ashore on moonless nights or dropping into jungle clearings armed with silencer-equipped weapons, infrared night scopes, handguns, and fighting knives, Puy-Montbrun's commandos ambushed enemy patrols, kidnapped or eliminated Vietminh political officers and cadre, and acted as first in, last out support for more classic operations. The insecurity created by the GMCA became a constant irritant to Giap and his planners.

In the mountains the French GCMA cadre lived with the tribesmen, learning their language, culture, and mores. They subsisted on the local diet, including portions of sticky rice and the occasional pork or chicken. On long treks into enemy territory, snake, monkey, wild pig, or forest deer might be added to the diet. They drank green tea and *choum*, the local rice wine. Tenuous radio links with the outside world brought in rare supply drops, including army rations of bully beef and pastis, cognac, and vinogel, a jellylike concentrate of wine to be mixed with water.

Some GCMA officers and noncoms spent years in the jungle. They taught the partisans small-unit tactics and how to use modern weapons and radios. They learned fieldcraft and the traditional techniques of guerrilla warfare from the tribesmen. Some took tribal women as wives, thus strengthening close ties to their allies. Marriage to the daughter of a tribal headman was considered a judicious move. But the men of the GCMA were not living an isolated, paradisiacal idyll. Malaria, fevers, and dysentery were common. Cuts and scratches festered quickly in the jungle. Proper medical care was unavailable, and otherwise treatable wounds could prove fatal.

Caporal Chef Robert Blondeau of the GCMA, a radio operator with a three-man team in command of a T'ai partisan company in the region of Lai Chau, remembers his team leader with fondness.

> Lieutenant David was a larger-than-life character who was on good terms with Deo Van Long. He was an adventurer, a true *filibustier*. He was a hard drinker who smoked two or three pipes of opium a day, but a true leader, worshiped by his men. He spoke T'ai and other tribal languages, wore no insignia of rank, dressed in shorts, and often went barefoot. With his education he could have been at home drinking tea in a Prince of Wales suit. He always wore the red beret of the parachutists; it was the only uniform item that told you he was a soldier.
>
> Once General Cogny arranged a meeting with some visiting British officers from Malaya. David greeted them in his shorts, stripped to

the waist and barefoot. The British stared at him in disbelief. Finally one of them asked, "But where are your shoes?"

The operational parameters of Blondeau's team were broad, allowing considerable scope for improvisation.

> Our job was to bring the T'ai population back to the Lai Chau region and to form maquis to fight the Vietminh. I was in the mountains for two and a half years. It was an adventurous life. We felt we were doing something worthwhile. We had excellent relations with the T'ai. Our orders came from Cogny's headquarters in Hanoi and from Deo Van Long. No one day was like another. We were always on the move and never stayed in one sector more than fifteen days. We received airdrops of food and supplies, but mostly we lived like the T'ai and ate rice. Salt and opium served as money, and our partisans were paid in air-dropped salt.

It was a war without quarter. Members of the GCMA had been labeled as "pirates" by the Vietminh. If captured, the best they could expect was a quick death after a violent interrogation. But summary justice in the jungle was not all one-sided.

Blondeau was northwest of Dien Bien Phu with a Meo commando group in early 1953.

> We were attacked, and the Viet took the mother of a Meo prisoner. That afternoon the Meo turned in all their arms. When I asked them why, they said, "We don't want to lose French arms while settling a personal matter." They sat by the fire that night sharpening their knives. The sound kept me awake. They were gone before dawn. A few days later they returned with the heads of five Vietminh in a bloody piece of tenting.

Punishment in the mountains was quick and without reprieve. "We had two Vietminh prisoners, regionals," Blondeau explains. "Two kids about ten or twelve brought them a meal of rice in a musette bag. We searched the bag and found a grenade. All four were shot on the spot. We left them where they fell before moving on."

Such incidents were light-years away from the sanitized atmosphere of General Navarre's headquarters in Saigon. Military traditionalists with little understanding or sympathy for special operations held the key positions in the French Expeditionary Corps. GCMA officers often had to fend for themselves and improvise. At one point Captain Puy-Montbrun unofficially "recuperated" a number of Sten submachine guns. For GCMA purposes, he needed silencers for the Stens.

Such nonregulation items were unavailable, but Puy-Montbrun stepped out of channels and took his problem to a friend, M. Perrier, the director of the Saigon Police. The silencers were produced by the police-arms workshop, and the giveaway chatter of the noisy Stens was considerably reduced. Puy-Montbrun's men, the ultimate masters of stealth, sometimes used a crossbow. "Imagine," he recalls with a laugh, "if I'd told the headquarters' operations division that!" Later, Puy-Montbrun, assigned as the deputy commander of a newly formed helicopter unit, suggested that armed choppers could be used to good effect. He was told that firing from helicopters would be both impossible and impractical. "No one in the [French] High Command," Puy-Montbrun laments, "could see further than his pencil."

Like many battle plans, the detailed orders for Operation "Pollux" represented the best effort of headquarters. The three-phase withdrawal from Lai Chau had begun as early as November 15, when a detachment of partisans began an eighty-kilometer forced march south along the piste Pavie to arrive at Dien Bien Phu on November 24. The following day, the first C-47 touched down on the airstrip, opening the way for the airlift of regulars from Lai Chau to Dien Bien Phu. The T'ai rearguard, scheduled to make their way out on foot, were not so lucky. The Vietminh had arrived at Lai Chau much earlier than projected in the planning for Operation "Pollux." They, too, had their "loyal" T'ai scouts to guide them through the mountains, and some of the enemy's regulars had been recruited from the jungle tribes.

The partisans of the rearguard slipped away from Lai Chau in small sections through territory already infested with the enemy. The long march south was a constant ordeal, a deadly game of hide-and-seek along narrow forest trails, where the heavy silence could be broken by a snapping twig and the play of light and shadow conjured up nonexistent threats. But the real threats were there, erupting as sudden fire from well-set ambushes or the bracketing blast of exploding mortar rounds. The GCMA had received orders to provide cover to the withdrawing partisans, but they, too, had become the hunted. The 316th Vietminh Division rushed to cut the escape routes.

Robert Blondeau had been captured after a Vietminh attack on a post held by his partisan group, but he later managed to escape with two wounded men. "We hid from Viet patrols for twelve hours," he recalls. "As the enemy was chasing the Lai Chau garrison in a southwesterly direction, I decided to head north." The three men moved through the jungle for five days without water, almost dying from thirst.

One morning, as Blondeau rested in the undergrowth at the edge of Provincial Route 41, he noted some unexpected movement. "The entire road got up and moved!" He had almost blundered onto a well-camouflaged Vietminh battalion. Heart pounding, he watched as the heavily armed *bo doï* ended their break and moved on toward Dien Bien Phu. Exhaustion and the lack of food and water were having their effect on the three escapees. They were gripped by fever, hallucinations, and delirium. Blondeau awakened in the middle of the night to find himself shouting incoherently. They finally reached a French post, but there was no flag, no sign of life. They did not know whether it had been occupied by the enemy until an observation aircraft appeared and dropped a message attached to a streamer. Elated that the post was still in French hands, Blondeau led his wounded charges out of the jungle only to come under automatic-weapons fire from the nervous garrison. Luckily, one of the wounded men was black. The presence of an African among the ragged trio convinced the post's commander that he was dealing with members of the French Expeditionary Corps, and he ordered his men to cease fire.

A helicopter soon chuffed in over the trees to evacuate the wounded to Dien Bien Phu, but Blondeau's ordeal was not over. The departing chopper was still a distant spot in the sky when the enemy attacked. Unwilling to give away their positions, the Vietminh had allowed the escapees to pass through their lines and the helicopter to come and go before launching a two-battalion assault on the post. The garrison, including Blondeau, managed to disengage, leave the post, and begin the long trek south with the Viet at their heels.

Fortunately for the garrison, a T'ai noncom, chief of a partisan commando group, was there to guide them through the jungle. Adj. Luong Van Ou had been trained as a parachutist, a radio operator, and a medic. He was a veteran of numerous special missions in northwest Vietnam. The small, wiry soldier had the self-assurance and modesty of a true survivor. The escape of the harassed column now depended on his tracking skills and ability to second-guess the enemy. He had been leading the mixed detachment through the jungle for seven days without food when one of those curious incidents that seldom find their way into official reports occurred. "We were starving," Luong Van Ou explains.

At 1100 one morning a "Dakota" [C-47] appeared and dropped supplies to us. The Viet were on a high hill nearby and saw the drop. They, too, hadn't eaten for days. There was a race for the DZ, and we arrived at the same time. We fought over the food, pulling and tugging at the containers, using our fists and kicking each other. Everyone was so tired and hungry we forgot about using our weapons. They finally went off, dragging their share. We ate and slept that night. They attacked us the next morning. It was the first of eleven ambushes.

Luong Van Ou shakes his head, remembering the scuffle for food on the DZ. "I tell that story to people," he murmurs, "but they don't believe it."

As Luong Van Ou led the column south, they picked up French, Moroccan, and Algerian stragglers from other units that had been overrun. They moved day and night, fighting off continual attacks. The same drama was being enacted on other trails where similar groups were attempting to reach Dien Bien Phu. There were still many days of privation and death ahead.

At Dien Bien Phu the defensive "hedgehog" was growing bristles. The air bridge from Hanoi was now functioning. C-47s, Bristol 170 "Freighters," and requisitioned civilian aircraft were tailing each other at short intervals onto the metal-topped runway, talked down from a precarious, stilted control tower on the edge of the strip. Unloading crews manhandled the cargoes onto waiting trucks before the empty aircraft taxied into position for takeoff. Despite their aversion to pick-and-shovel work, the paras had done a creditable job of digging in and laying more fields of barbed wire. Engineer officers, their eyes on the clock and the calendar, were supervising the effort and planning more elaborate permanent bunkers, dugouts, fire bases, and communication trenches. They were already expressing concern over the paucity of local hard timber for construction and the time that it took to receive building supplies requested from Hanoi. Batteries of the Colonial Artillery had arrived to install their 105-millimeter howitzers in sandbagged positions not far from the strip.

By December 8, three of Brigadier General Gilles's para battalions, the First Colonial, the Sixth Colonial, and the Second Battalion of the First Regiment of Chasseurs, had begun an airlift out of the valley. The Fifth Bawouan was scheduled for a later departure. Gilles was not pleased at having to leave the First BEP and the Eighth "Shock" Battalion behind, but at last he would be able to leave Dien Bien Phu and turn over his command to his successor. Col. Christian Marie Ferdinand de la Croix de Castries had been handpicked by General Navarre to command the entrenched camp. Like Navarre, de Castries was a cavalry officer, with all the traditional panache that that title implied. He had fought with distinction early in World War II, been captured by the Germans, and escaped. He later commanded armored units under Navarre's orders in France and Germany. His early assignments to Indochina in 1946 and 1951 had added to his reputation for dash and courage. His battle wounds and citations proved that his aristocratic aplomb was not merely the pose of a military fop. Just prior to his Dien Bien Phu assignment, de Castries had commanded a *groupe mobile* in a "hot" zone of the delta.

Colonel de Castries arrived in the valley sporting a shooting stick, a foulard, and the red *calot*, or peaked overseas cap, of his old cavalry regiment, the North African spahis. After a briefing in the CP, General Gilles took de Castries on a tour of his new command, pointing out the fortified positions, the support installations, and the topography. They did not have much in common, but they did share a dislike for static, defensive warfare. Navarre had selected de Castries to activate his plan for offensive action against the Vietminh, using Dien Bien Phu as a base. He had also promised de Castries to send tanks to spearhead his mobile operations. The fact that the paras were being bloodied even during routine patrols outside the defense perimeter indicated the fragility of such grandiose plans. A major effort to rescue one of the T'ai units retreating from Lai Chau would soon underline the dangers of such an illusion.

Colonel Langlais had returned to Dien Bien Phu on December 8 with de Castries to take command of the remaining battalions of the airborne battle group. He still favored his half-healed broken ankle, but he had talked his way past the doctors. Although he managed to hide the real pain that he was suffering, his staff quickly found him a mountain pony to ease his movements. Two days after his arrival, Langlais was ordered to move north with his three para battalions to rescue a T'ai company surrounded at Muong Pon, eighteen kilometers north of Dien Bien Phu.

The next morning, while the Eighth "Shock" Battalion struck off into the jungle for a trek that would bring them in position to the enemy's rear, the First BEP of the Foreign Legion and the Fifth Bawouan started their march along the piste Pavie. The Vietminh were waiting only 300 meters beyond the forward French observation post. Lieutenant Roux, a platoon leader, had never heard such heavy firing.

> They had as many submachine guns as we did, and, in addition, theirs—I think they were Skodas—had a higher rate of fire. There was no question of maneuvering. The point platoon drove back the Viets. We waited on the trail, flat on our stomachs, because there was too much iron flying. We couldn't see ten meters ahead. We didn't know where our friends or the Viet were. For the moment it was impossible to fire or do anything. I had to calm some of my Vietnamese [paras] who had already cocked their submachine guns and sent some bursts into the surrounding bush to build up their courage.

When the Vietminh withdrew, the First BEP evacuated their casualties and continued toward Muong Pon. The presence of the enemy forced the column off the road, and Langlais decided to progress along the difficult mountain ridges. His paras began a race against time to save the beleaguered company. As Lieutenant Roux's platoon struggled up a steep slope, a small group of French paras appeared, returning from a jungle patrol. "The Viets are right behind us," they warned. "Enjoy yourselves." Once again the jungle proved an indomitable enemy. The morass of intertwining vines, fallen trees, thick, high buffalo grass, and impenetrable stands of bamboo slowed progress to a crawl. But Langlais kept his men moving, cutting through the green wall with machetes and entrenching tools, driven by the continued radio appeals for help.

On the morning of December 13, the exhausted relief column was close enough to Muong Pon to hear the rattle of firing. Then the firing stopped. When the paras entered the village later that day, they found it deserted, the huts smoldering. The Vietminh had pulled out, taking most of the dead and the wounded and prisoners with them. The Eighth "Shock" Battalion arrived to join the column on December 14. Langlais and his men were bitterly disappointed. They had come so far, they had made such an effort, and their mission had failed.

Now the isolated battalions faced the trek back to Dien Bien Phu. The Vietminh, well aware of the relief force's arrival at Muong Pon, soon brought the paras under heavy machine-gun fire and launched assaults designed to fragment the column. The ridges and gorges echoed to the din of small-arms fire as the paras fought their way south. The Fifth Bawouan was almost overrun. A fierce enemy assault matched Vietnamese against Vietminh in vicious hand-to-hand fighting. Langlais managed to relay a desperate request for air support through the hovering spotter plane, and a flight of fighter-bombers roared in over the trees to lay a searing curtain of napalm on the attackers. But the contact between the Vietnamese paras and the Viet had been so close that the Fifth Bawouan lost some men in the flaming holocaust.

After fighting their way to the top of a hill, Lieutenant Roux's platoon of the First BEP found themselves facing a reinforced enemy heavy-weapons company. Roux reported hearing the sound of bamboo being cut. He was told that the enemy were probably preparing litters for their wounded. Although he would have liked to believe that analysis, the lieutenant asked for artillery fire on the enemy positions. The guns were almost out of range, and the requested bombardment was meager and disbursed. As Roux's platoon left the hill, the Vietminh broke cover at 500 meters in hot pursuit. The bamboo chopping that he had heard had been their preparation for the assault. Roux directed machine-gun fire into a human wave of attackers. "We didn't have to aim," he stated. "Every shot hit its target." The para battalions leapfrogged each other, sharing the point and the rearguard, trying to keep their withdrawal orderly and making the enemy pay dearly for each attack. The two batteries of 105-millimeter howitzers in support of the operation laid a barrage behind the rearguard and pounded the jungle and hills surrounding the trail.

During a pause, while the chaplain prayed briefly over the hastily dug graves of the First BEP's dead, Lieutenant Roux and his men saw a group of Foreign Legion prisoners on the hill opposite. They were being led off by the Vietminh, hands tied behind their backs. Moving at night with the rearguard through a "sea of bamboo," Roux lost contact with the noncom in front of him. "I was haunted by the thought of finding myself nose to nose with the Viet in waiting on the next hill." Passing through a pitch-black gorge, the paras broke off chunks of phosphorescent, decayed logs and fixed them to their packs so that the men could follow each other. Entering the Muong Thanh Valley, they stopped at the river to drink from their helmets. Then they crossed two kilometers of rice paddies and reentered the defense perimeter of Dien Bien Phu. After being greeted with a glass of pastis and a plate of *bifteck-frites*, Roux sought out his bedroll and fell asleep. "But in my sleep I was still marching. That night trek had been exhausting. In a few hours we'd retraced the distance it had taken us two days to cover. I didn't stop marching till I awoke the next morning."

Colonel Langlais limped back into Dien Bien Phu grim-faced and angry, realizing how close his paras had come to disaster. The First BEP alone had suffered twenty-eight dead or missing and twenty-four wounded. One did not have to be a graduate of Saint-Cyr or the École de Guerre to see—in light of this abortive and costly sortie—that Navarre's plan for ranging the countryside in pursuit of the enemy was an optimistic dream. But the French High Command seemed numb to its implications. Colonel de Castries's tanks were being prepared for airlift, and an operation to prove that the strongpoint had not been isolated was imminent.

The survivors of the Lai Chau rearguard filtered into the valley during the next few weeks. Three French officers, thirty-four noncoms, and over 2,000 partisans of the rearguard had begun the march. One French officer, nine noncoms, and 175 partisans reached the safety of Dien Bien Phu. The remnants of the T'ai regular battalions and the partisans were depressed and bitter. Despite previous French promises, they had been forced to leave their homeland. Although some dependents had shared the grueling march, entire families had been left behind in the now-unprotected villages.

Many tribesmen reported as missing had elected to slip into the jungle in an attempt to protect their wives and children. The escapees led by Adj. Luong Van Ou did not reach Dien Bien Phu till January 1, 1954.

The tightening of Giap's ring of steel around Dien Bien Phu emphasized the strongpoint's dependence on air supply and tactical support. From the eight of December, four air force F8F "Bearcat" fighters were based on the airstrip, along with one helicopter and six light observation-liaison aircraft. The proximity of the fighters had contributed to the survival of Lieutenant Colonel Langlais's paras, and their presence gave everyone an added sense of security. More "Bearcats" would soon join "Air Base 195." But air force commanders in Vietnam, unenthusiastic about Operation "Castor" from the beginning, were not reassured. The lack of weather reports from the mainland of China and imprecise, dated maps of the region were reducing operational efficiency. Fears that the dense rains of the Tonkinese *crachin* would often delay takeoffs until noon or later were proving only too true. The air force reported: "Conditions on one slope of the Annamite Mountain Chain are never the same as [on] the opposite slope. It is rare that both the take-off zone and the operational zone benefit from good weather." This simple truth was serious enough for the transport fleet, but a no-fly situation could have tragic consequences if bombers and fighters were grounded when they were needed for close and immediate air support.

The increase in the enemy's antiaircraft capability was even more troubling. In a secret operational report to Paris covering the month of December, Gen. Henri Charles Lauzin, chief of the French air force, Far East, had noted, "As predicted at the end of October, the number of the enemy's AA weapons increased considerably. Still limited to 20mm guns, this AA was particularly active and accurate." The same report recorded enemy hits on twenty-four fighters, four bombers, sixteen transports, and nine observation aircraft. Lauzin pointed out that the required repairs had meant the loss of 470 flying hours. General Dechaux's Northern Tactical Air Group was already stretched thin, responding to requests for air support at Dien Bien Phu, in northern Laos, in the Tonkin Delta, and north of Hanoi. Air force fighters and B-26 bombers were bolstered by navy "Helldiver" dive-bombers and "Hellcat" fighters from the French aircraft carrier *Arromanches* operating offshore in the Gulf of Tonkin. The heavy bomb loads of eight land-based "Privateer" bombers capable of long-range missions added "punch" to the navy's contribution.

The need to interdict the movement of Vietminh troops and supplies toward Dien Bien Phu and attack the enemy engineers and *dan cong*, or civilian labor detachments, working on Provincial Routes

13 and 41 now put a heavy strain on air force and naval air capabilities. Officially, the French could list 173 combat aircraft and close to eighty transport planes. In reality, mechanical failure, enemy action, normal repairs, engine-part delays, personnel losses, and illness cut the actual airborne figure by almost half. Like doctors on continual emergency duty, the overworked aircrews dragged themselves to their aircraft whenever the *crachin* lifted to fly bombing, strafing, and resupply missions. The pilots did not have to watch their tail or scan the sky for enemy aircraft. Their nemesis lay below. A dense, challenging, green-gray canopy of jungle stretched to the horizon, concealing both targets and enemy antiaircraft batteries.

In late December the French High Command made a last attempt to prove that Dien Bien Phu could still be reached by land. Lieutenant Colonel Langlais and his paras were ordered to move southwest of Dien Bien Phu on December 21 and cross the Laotian border to link up with a column of Franco-Laotian troops at the village of Sop Nao. Langlais's portion of the operation was named Operation "Régate" ("Regatta"), and the long, northward march of the other force was labeled Operation "Ardèche" (a French department). On December 23 the Laotians, Moroccans, and Legionnaires of Operation "Ardèche" and the paras of Operation "Régate" met in Sop Nao. Their junction was covered by a group of journalists specially brought in by chopper for the event. Colonel de Castries was also present, having landed the previous day on a short strip hacked out of the jungle to accommodate his light liaison aircraft. Cameras clicked and whirred, but the brief ceremony could not hide the truth.

The 200-kilometer trek of the Operation "Ardèche" column had been a painful ordeal. Harassed by pro-Communist Pathet Lao guerrillas and forced to fight a pitched battle with a battalion of the 148th Vietminh Regiment for the key village of Muong Khoua, the exhausted soldiers looked more like survivors than victors. Many were suffering from fever, including typhoid, or dysentery. Brigitte Friang, a tanned and petite French government war correspondent and former Resistance member, had parachuted in to join the column. She was struck by the fact that the emaciated troops reminded her of her fellow inmates in the wartime Nazi death camps.

Langlais's paras, although their route had covered only fifty kilometers, had found the jungle march equally difficult. Once the ceremony had ended, de Castries and the journalists left. The two columns parted. The paras took a different return route to Dien Bien Phu, constantly shadowed by the enemy. Dixie Reese, a photographer from the American Aid Mission in Saigon, who had always wanted to try his hand as a war correspondent, had joined the paras at Sop Nao. Boarding a medevac helicopter with little notice, he had arrived in the jungle wearing a necktie and polished oxfords and carrying two cameras, a bag filled with photographic equipment, and a bottle of sour-mash bourbon. The two-day return march with the paras convinced Reese that there must be easier ways to cover a war. The column shuffled through the defensive wire surrounding Dien Bien Phu on the day after Christmas.

Army information officers in Saigon and Hanoi announced the troop linkup with enthusiasm, as if the hollow maneuver had been a victory of some kind. But no amount of official tub-thumping would ever convince the men who had participated in Operation "Régate" and Operation "Ardèche" that their effort had been worthwhile. From now on the paras would fight their battles in the valley of Dien Bien Phu and the surrounding hills.

3

Movement
in the Mountains

*"We could choose our time to attack or to rest while the enemy
had to remain dug in, living in fear of an attack and the
anguish common to all troops under siege."*
General Vo Nguyen Giap in his book Dien Bien Phu

General Giap had made his decision. Every French move had
confirmed Navarre's intention to remain at Dien Bien Phu. Here,
finally, was the opportunity to destroy some of the enemy's best battalions in a favorable tactical situation. The isolated jungle trails suddenly teemed with activity. The sounds were those of movement, the
soft, steady padding of sandaled feet and the occasional clank of
metal. Snakelike files of coolies wound down the steep slopes,
crossed ravines, and passed newly constructed, thatch-roofed checkpoints. Some of the coolies were stripped to the waist, and sweat
glistened on their bare chests. Heavy loads pressed down on their
makeshift shoulder padding, and the muscles of their straining
calves swelled and twitched with their efforts. They came singly and
in teams of two or four: one man with a mortar baseplate high on
his shoulders, strapped into a crude bamboo carrying frame; two
men struggling, sinking ankle-deep into the churned mud of the
trail, with a wheel slung between them on a swaying carrier pole;
four men passing, stepping carefully, the muscle-tearing weight of a
breechblock bearing them down, sucking the breath from their
lungs. The checkpoint huts sagged with dampness, and thin shreds

31

of thatching hung over the doorless entrances. Relief crews squatted nearby, eating sticky rice and waiting for the order to shoulder another load. Vietminh sapper officers in tan uniforms, wearing cloth-covered sun helmets, conferred beside the trails with political cadres garbed in peasant black, with checked cotton scarves knotted around their necks. Wooden sledges drawn by small mountain ponies skidded by, bearing the weight of squat, dismounted seventy-five-millimeter howitzer barrels or mortar tubes. Long files of bicycles, each loaded with up to 200 kilograms of rice, and cyclos carrying everything from radio equipment to vegetables were pushed along the tortuous roads and trails.

This was a general mobilization, a modern-day manifestation of the ancient Vietnamese saying "In time of conflict or menace, all the population—men, women, old people, children—will become soldiers." The major effort to support the move on Dien Bien Phu reached far beyond northwest Vietnam. Delta rice was spirited past French outposts by sampan, and medicines purchased on the black market in Hong Kong and Bangkok were backpacked in from the border regions and the coast. Even segments of bombed-out rail lines were reestablished. An unnamed French general, writing in a secret report on Indochina requested by the Far East High Command (responsible for all French forces in Asia) in 1955, stated, "They [the Vietminh] used small rail cars pushed by coolies running barefoot along the track bed. Each coolie pushed for a distance of 10 kilometers. . . . Jeeps were mounted on rail car wheels. In addition the Vietminh used horses, sampans, wagons and bicycles."

The main supply line started at the Chinese border, took Provincial Route 13 to the Red River, and branched onto Provincial Route 41 to the main Vietminh supply depot of Tuan Giao, eighty kilometers northeast of Dien Bien Phu. Smaller feeder trails were also used to move men, equipment, and matériel. Elements of the 308th Division had already passed on their way south. The 312th and the 351st, with its heavy artillery and engineers, were following at the marching rate of thirty kilometers a day and more at night. Giap's uniformed regulars wore cheaply made tennis shoes or sandals and woven sun helmets netted and covered with a camouflage of small, leafy twigs. They carried their individual weapons: captured French and drum-fed Chinese submachine guns, Chinese or Soviet carbines, and modern Czech automatic rifles. Stumpy Chinese stick grenades protruded from the multiple pockets of their carrying sacks. Cloth sausage rolls holding fifteen kilograms of rice were slung over one shoulder, and canteens hung at their waists. Enameled cups emblazoned with the red flags of China, the USSR, and the Vietminh were attached to their packs. The bo doï's average age was from eighteen to twenty years. Most of their officers were in their mid- or late twenties. The columns left the trail during breaks in the march to seek cover in foliage-screened gulleys and heavy bush. The Vietminh infantry had a healthy respect for the destructive capacity of patrolling French aircraft. They kept their heads down, showing only the top of their camouflaged helmets. The Vietminh art of camouflage was highly developed and systematic. "Approaching a danger zone," one French officer wrote in the French High Command report, "each Vietminh soldier picks leaves and foliage of matching colors and places them in the small disk on the pack of the man in front of him." An air force officer also attested to the enemy's camouflage skill. "In my career [as a pilot] I've flown over Moroccan, Italian, German, and even British adversaries, but I have never felt such a sensation of flying over a vacuum as above Vietminh territory."

Although some of Giap's men were veterans of jungle warfare or had come originally from the mountains, many were from the cities and deltas. They faced the same disorientation and hardships in the tropical forest as their French enemies. Although the way stations and checkpoints were sometimes supplied with medicines, the stocks were low. Malaria, typhoid, dysentery, and jungle fevers, coupled with exhaustion, took their toll of the city dwellers. Political officers continually checked the morale of the men, reiterating the importance of their patriotic task, reminding them of their goal, and leading them in marching songs: "It's raining, our clothing is soaked, but not our hearts."

Col. Bui Tin was a twenty-seven-year-old battalion commander in 1954. Joining the Vietminh in September 1945, he had served in central Vietnam and later as a sentry at Ho Chi Minh's headquarters in Hanoi prior to the outbreak of the Franco-Vietnamese conflict. He recalls the grim toll of noncombat deaths and injuries.

> Our men died in many ways. They lost their way, they fell from high bridges, [they] suffered from appendicitis, and venomous snakebites often meant instant death. Tree falls during typhoons crushed them in their hammocks. Flash floods were very dangerous. There were fevers, malaria, even tiger attacks, and the small jungle leeches attached themselves during the night so a man would awake weakened and covered by his own blood.
>
> We took what precautions we could. General Giap issued special orders on hygiene that were distributed to our units. Drinking water was to be boiled. The troops were to use clean socks after washing their feet in warm water and salt. They should have hot rice with adequate meat and vegetables at least once a day and sleep at least six hours every night. Giap also ordered that hair should be kept short, nails trimmed, and uniforms changed every two or three days.

If the French resupply effort relied on the air force, Giap's offensive preparations depended on the Vietminh engineering detachments, the *dan cong* labor units, and a mass of coolie porters. One of the prime tasks of the engineer officers was to plan and carry out the widening and reinforcement of roadways to support the passage of truck-towed artillery and heavy loads of ammunition. Giap could muster close to 600 Soviet "Molotova" two-and-a-half-ton trucks, a number of American Dodge trucks captured by the Chinese in Korea, and some heavy tractors. The captured American trucks were not the only U.S. equipment in Vietminh hands. Most of their artillery was of U.S. origin. A number of seventy-five-millimeter mountain howitzers captured from Chiang Kai-shek's Nationalist army had been turned over to the Vietminh when the border opened. These had already been in action against the French since late 1950. American 105-millimeter howitzers captured in Korea would supply the Vietminh with additional firepower.

The engineers were also charged with improving existing bridges or building new ones. Log bridges were constructed under the surface of a stream to hide them from French aircraft. Treetops were pulled together with ropes and cables to screen the roads, trails, and bridges. Vehicles were covered with fresh-cut, leafy branches. Tire tracks were obliterated with palm fronds once a truck had passed. Camouflaged antiaircraft positions were dug in to cover difficult stretches of road, including narrow passes and river crossings. A primitive but effective air-warning system put spotters in the trees and on high promontories. Their signals could fill the trails with the clanging of alarm triangles or the shrilling of whistles. The main roads were divided into sections, and each section had its allotment of thirty or forty trucks. The coolies assigned to each section were divided according to their tasks: loaders and unloaders, road-repair squads, and special companies of porters to fill in for the trucks when air attacks knocked out sectors of the road.

French air strikes were a constant hazard. When reconnaisance flights or GCMA patrols reported definite sightings, the air force and naval aircraft pummeled the targets with high-explosive, antipersonnel bombs and napalm. Pilots targeted those sections of road that were the most difficult to repair, particularly along hillsides, where one or two hits could create landslides. To their surprise and frustration, a photo reconnaissance mission two or three days later would often report the cut repaired. The airmen had also noted a steady improvement in Vietminh antiaircraft capability. Their debriefings mentioned the escalation in enemy firepower. The Soviet heavy machine guns that posed a considerable threat had been reinforced by thirty-seven-millimeter antiaircraft guns. Some pilots were sure that they had been under fire from forty-millimeter weapons. Such hazards were supplemented by a curtain of automatic-weapon and rifle fire. The Vietminh had been schooled in directing concentrated small-arms fire at low-flying aircraft, learning to lead targets to compensate for their speed. Though not effective at normal flying altitudes, this tactic could be dangerous on strafing and bombing runs. Some sectors of the road suffered more than others, and casualties among the *dan cong* were often high. There was a shortage of qualified doctors along the trails, but medical students and aid orderlies filled the gaps as best they could, working with a minimum of surgical equipment and a limited supply of drugs.

The political cadre increased its propaganda efforts in a major effort to maintain morale. General Giap was careful to ensure that the *dan cong* were included in his many messages to his troops. Individual *dan cong* killed in action were lauded as heroes of the revolution. Not all the labor force worked with the enthusiasm of true believers. Ablebodied tribal villagers, men and women unlucky enough to find themselves in the path of Giap's advance, were enlisted in the "people's war" as road workers and coolies. From the 35,000 coolies working at the start of the campaign, the number would rise to over 70,000 before the battle ended. Estimates put the number of those involved in the "battle of supply," including uniformed transport and quartermaster units, at close to 300,000. Their efforts would accomplish the monumental task of supporting Giap's assault force of 47,500 men during a six-month campaign over some of the world's most difficult terrain and under constant enemy harassment. They would also accomplish the clandestine movement through the jungle of 144 artillery pieces, thirty-six antiaircraft guns, and a number of twelve-tubed "Katyusha" rocket launchers and the ammunition to go with them. The French High Command had already declared such transport impossible because of the mountains, the lack of passable roads, and the enemy's primitive logistics. If such a miracle ever did take place, they were confident that any Vietminh guns appearing at Dien Bien Phu would be neutralized quickly by artillery fire and air strikes.

Since mid-December Vietminh forward observers and scouts, hidden in the tall elephant grass and bamboo of the hills, had kept the valley under surveillance. They watched as the air bridge delivered reinforcements and more artillery, confirming Navarre's intention to remain at Dien Bien Phu. They also noted the continual clearing work going on in the valley as the garrison cut trees and brush in and around the fortified positions. For the French, it was standard military procedure to open fields of fire and deny close cover to the enemy. For the Vietminh, it meant that the French were stripping themselves naked, forgoing all concealment and revealing clumps of tall radio antennae that marked the exact locations of their principal CPs.

In the valley below, Colonel de Castries was taking a personal interest in the cleanup work. The comments of an officer of the newly arrived Fifth Battalion of the Seventh Algerian Rifle Regiment (Septième Régiment de Tirailleurs Algériens) reveal that not everyone agreed with the clearance orders. "De Castries insisted during his visit that all scrub foliage be cleared immediately," the officer complained. "Our commanding officer argued that the Vietminh—less than 2 kilometers distant—would be able to observe the installation of the entire strongpoint and identify the emplacement of the command posts of the battalion, the companies, and our weapons positions. De Castries insisted." The officer added his own opinion on the incident. "The choice of a cavalryman to defend an entrenched camp was not judicious. The days of mounted charges had passed."

By late December the first platoon of three U.S.-supplied M-24 "Chaffee" tanks airlifted to Dien Bien Phu were ready for action. They had been delivered in two sections—chassis and turret—and reassembled laboriously with a block-and-tackle rig. A total of ten M-24s would soon make up the squadron. Colonel de Castries now had his promised "chargers" even if their operational territory was being reduced daily.

Dien Bien Phu was taking on the aspect of a military city with its own character, rules, and procedures. It was one giant construction site as strategically placed strongpoints were established and manned. Most of these positions were on low hills within the valley. In good weather, construction activity produced hanging veils of gritty dust. High winds could produce windstorms and zephyrs that drove the grit into mechanical equipment and clogged engines. Sudden rains infiltrated the bared soil, producing a sticky, ochre mud that turned the roads into skid paths, destabilized the fortifications, and created concern for what could happen during the *crachin* rains due in February and March. The hard-pressed engineers concentrated on obvious priorities. The central CP, the hospital, the communications center, and the water-purification unit were located underground in log-braced shelters covered with steel sheeting, sandbags, and several layers of earth. Each infantry battalion worked on its own shelters, dugouts, trenches, and weapons emplacements with engineer supervision and support. Much of the hard labor was performed by captured Vietminh designated as *prisonniers-internes militaires,* or PIM. The PIM, the majority of whom had been captured in previous campaigns, whether attached to the pooled work force or remaining with the unit that had captured them, presented a unique case study in wartime human relations. They appeared to have abandoned the dialectical indoctrination of their Communist cadres for a pragmatic acceptance of their own sort and a desire to survive. The work details were long, arduous, and often dangerous, but the PIM lived from day to day. Some PIM detachments had been with a French unit over a long period of time and had almost become an integral part of its companies or battalions. Many were known by name to the French officers and noncoms with whom they had shared long marches and bloody encounters. Some former Vietminh soldiers filled a role equivalent to that of prison trustees and were given an ethereal, unofficial authority in the PIM community. The PIM were to play an important support role in the approaching battle.

The engineer officers gritted their teeth when patrols and sorties took combat troops away from their tasks, delaying the urgent construction work. Engineering matériel was slow in arriving, and what did arrive was far short of the garrison's needs. Some units had neither the skills nor the experience needed for the work, and it showed. Most of these troops had long enjoyed the advantage of superior firepower and air support in clashes with the Vietminh, and few had been exposed to extensive enemy artillery fire. The array of weapons and fighting units at Dien Bien Phu tended to create a false sense of security.

Pierre Schoendoerffer, a young army cameraman who had arrived in early December, was overwhelmed by his first sight of the fortifications. "It's not possible the Vietminh can take a place like this," he told himself. But some veterans soon burst his bubble of optimism, pointing out defects in the defenses and describing Dien Bien Phu as purely a theatrical decor. "We had to clear growth, dig holes, dig, and dig again," Schoendoerffer would later write. "There was a certain lassitude: we had already dug so much, at Hoa-Binh in 1951, at Na-San, Sam Neua, Lai Chau, and the Plain of Jars in 1952, and now we had to keep digging."

But the old soldiers had no such qualms. First Sergeant Bleyer of the Foreign Legion was ordered to install his platoon at the strongpoint baptized "Béatrice" on a series of hills to the northeast of Dien Bien Phu.

> We immediately went to work, clearing brush, cutting trees and building the most solid blockhouses possible, each platoon competing with that intensity particular to the Legion. I could only encourage my men. Having had a little experience during the Russian campaign, I knew the damage that could be done by artillery. My legionnaires— terrific lads—were also well aware of the risks we were running.

Some Legion units used their flamethrowers to burn away the scrub in jets of fire, and the stench of ignited fuel oil hung over the positions. When the dugouts were completed, the hard labor continued. Extensive wire fields were constructed to act as "wave break-ers" during heavy-infantry assaults and channel the attackers into prepared fields of fire. Mines were laid, booby traps set, and canisters of napalm placed, ready for detonation during enemy attacks.

By the twentieth of December, the bulk of the Ninth Groupe Mobile had been airlifted to Dien Bien Phu. GM-9 consisted of two battalions of the Thirteenth demi-Brigade of the Foreign Legion and a battalion from the Third Algerian Rifle Regiment. The arrival of the Thirteenth demi-Brigade was an event akin to the battlefield appearance of Napoleon's "Old Guard." Although the paras of the Legion's First BEP were still in the valley, the presence of the Thirteenth, a traditional line unit, lent a reassuring permanence to the mountain fortress. The Legion had been part of Indochina's military history since the late 1800s. Legionnaires had spearheaded France's colonial conquest of Indochina and participated in the early campaigns against the Black Flag pirates in Tonkin. These included the siege of Tuyen Quang in 1884, when two Legion companies held out for four months against an attacking force of 20,000 Chinese. The more recent honors of the Thirteenth demi-Brigade included the World War II battles of Narvik in Norway and Bir Hakeim in the Libyan Desert. Its solid reputation in Indochina was well established. The Algerians of the Third Rifle Regiment were also dependable troops with a good combat record.

Lt. Col. Jules Gaucher, the Legion officer commanding the Ninth Groupe Mobile, was a legend in his own right. Tall, tough, and iras-cible, the forty-eight-year-old Saint-Cyr graduate had been in Indochina since 1940. Ranging the mountains and deltas at the head of his Legionnaires, he had fought the Japanese, the Vietminh, bands of tribal pirates, and a marauding force of Chinese Nationalist troops. He was no stranger to Dien Bien Phu, having carried out a delaying action there in 1945 against the Japanese before leading his men to safety over the Chinese border. The hard-drinking colonel and his staff, a sort of Legion "mafia," had an equally bellicose reputation for punch-ups in the bars and *dancings* of Hanoi and Saigon during their rare periods of R and R.

Each day brought more reinforcements to Dien Bien Phu: Legion, Algerian, and Moroccan infantry battalions; colonial artillery batteries with a large number of black African gunners; more engineer, signal, and supply units; surgical teams; air force detachments; and intelligence units. There were even sections of the Garde Républicaine and the *gendarmerie* attached to the central headquarters. By Christmas Eve there were 10,910 French Union troops in the valley. All of these troops were fed into the now-established defense system of eight strongpoints linked by radio and field telephone. "Gabrielle" was the farthest north of the village and airstrip, bordering the piste Pavie; "Anne-Marie" was just northwest of the airstrip; "Béatrice" was northeast of the airstrip, at the jungle's edge, where it dominated Route 41; "Huguette" was to the west of the airstrip, and "Dominique" to the east. "Claudine," the central CP, was located in the village itself, southwest of the airstrip, and "Eliane" was to the east, straddling Provincial Route 41. "Isabelle" and a small emergency airfield were located six isolated kilometers south of the other fortifications. The strongpoint "Françoise," west of "Claudine," would be abandoned early on, and secondary positions, such as "Opéra" and "Junon," would be established according to the needs of battle. Although the strongpoints were meant to be mutually supporting, they did not, according to the popular image, form a solid defensive ring around Dien Bien Phu. The origin of their female names remains a mystery. A rumor persists that Colonel de Castries, renowned for his amorous adventures, had appropriated the names of his mistresses. A more sober explanation is that de Castries's headquarters, wishing to change the original alphabetical designations of the positions, had come up with the more distinctive, easily identifiable designations. Whatever the reason, visiting American and British officers found such nomenclature amusing.

There was, however, a real feminine presence at Dien Bien Phu. Pauline Bourgeode, de Castries's secretary, had accompanied the colonel to the fortress. Some members of the Royal T'ai Ballet from Lai Chau, unlucky enough to have missed a flight to Hanoi, shared the shelters of the T'ai detachments. The wives and children of certain Meo and T'ai intelligence operatives were housed in the GCMA position. The Foreign Legion had flown in a number of Vietnamese and Algerian prostitutes, members of two BMC (Bordels Mobiles de Campagne—Mobile Field Bordellos). This tradition had emerged during the Legion's long service in the isolated forts and outposts of the North African desert, where *le cafard*, a depression born of solitude, boredom, and frustration, often led to violence or madness. Since then, the BMC had become as much of a tradition as the Legion's belief that a Legionnaire should be fed a hot meal whenever possible and never be without his *pinard*, the throat-rasping, army-issue red wine. The women of the BMC, like the PIM, were fated to remain at Dien Bien Phu throughout the siege.

General Navarre had decided to make a Christmas visit to the garrison at Dien Bien Phu. Each battalion had organized their own celebration around a spindly, makeshift Christmas tree decorated with colored paper, bits of cotton, and whatever could be found to give the impression of ornaments. Word of the general's presence soon spread from one strongpoint to the next, and some troopers, previously critical of the "air-conditioned general," were pleased by the commander in chief's gesture. Witnesses at the *pot*, or drinks party, offered by Colonel de Castries to mark the visit were less enthusiastic. Navarre appeared as cool, distant, and preoccupied as ever. His brief speech to the gathering of selected officers and men was uninspiring. Pierre Schoendoerffer, who had been filming the general's visit, insinuated himself into a briefing at de Castries's CP. Before being chased out by zealous staff officers, he heard Colonel Piroth, de Castries's artillery commander, assure General Navarre that "no Vietminh cannon would be able to fire more than three rounds without being located." Navarre remained skeptical and expressed his concern at the number of Vietminh supply trucks reported on the road. "We can't cut the trails," he said, but many officers disagreed.

There is little doubt that the general did have a lot on his mind. Operations "Régate" and "Ardèche" had proved the impossibility of maintaining a viable overland link with Dien Bien Phu, repeated appeals to Paris for reinforcements and additional supplies remained unanswered, and intelligence reports were painting an increasingly gloomy picture of the enemy's preparations and capabilities. Four days after his visit to Dien Bien Phu, Navarre ordered Major General Cogny to prepare top secret contingency plans for the possible evacuation of Dien Bien Phu. Navarre cited two situations that could force the evacuation: collapse of the defenses under heavy attacks carried out "with modern means not heretofore used," or "suffocation" of the strongpoint caused by interdiction of the airstrip by enemy artillery or antiaircraft fire. Navarre's order emphasized that, in either case, Dien Bien Phu should not be evacuated until the last moment. The two plans—Operation "Ariane," providing for the rescue of the withdrawing garrison, and Operation "Xenophon," the fighting sortie of the garrison to the south—were not be be revealed to the commanders at Dien Bien Phu. At about the same time, Navarre received a secret telegram from Major General Cogny informing him that elements of the Vietminh 308th and 316th Divisions had established observation posts and defensive positions to prevent any French withdrawal from Dien Bien Phu and oppose the sortie of deep-reconnaissance patrols. The seriousness of this new enemy implantation was obvious. The Vietminh elements consisted of "4 battalions of infantry and 2 anti-aircraft companies on the west slope; 4 or 5 battalions of infantry and 2 anti-aircraft companies facing east." Another terse telegram to Hanoi headquarters in early January requesting air support revealed the extent of enemy activity close to the fortified camp.

FM: GROUP OPERATIONAL NORTHWEST
TO: GROUND FORCES NORTH VIETNAM
SECRET
FOR OPERATIONS DIVISION

REQUEST 12TH JANUARY 1954—STOP—SOON AS WEATHER FAVORABLE—STOP—MASSIVE BOMBARDMENT BENEFIT G.O.N.O. [GROUPE OPERATIONAL

NORD-OUEST—GROUP OPERATIONAL NORTHWEST]—STOP—2,000 V.M. [VIET-
MINH] INSTALLING AND DIGGING TRENCHES IN WOODED ZONE AT 3KM
NORTHWEST OF BAN TAU [VILLAGE]—STOP

The telegram went on to list the grid coordinates and warn that friendly-troop positions were four kilometers south of the objective. A penned note scribbled at the top of the received telegram by a headquarters officer in Hanoi stated: "This affair should be handled this morning by 3 B-26 with 500 pound bombs and followed up by fighters from Dien Bien Phu and Xieng Khoang [in Laos]."

High-ranking officers from artillery headquarters in Hanoi, civilian officials, and some experienced war correspondents had expressed concern during their visits over the possible inadequacy of Dien Bien Phu's artillery. The artillery commander, Col. Charles Piroth, inevitably responded with a hearty optimism. Piroth, at forty-eight, was an experienced gunner. He had lost his left arm during the campaign of Italy but had recovered enough to command an artillery regiment in the Indochina War. He was a stout, outwardly cheerful officer whose presence could lighten the atmosphere at any mess table. Although all his guns were not yet in place, Piroth knew he would soon have the firepower of twenty-five 105-millimeter howitzers, four 155-millimeter howitzers, and sixteen 120-millimeter mortars at his disposal.

Colonel Piroth's optimism continued even in the face of intelligence reports on the movement of enemy guns and large stocks of ammunition. His gun emplacements, open pits with shoulder-high, sandbagged redoubts designed to allow "all-azimuth" firing, were better designed for the old colonial campaigns against rebellious, lightly armed tribesmen than against a well-trained, artillery-equipped enemy force. Effective counterbattery fire by Piroth's guns would depend on the establishment of durable forward artillery observation posts and the six light observation planes based on the airstrip. Thus, a senior officer with a crucial role to play in the defense of the French position appeared blind to the ramifications of a worst-case scenario. The possibility that his observation posts might be overrun or the airstrip rendered unusable seemed not to have entered his mind. But even if such situations did concern him, he maintained his positive approach and made no apparent move to remedy the situation. However, Piroth was not alone. Underestimation of the enemy was to be a shared sin.

Colonel de Castries and his staff found too much of their valuable time devoted to official inspections and VIP visits. Their military and civilian visitors would be flown into Dien Bien Phu in the morning for a briefing, a tour of the most accessible strongpoints, and then a quick, informal lunch before the return flight to Hanoi.

Lt. Gen. John "Iron Mike" O'Daniel, the U.S. Army commander in the Pacific, who would soon take over the U.S. MAAG Mission in Saigon, was one of these visitors. He made polite public noises about the French installation but privately shook his head in disbelief over the fish-in-a-barrel aspect of the valley positions.

Dien Bien Phu had become a focus of world attention as a bastion of "free world" resistance to Communist aggression. The French government, facing a growing antiwar sentiment at home, was pushing for favorable press coverage, and the army was doing its best to put its best foot forward. Luckily for the army information officers, most journalistic visits to Dien Bien Phu were short and comparatively painless. It was a wait-and-see situation, and many Western newsmen were on a first-time visit to Indochina. The old hands were not as easily impressed. Some, with experience in Korea as well as Vietnam, noted that the Korean War principle of "taking the high ground" had been ignored at Dien Bien Phu. Their hosts pointed out that the strongpoints were located on hills and the Vietminh would have to attack the French positions from the valley floor. This argument failed to impress seasoned war correspondents who regarded the surrounding jungle-covered mountains as the real threat. Above all, they questioned the logic of carrying out an "offensive" campaign against the Vietminh by digging into static, defensive positions. To avoid French army censors, many British and American correspondents filed their pithier reports after leaving Indochina.

One group of journalists, writers, photographers, and cameramen wore uniforms as members of the army's Information and Press Service. Cameraman André Lebon and photographer Daniel Camus had jumped into Dien Bien Phu with the assault force. Pierre Schoendoerffer, Jean Péraud, and Jean Martinoff joined them later. They were a young, swashbuckling lot, recording the war from the front lines. These correspondents held noncom rank and were issued Colt 45s that they seldom carried, preferring to use concussion grenades for disengagement in tough situations. Their graphic images of Dien Bien Phu remain among the best and most moving military coverage since World War II.

All of the Dien Bien Phu garrison and the visiting VIPs and journalists were dependent on hard-working army cooks for their nourishment. From the beginning the Indochina campaign had presented special problems to quartermasters and cooks alike. The racial and religious diversity of the French Union Forces called for special procurement and delivery. This requirement was doubly difficult to fulfill by air transport. The North African riflemen habitually consumed an abundance of lamb. They required grain for couscous, *harissa* hot sauce to go with it, and mint for their tea. Troops from West Africa had a taste for yams, coconuts, and hot peppers. The Vietnamese of the National Army and those serving with French units were fond of pork, plentiful rice, noodles, and *nuoc mâm*, the fermented fish sauce. The Foreign Legion's cooks, faced with a veritable tangle of culinary cultures, attempted to provide the Legionnaires with solid nourishment as varied as their supplies and imagination would allow. To complicate matters, there were a number of traditional military or religious feasts calling for special menus. The Legion counted on having *boudin*, a rich blood sausage, for their annual celebration of Camerone, a famous Legion battle in Mexico in 1863. The North African troops looked forward to a *mechoui* feast of spitted roast lamb at the end of the Muslim Ramadan fast.

The French Expeditionary Corps was a hard-drinking army. A jolt of pastis or another aperitif was common before a meal. Wine and beer were served with food. Cognac, rum, eau-de-vie, and other *digestifs* were often available in the officer's mess. Although the dugout ambience at Dien Bien Phu was rustic and the promise of action did not allow overindulgence, the air bridge to Hanoi kept the tradition alive and bottles on the table.

Colonel Langlais's paras continued their probes outside the defense perimeter. Vietminh camouflage and trail discipline had rendered de Castries's observation and spotter aircraft all but blind. To locate the Viet, to gauge his strength, and seek any signs of an imminent attack, the infantry had to track the enemy, make contact, and take prisoners. Excerpts from a written account of a reconnaissance patrol on January 12, 1954, by an officer of the First BEP describe this deadly game of hide-and-seek.

"Isabelle" had already been harassed [by the enemy] and our reconnaissance would cover the region west of "Isabelle," an approach route open to the Vietminh. We left [Dien Bien Phu] at 0400 to be in place by daybreak. At dawn the 1st BEP moved on Ban Phu, which it occupied at 0900. At 1000, the Bn. reached Ban Co Hen and at 1100 Ban Lung Con. There were no villagers to be seen, having been evacuated or pulled back to the French outposts. The abandoned villages had been destroyed, burned, and showed no signs of occupation. The plain between Dien Bien Phu and "Isabelle" was not held by the Viet, at least in daylight.

At 1330 the 3rd Company reached Ban Huoi Phuc, abandoned like the other villages. Lieutenant Brandon advanced through a break in the bush, compass in hand, to get a bearing. A bullet smashed the compass, wounded Brandon's hand, and damaged his wedding ring. The Viets opened heavy fire, wounding Legionnaire Bruck of the 1st Platoon in the arm. . . . The Vietminh disposition seemed to consist of a small unit in the nearby paddy supported by what must have been a heavy Company hugging the flanks of a hill about 400 meters ahead. The 57mm recoilless rifles took care of the distant objective while the 2nd and 3rd Companies mopped up in the paddy. . . . At the same time the Bn. came under well prepared fire from 81mm mortars, adjusted on the center of our position, that caused serious damage. Major Verguet disappeared in smoke from the explosion of a shell less than two meters away. Verguet remained standing, stunned, without apparent wounds. Thirty meters from there, fragments from the same shell killed 2nd Lieutenant Nenert and wounded 2nd Lieutenant Thibout.

The list of casualties from this mortar fire provides an insight into the makeup of the First BEP.

2nd Platoon/4th Company; wounded, Adjutant Martin, Senior Corporal Zivkovic, Corporal Do Van Kinh, Legionnaires Larensac, Mlekusch, Ahlgrin; the Vietnamese volunteers Nguyen Van Mui, Do Van Phong, Tran Van Thay, Nguyen Van Ngai: 1st Company; dead, Legionnaire Pittak, wounded, volunteers Than Trong Phong and Pham Van Vinh.

The seriously wounded were evacuated by helicopter, and the battalion began its return march. The column's scouts, noting suspicious movements ahead, signaled an alert. Suddenly, a patrol of White T'ai partisans appeared on the trail. They had left their positions at Dien Bien Phu without notifying headquarters. Since the paras had been told that there were no friendly forces in the area, the careless T'ai had come close to being wiped out.

Nearing Dien Bien Phu, the battalion came under automatic-rifle fire. One slug ripped into a Legionnaire's mouth and exited the nape of his neck. "Despite everything, he came out of it without a serious wound." Two lieutenants and a corporal were also hit. The Vietminh were driven off, leaving one of their wounded behind. They had obviously been preparing to ambush the T'ai on their return to Dien Bien Phu. The First BEP reentered the security of the defense perimeter at 2340. "Colonel Langlais received us coolly," the lieutenant recorded. "He considered the noise of our return too loud." The patrol had confirmed a sizable Vietminh presence to the west of "Isabelle" that gave every indication of permanence. The First BEP had suffered five killed and thirty-three wounded on the patrol, including one officer killed and five wounded. Vietminh losses were sixteen dead, left on the ground, and one wounded, taken as a prisoner. In cold military jargon, the French had suffered "light" casualties, but such continual, gnawing attrition of their elite units would eventually cut overall effectiveness and affect morale.

While his regulars closed on Dien Bien Phu and the flow of supplies for a major offensive continued, General Giap moved to throw the French off balance and drain off more of their military resources. Seven battalions from his Vietminh 304th and 325th Divisions sliced into central Laos, linking up with their Pathet Lao allies. It appeared to be a major effort to cut Laos in half at its narrowest point. With everyone concentrating on Dien Bien Phu, this move caught the French by surprise, and the town of Thakhek had to be evacuated. General Gilles and his airborne forces were flown into Laos and set up shop at the French base at Séno, not far from Savannakhet. Major Bigeard and Major Bréchignac were soon leading their battalions into the flat jungle wasteland in search of the enemy. They found them on January 5 at the village of Ban Som Hong. After two days of hard fighting that cost the Vietminh 400 dead, the paras returned to their base. Shortly thereafter, Giap's offensive ran out of steam, but he had managed to "liberate" certain areas of Laos and draw French units from the hard-pressed delta.

Giap was not the only general planning offensive action. In mid-December, despite early signs of the Vietminh investiture of Dien Bien Phu, Navarre had issued orders for Operation "Atlante." This ambitious strike into Vietminh-held territory of south-central Vietnam included an amphibious landing on the coast at Tuy-Hoa on January 20 and a sweep by more than thirty infantry battalions with supporting artillery and armor through Vietminh Interzone V. The objective was to inflict casualties on the 30,000 Vietminh troops defending the zone, secure the Plateau Region of the Central Highlands, and allow the newly mustered "light battalions" of the Vietnamese National Army to be tested in battle. Operation "Atlante" was to prove once again the French High Command's inability to understand and cope with guerrilla warfare. After a few brief clashes, the Vietminh followed the basic tenets of guerrilla tactics and faded into the hills, leaving snipers, mines, and *punji* traps to deal with the enemy. Operation "Atlante" became one long, thirsty promenade under a blazing sun. In the end, the Vietminh would counterattack on the plateau, ambushing and wiping out an entire *groupe mobile* made up of French troops who had made a name for themselves fighting with the U.S. Second "Indian Head" Division in Korea. Navarre was even forced to deplete the force of paras that he was holding in reserve for Dien Bien Phu to blunt the enemy drive.

Major General Cogny, who had seen his plan for an offensive toward the Vietminh base depots and supply lines northwest of the delta refused by Navarre, fulminated over Operation "Atlante," particularly since it was drawing aircraft and troops from his larder. Two days before the first French troops splashed ashore at Tuy-Hoa, he sent a secret/urgent telegram to Navarre relaying the latest intercepts of Vietminh radio traffic. The first mentioned 2,000 105-millimeter shells and 3,000 eighty-two-millimeter mortar rounds on the way to the Vietminh supply center at Tuan Giao, northeast of Dien Bien Phu. The second message to Navarre contained even more ominous news.

MOST SECRET/EXTREMELY URGENT
RESERVED/COGNY TO NAVARRE

. . . REGARDING LOGISTICS, SHIPMENT OF 130,000 CARTRIDGES SCHEDULED FOR TUAN GIAO. SO FAR, SINCE 13 JANUARY, 7,000 82MM MORTAR ROUNDS [INCLUDING 3,000 MENTIONED IN PREVIOUS TELEGRAM], 3,000 SHELLS FOR 37MM ANTI–AIRCRAFT AND 9 TONS OF EXPLOSIVES ON THE WAY. VM 316TH DIVISION ASKS THE 98TH RGT. TO SEND THEM SPECIFIC DOCUMENTS BEFORE JANUARY 20. THIS REFERS, WITHOUT DOUBT, TO REPORTS COVERING A STUDY OF OUR POSTS [AT DIEN BIEN PHU] PREVIOUSLY REQUESTED FOR JANUARY 18.

4

A Watchful Ally

*"NAVARRE SAID LOSS OF DIEN BIEN PHU OR EVEN AS MANY AS TEN
BATTALIONS OF HIS BATTLE CORPS WOULD NOT PREVENT HIM MOVING
ON TO EVENTUAL VICTORY."*

U.S. Ambassador Donald Heath
in secret telegram to the State Department,
January 3, 1954

If the world was watching the buildup to the battle at Dien Bien
Phu with varying degrees of interest, the U.S. government was monitoring the situation on a day-to-day basis with all the means at its
disposal. The Eisenhower administration had a direct political and
military stake in the battle's eventual outcome. Dien Bien Phu was
shaping up as a crucial test of France's ability to hold Indochina and
parry what was seen as the main Communist thrust into Southeast
Asia. Success or failure in Indochina would deliver a judgment on
the U.S. policy of supplying economic and military aid over a period
of four years (then standing at 80 percent of the war's cost) in support of the French effort. The ripple effect of the Indochina War had
a direct bearing on American foreign policy in Europe, where the
cold war was now more than lukewarm. Washington considered
France's continued membership in the NATO alliance essential to
Western Europe's survival and had watched uneasily as successive
French governments tried to cope with the unpopular and distant
war in Indochina. France was exhausted from its role as a "free
world" rampart against Communism in Southeast Asia. Under political and public pressure at home, French policy was moving inex-
orably toward a negotiated settlement. Policymakers in Washington,

considering such an outcome both undesirable and dangerous, continued to hope for a favorable military solution and were doing their utmost to ensure that the French received what they needed at Dien Bien Phu and elsewhere in Indochina.

The State Department, the Department of Defense, and the CIA required accurate, timely reports and practical recommendations from the field on which to base their policies and planning. The American embassy, the U.S. MAAG, the American Aid Mission, the CIA station in Saigon, and the consulate in Hanoi were the prime purveyors of this information. Prior to the development of satellite communications, the advent of "shuttle diplomacy," and policy-making via scrambler telephone by presidents and secretaries of state, the U.S. government depended largely on carefully drafted reports from its overseas professionals. Urgent and important information moved by coded telegram. Less urgent, more detailed dispatches arrived by diplomatic courier or were air-pouched to Washington.

Donald Heath, a short, wry career diplomat with a penchant for wide-brimmed fedoras, was the American ambassador in Saigon. As the chief of the U.S. diplomatic mission in Indochina, he signed off on all substantive outgoing communications. The ambassador, his political section, and Paul Sturm, the U.S. consul in Hanoi, supplied Secretary of State John Foster Dulles with a stream of concise information on Dien Bien Phu. The CIA station chief supplemented this reporting with his own back-channel messages to his boss, Allen Dulles. Some of his undercover intelligence officers, emulating their wartime Office of Strategic Services predecessors in Indochina, were operating close to the action.

Excerpts from embassy telegram traffic for the month of January 1954 reveal the extent of official U.S. reporting at the time.

• January 5. A secret telegram to the secretary of state reported Ambassador Heath's conversation on Dien Bien Phu with Maurice Dejean, the French high commissioner in Saigon. "AS REGARDS SITUATION IN NORTH, DEJEAN HAD JUST COME FROM VISITING DIEN BIEN PHU WHICH HE DESCRIBED AS MANY TIMES STRONGER THAN NASAN [sic] HAD BEEN AND UNDER COMMAND OF COL. [DE] CASTRIES WHOM HE CONSIDERS ONE OF BEST OFFICERS IN ENTIRE FRENCH ARMY." After predicting heavy Vietminh losses in the event of an attack and discussing a possible Vietminh incursion into Laos, Dejean came up with "HIS PRIVATE SOLUTION FOR ACCELERATING VICTORIOUS CONCLUSION OF WAR. THIS WOULD EXPAND FOREIGN LEGION BY SIX NEW REGIMENTS RECRUITED ALMOST ENTIRELY FROM GERMANY." Dejean told Heath that "PROVIDING FUNDS COULD BE FOUND TO PAY NEW LEGION UNITS AND MATERIEL TO EQUIP THEM, THERE WOULD BE NO DIFFICULTY AT ALL IN RECRUITING THESE NEW LEGION DIVISIONS IF

'ADENAUER WOULD LOOK THE OTHER WAY.'" Dejean then told Heath that he had "PUT THIS IDEA BEFORE NAVARRE, WHO HAD FOUND IT INTERESTING BUT WISHED TO CONSIDER IT FURTHER."

• January 8. A secret/Nodis (no distribution) telegram from Heath to the secretary of state mentioned a tentative French request to Maj. Gen. Thomas J. H. Trapnell (a veteran of Bataan, then chief of U.S. MAAG, Saigon). The French were thinking of asking for "AMERICAN PILOTS TO FLY 12 C–119'S ON SUPPLY TASKS." The telegram mentions that "17 US C–119'S [ARE] ON LOAN TO FRENCH AT THIS PRECISE MOMENT" and informs Washington that Maurice Dejean had invited an American Air Force general from Tokyo to visit Indochina at the end of the month.

• January 15. A secret telegram to the secretary of state and the American embassy in Saigon from Hanoi detailed Consul Paul Sturm's conversation with Major General Cogny on Dien Bien Phu. Cogny told Sturm that Vietminh attack was not expected till late January and explained the tactical situation.

PATROLS HAVE PROVED DIEN BIEN PHU TO BE SURROUNDED ON ALL SIDES BY ENEMY FORCES LYING JUST OUTSIDE ARTILLERY RANGE. RECONNAISSANCE IN ANY DIRECTION NOW PROVOKES STRONG ENEMY REACTION. COGNY SAID IT IS CERTAIN THAT DIVISIONS 308 AND 316 ARE IN VICINITY OF STRONGPOINT; THERE ARE STRONG INDICATIONS, BUT NOT PROOF, THAT DIVISION 312 IS LIKEWISE IN AREA. . . . REGARDING VIETMINH ANTI-AIRCRAFT GUNS, COGNY SAID PILOTS HAVE REPORTED [THAT] BURSTS OF SHELLS FIRED AT THEM INDI- CATED WEAPONS OF 37 OR POSSIBLY 40 MM.

The far-ranging discussion between the French general and the American diplomat covered the supplying of Dien Bien Phu (sixty DC-4 and twenty "Flying Boxcar" flights daily), the arrival of French artillery and tanks, Vietminh plans for Laos, and the shortage of reserves that kept Cogny from striking deep into the enemy strongholds around Yen Bay and Thai Nguyen. Sturm ended his telegram with the cogent comment:

COGNY APPEARED LESS CONFIDENT DURING INTERVIEW WITH REGARD TO OUTCOME OF EVENTUAL ATTACK ON DIEN BIEN PHU THAN HE HAS BEEN HITH- ERTO, TENDING TO QUALIFY HIS STATEMENTS WITH SUCH REMARKS AS "AT LEAST I THINK SO." THERE IS NO DOUBT THAT IF THREE ENEMY DIVISIONS, SUPPORTED BY ARTILLERY AND ANTI-AIRCRAFT, ARE THROWN AGAINST DIEN BIEN PHU, STRONGPOINT'S POSITION WILL BE CRITICAL.

• January 21. A secret telegram to the secretary of state relayed the substance of a meeting between Ambassador Heath and Marc Jacquet, secretary of state for the Associated States of Indochina.

JACQUET TOLD ME YESTERDAY THAT IN HIS VIEW IT WAS ABSOLUTELY NECES-SARY FOR NAVARRE TO PRODUCE SOME VICTORIES WITHIN NEXT FEW MONTHS OR PRESSURE OF OPPOSITION IN FRENCH PARLIAMENT TO CONTINUATION OF FRENCH EFFORT IN INDOCHINA WOULD FORCE ANY GOVERNMENT IN POWER TO INITIATE NEGOTIATIONS WITH HO CHI MINH. . . . JACQUET SAID BEST THING THAT WOULD HAPPEN WOULD BE FOR VIETMINH TO ATTACK DIEN BIEN PHU AS THEY ARE EXPECTED TO DO AND HAVE FRENCH INFLICT A BLOODY DEFEAT ON THEM. THAT WOULD GREATLY DIMINISH FRENCH OPPOSITION TO WAR IN INDOCHINA.

Jacquet then spoke of eventual U.S. participation in the war.

. . . HE SAW NO POSSIBILITY OF DECISIVE DEFEAT OF VIETMINH UNLESS THERE WERE EVENTUALLY AMERICAN PARTICIPATION, SAY IN FORM OF "FOR-EIGN LEGION" WITH AMERICAN FLYERS, MECHANICS, AND TECHNICAL WAR-FARE SPECIALISTS. . . . FRENCH GOVERNMENT HAD VERY SERIOUSLY CONSID-ERED AMERICAN GOVERNMENT FORMATION OF SO-CALLED "FOREIGN LEGION" OF AMERICAN FLYERS AND SPECIALISTS BUT HAD REFRAINED FROM FORMU-LATING DEMAND ON [BASIS OF] "INFORMATION" THAT SUCH A REQUEST WOULD CAUSE DIFFICULTIES FOR AMERICAN GOVERNMENT AND BE TURNED DOWN.

In addition to these high-level interviews, embassy, consular, USIA, and American Aid Mission officers were traveling in Vietnam, Cambodia, and Laos, gathering information on everything from rice-crop yields to the views of field-grade French officers, Indochinese politicians, and newspaper editors. Having already covered seven major military operations in Indochina as a USIA war correspondent, I had been at Dien Bien Phu during Operation "Castor" and had also covered Operation "Atlante" and the French riposte to Giap's push into central Laos. Officers from the U.S. MAAG in Saigon were carrying out regular end-use missions, visit-ing French and Vietnamese units in the field to check on their use of U.S.-supplied equipment. They also reported on the readiness and morale of French and Vietnamese units. Military specialists and intelligence experts from the U.S. Pacific Command made reg-ular visits to Indochina. Some U.S. Army officers actually spent time on the ground at Dien Bien Phu as observers, offering advice when possible. They were to leave discreetly when the real battle was joined. The arrival of a battery of U.S. quad-.50 antiaircraft weapons (four .50-caliber machine guns on a swiveling, electrically operated mount) originated from a suggestion by one of these temporary visitors. After some bureaucratic wrangling over the unorthodox use of antiaircraft weapons for ground combat, the recommendation was approved by General Navarre. The quad-.50s were to prove as lethally effective against Vietminh ground assaults as they had against the attacking Chinese in Korea.

Since early January the strongpoints at Dien Bien Phu had been fully manned: the Third T'ai Battalion and a Legion mortar company at "Anne-Marie"; the Third Battalion of the Thirteenth Legion demi-Brigade at "Béatrice"; the First Battalion of the Thirteenth Legion demi-Brigade, the First BEP and the Eighth "Shock" Colonial Parachute Battalion and artillery, two tank platoons, a Legion heavy-mortar company, and security, intelligence, medical, and service units at the CP at "Claudine"; the Third Battalion of the Third Algerian Rifle Regiment, artillery, and quad-.50s at "Dominique"; the Fifth Battalion of the the Seventh Algerian Rifle Regiment and a Legion mortar company at "Gabrielle"; the First Battalion of the Fourth Moroccan Rifle Regiment at "Eliane"; elements of the Second T'ai Battalion and the First T'ai Partisan Group at "Françoise"; the First Battalion of the Second Legion Infantry Regiment and quad-.50s at "Huguette"; and the Third Battalion of the Third Legion Infantry Regiment, the Second Battalion of the First Algerian Rifle Regiment, one tank platoon, artillery, and a T'ai partisan company at "Isabelle."

The label "strongpoint" can be misleading in describing these fortified installations. In reality, they often consisted of several numbered, mutually supporting positions occupying a group of hills or high ground of varying elevation. Some had unique physical features. "Gabrielle," rising from the plain like a warship under full steam, had quickly earned the naval sobriquet of "the destroyer." The CP at "Eliane" was dug into the ruins of the regional colonial governor's house, leveled by the engineers with explosive charges during their clearing operation. A thick tree stump rose like a giant bare thumb not far from Lieutenant Colonel Gaucher's CP at "Claudine." The troop composition of these strongpoints would change according to the arrival of reinforcements and the needs of battle.

By January 5, General Giap and his chief of staff, Gen. Hoang Van Thai, had moved their CP to a cave near a waterfall about twenty kilometers from Dien Bien Phu. The cave, under fifteen meters of solid rock, was surrounded by jungle cover, and huge boulders concealed the entrance. A camouflaged tent was pitched near an out-door working area, where a large, flat-topped stone sometimes served as a map table. The Vietminh commander was planning a general attack for January 25. One of his primary concerns was to see that his artillery was in place and ready to fire. The artillery pieces had arrived close to Dien Bien Phu over five newly construct-ed roads, but the trucks could tow them no further without drawing the garrison's attention. Each heavy gun now had to be moved up the steep jungle hills and into position by hand, with the use of block and tackle, thick ropes, and braking chocks to keep them from thun-dering back down the slopes. Progress was measured in yards dur-ing seven days and nights of nonstop hard labor. Gen. Tran Do, a division commander, wrote of the arrival of the guns and the "silent battle" of the *keo phao*, or "cannon pulling."

> They [the infantry] sought every opportunity to approach the artillerymen to talk and learn more about the [truck-towed] guns. When they returned to their units they reported in a low voice, "Mother vehicles pull young ones."
>
> The ten kilometer track was so narrow that if a slight deviation of the wheels had taken place, the gun would have fallen into a deep ravine. The newly-opened track was soon an ankle-deep bog. With our sweat and muscles we replaced trucks to haul the artillery into position. . . . We ate only rice—sometimes undercooked or overdone . . . the kitchens had to be smokeless by day and sparkless by night. To climb a slope, hundreds of men crept before the gun, tugging on long ropes, pulling it up inch-by-inch. On the crest the winch was creaking, helping to prevent it from slipping. . . . It was much harder descending the slope. . . . The gun was all the heavier, the track full of twists and turns . . . steering and jamming [the wheels] were the work of the artillerymen. Infantrymen worked with the ropes and windlass. Entire nights were spent laboring by torchlight to gain 500 or 1,000 meters.

Although the trail had been camouflaged carefully, Tran Do found that the foliage was often too old.

> Twigs and leaves withered and were in a tangle . . . the enemy sus-pected something. During the day, reconnaissance planes buzzed overhead making constant dives while the fighters strafed and bombed. At night, enemy artillery was very active and its shelling sometimes caused many casualties among the workers . . . each time an enemy shell was lobbed, a shower of splinters followed the sparkling explosion and the trees split. The heroic haulers had to lie flat on the ground for a few seconds, not losing their hold on the ropes, even if their hands were bleeding. . . .

When the guns were finally in place, the ammunition had to be man-handled up to the emplacements.

These were days of serious introspection for General Giap. He had hoped to attack before the French defenses were completed, adhering to his maxim of "mobility, flexibility, and surprise." But the intelligence reports on the French fortifications were not encouraging. Col. Bui Tin recalls:

> General Giap told me he couldn't sleep the night of January 24. He was trying to assess the situation and ask himself, "Can we win or not?" He said he faced three major problems:
>
> The extent of the battlefield. Na-San had been comparatively small, but Dien Bien Phu was fifteen times larger. How can we cope? Our forces were not trained to operate over such a large expanse.
>
> The size of the Vietminh forces. Up to then, the largest battle had involved one reinforced division and two regiments. Now we had more than five divisions. Are we capable of the necessary control?
>
> The question of time. Before, the longest battle had lasted twenty hours. Most began at night and ended in the early morning. Would we be able to handle a drawn-out battle?
>
> We had hoped to attack quickly, but after three months the situation at Dien Bien Phu had changed. It was stupid to think that tactics approved in December could be used in January, when French forces had doubled in strength and fortifications had improved with more barbed wire and more artillery. An attack now would be an "adventure." Giap reflected on what Ho Chi Minh had said: "General, I give you full authority to decide—on one condition—if an attack is launched, you must win. If you are not certain of victory, do not launch the attack." Thinking of his responsibility to Ho Chi Minh, to the people, and to the army, Giap decided to cancel the attack, convinced that if the old tactics were used, defeat would be certain. Instead, he issued orders calling for thousands of shovels and spades.

On March 18, 1991, during an interview in Ho Chi Minh City, General Giap told me of that fateful night.

> I can say the army I commanded was extremely well disciplined. Our disposition was in place at Dien Bien Phu and ready to open fire, but I gave the order to pull back. The decision was made because the situation had changed. I decided to change our method of combat and to pull back immediately. So we withdrew. They [my troops] weren't happy . . . not happy at all . . . [chuckle].

Their reaction was understandable. Giap's *bo doï* and the supporting *dan cong* had outdone themselves preparing for the January assault, and the political cadre had harangued them continually on the importance of the coming action and the determination and sacrifices expected of them. But the Vietminh troops did not have time to brood over their disappointment. They now faced the arduous task of moving many of the guns down the hill from their provisional emplacements. General Giap had decided that the artillery positions would have to be more carefully prepared, that more ammunition would have to be on hand, and that supremacy in men and firepower would be essential before launching an attack in accordance with his maxim of "steady attack, steady advance."

Meanwhile Giap worked on the first phase of his attack plan that would call for the destruction of "Beatrice," the strongpoint dominating Route 41 to Tuan Giao, "Gabrielle" astride the piste Pavie, and "Anne Marie" protecting the northwest approach to Dien Bien Phu.

Many of the Vietminh seventy-five-millimeter and 105-millimeter guns were now painstakingly installed in casemates sunk into the forward slope of the hills surrounding the valley. This practice was contrary to the basic rules of classic artillery deployment, in which howitzers traditionally fired from the reverse slope, lobbing their shells up and over the ridge line. This radical positioning would allow the Vietminh guns to fire "down the tube" at stationary French targets. Some gun positions were dug deep and narrow enough to allow the placement of only one cannon, preserving the integrity of the rock as protection from enemy air attacks and artillery fire. Only the cannon's mouth protruded from the camouflaged firing port when the cannon was engaged. Artillery officers and their Chinese advisers had spent weeks mapping the exposed French positions. Individual batteries and guns were given the coordinates of specific targets. Their fire missions covered the valley: strongpoints; CPs; artillery emplacements; the two small spans over the Nam Yum River, one of them an engineer-constructed Bailey bridge; and the airstrips. Dummy guns were built and readied for positioning in decoy emplacements to draw enemy fire and air attacks.

Beginning on January 26, the Vietminh began to shell different points in the valley with what appeared to be a lone seventy-five-millimeter howitzer. These desultory bombardments in the late afternoon or early evening were usually brief and comparatively ineffective. The reassuring rumor spread that this timid harassment represented the extent of the Vietminh's artillery capabilities. The bemused garrison could imagine the enemy gunners nervously loosing a few rounds before frantically dragging their piece undercover. The more cynical combat veterans had noted that the responding French artillery and scrambled fighters had been unable to knock out this potentially lethal source of irritation. In reality, the seventy-five-millimeter fire came from more than one howitzer and was serving as a ranging exercise.

At noon on February 3, a battery of seventy-five-millimeter guns marked Tet, the Vietnamese lunar New Year, by loosing a thirty-minute bombardment on the French positions. Colonel Piroth's guns quickly accepted this challenge, pounding the hills with high explosives. B-26 and fighter strikes were called in and tanks rolled forward to fire on the suspected gun positions. The minute research of military historian Jules Roy reveals that the French expended 1,650 105-millimeter shells and 158 bombs during their energetic riposte. When the firing, bombing, and strafing ceased, de Castries and his staff were convinced that they had destroyed the enemy guns. In reality, most of their targets had been the more easily discernible dummy emplacements, made realistic by the spaced explosions of controlled charges to approximate outgoing cannon fire. Giap had kept his 105-millimeter batteries silent, saving them for a later date.

On February 7, General Giap visited his artillery units to congratulate them on the work that they had done putting their guns into position, to caution them not to be intimidated by the enemy's artillery and aircraft, and to underline the importance of following orders. His words on this latter point hint at certain command problems. "Heroism and strict obedience to orders are the two fundamental characteristics of our troops in combat," he told his gunners. "Recently, thanks to your strict obedience to orders, you've been successful, and that's good. However, certain comrades have hesitated in the face of difficulties and have not completely carried out their orders with rigor and dispatch. Let them correct their deficiencies in order to move forward." After praising "many cadre" (officers) who had remained close to their men, helping move the guns and setting an example, Giap mentioned "a certain number" of officers who "have no real affection for their men and leave their posts at difficult moments." He accused such individuals of shirking their duty as cadre and recommended that they mend their ways. With his attack timetable now pushed back to late February or March, Giap detached the 308th Division from its siege role and sent it toward Luang Prabang.

Warned by previous radio intercepts and data gathered from prisoner interrogations, the French had been expecting the Vietminh to attack on or about January 25. For them, the sudden movement of the 308th was a puzzling surprise and a sure indication that the battle had been postponed. Any relief that might have been felt at this reprieve was tempered by frustration. Like the Vietminh, the French troops had been geared up and ready for action. The men in the dugouts and trenches were confident and had welcomed the prospect of ending their long wait. Above all, they wanted the test of strength over and done with. If the riflemen and gunners at Dien Bien Phu were deceived, the members of the French High Command were deeply disappointed. The attack that they had awaited for so long, the assault that would expose Giap's divisions to a hail of French shellfire and bombing, the happening that they had told their high-ranking visitors from Paris could well be the turning point of the war in France's favor, was now a nonevent.

Once again, troops badly needed elsewhere had to be flown in to bolster the defenses of the Laotian royal capital. Some observers speculated that Luang Prabang had always been Giap's primary objective and that the bulk of his divisions would soon follow the 308th while a reduced holding force contained Dien Bien Phu and its hemmed-in garrison. But the 308th, although it did descend the Nam Ou River to within ninety kilometers of Luang Prabang, was primarily on a spoiler expedition. Its prime task was to forestall the likelihood of any French withdrawal into Laos from Dien Bien Phu and discourage further attempts to form a land link to the fortress. The 308th Division wiped out the garrison at Muong Khoua, the post that the French had retaken during Operation "Ardèche," and rolled up some minor outposts before heading back in the direction of Dien Bien Phu.

Meanwhile, responding to orders from the French High Command, de Castries continued to push multibattalion combat patrols into the surrounding countryside to sniff out strong enemy implantations and locate and destroy Vietminh gun positions in the hills to the east. These patrols inevitably ran into hard enemy contacts a short distance from Dien Bien Phu. The exhaustion of the returning troops meant further delays in the task of improving their defensive positions. Previously, the patrols had clashed with mobile enemy units in temporary ambush positions. Now they were butting their heads against Vietminh infantry in solidly constructed pillboxes and trench networks. These emplacements were so well camouflaged that the point scouts or flank guards often moved past them unknowingly. The Vietminh took full advantage of the element of surprise, holding their fire until the optimum moment before raking the French patrols with automatic weapons, DK-Z 57-millimeter recoilless-rifle fire, and a hail of hand grenades.

In one abortive mission, Langlais led his paras, a Moroccan rifle battalion, and the Second T'ai Battalion toward Hill 781 due east of Dien Bien Phu. They expected to find enemy artillery on the reverse slope of the hill and destroy it. Langlais had brought along a Legion flamethrower detachment and a combat engineer section to help deal with any Vietminh fortifications in the patrol's path. Here again, the lessons in the manual did not match reality. No guns were found on the reverse slope, and before the patrol could scale the

heights to examine the slope facing Dien Bien Phu, it was knocked
on its heels by a vicious enemy assault. The Moroccans, true to their
reputation, fought "like lions," but the T'ai battalion faltered and
began to fragment. Langlais had to order another fighting withdrawal. The patrol dragged itself back to Dien Bien Phu with nothing to
show for its effort but more casualties. It had lost ninety-six officers
and men.

Such failures were nibbling away at the French garrison's confidence. They were also revealing shortcomings in individual units.
The T'ai battalions, accustomed to ambushes and small jungle
actions, were not meant to be used as regular line units. Although
individual T'ai soldiers often fought with bravery, they were not the
equal of veteran Vietminh regulars in a protracted, pitched battle.
The North African troops, who had fought with distinction in World
War II and had done well in Indochina prior to Dien Bien Phu,
were also showing signs of diminished efficiency. The Moroccan
riflemen had been shaken a year earlier by the dethronement and
exile of their sultan by the French government for his nationalist
views. This act had been both a political and religious affront to the
Moroccans, since the sultan was also the revered religious leader of
all Muslim believers in his country. Although the rank and file of
these colonial regiments had been traditionally apolitical, many of
them had been shocked by the French action. The Algerian units no
longer had the professional cadre that had made them efficient
fighting machines in World War II. Their losses had been heavy,
and the replacement cadre did not have the same quality as their
predecessors. Like the Moroccans, the Algerians needed officers
whom they knew and respected and who knew and respected them.
Moreover, many of these units were suffering from combat fatigue
and the frustrations of fighting a seemingly endless war in a hostile
countryside.

To complicate matters, the French were facing the problems of
growing nationalism and the thirst for independence in their North
African colonies. New recruits arriving in Indochina brought word
of growing discontent with French rule at home and reports of harsh
police methods used in quashing nationalist movements. The
Vietminh, ever alert to the importance of psychological warfare,
made a methodical effort to indoctrinate their North African prisoners with emphasis on the evils of colonialism and international capi-
talism and the virtues of revolutionary Marxism according to Ho Chi
Minh. The most susceptible North African prisoners were then given
the task of "educating" their newly captured countrymen under the
supervision of a Vietminh political cadre. One "hot" revolutionary
war was thus already fanning the embers of another.

De Castries continued the attempts to locate and destroy the Vietminh guns in the eastern hills with little success. In mid-February a major French operation involving six battalions continued over a period of several days. Colonel Langlais's task force of paras, Legionnaires, and Algerian and T'ai riflemen pushed their way through heavy undergrowth to drive the enemy from their bunkers and trenches. Some hill slopes had been hit with napalm, and the smoldering, ankle-deep ash still glowed at its core. Blackened branches hung from the charred trees, and the perspiring troopers took on the look of helmeted chimney sweeps. The swollen, roasted corpses of Vietminh dead lay half-buried in the hot ash, filling the thick air with the cloying odor of burned flesh. Explosives and flamethrowers were used on the enemy emplacements. The shrilling of a whistle brought Vietminh troops swarming from cover to the cry *"Tien liên!"* ("Forward now!"). The hand-to-hand fighting was bloody and merciless—individual contests of grunting, cursing men wielding trench knives, bayonets, rifle butts, and entrenching tools. During one hill climb in search of Vietminh bunkers, the Viet infantry surprised a Legion company by concealing their firing positions on the reverse slope and holding their fire until the winded attackers arrived on the hillcrest. There, silhouetted against the sky, the Legionnaires were decimated by a deluge of close-range automatic-weapons fire. Casualty reports sputtering over the field radios spoke of eighteen dead in one battalion, fourteen dead in another, and double those amounts in wounded.

Four of the hills had been "cleared" of the enemy, a number of blockhouses and bunkers had been destroyed, and Vietminh losses had been heavy. But clearing the hills meant little if they could not be secured. Once more the expenditure in dead and wounded had been too high a price to pay for such a mediocre result, particularly since Giap's guns had not been put out of action. On February 15, Langlais received the order to bring his bloodied, ash-smeared battalions back to Dien Bien Phu, leaving the contested hills to the enemy. A handful of troops from the hard-hit Third T'ai Battalion were listed as deserters. It was a warning of things to come.

The wounded from these sorties were being treated by the forty-two-bed (canvas cots and litters) Twenty-Ninth Mobile Surgical Detachment, located within the command complex on the west bank of the Nam Yum River. Each battalion had its *toubib*, or field surgeon, backed by a team of medics, to provide preliminary treatment of its wounded and to perform emergency surgery in urgent cases. One surgeon had already been killed in Operation "Castor." The seriously wounded were to be sent to the hospital for operations and from there to Hanoi by medevac C-47s rigged to take litters and manned by air force nurses. The key hospital components, including its operating, X-ray, and recovery rooms, had been sunk into the ground and protectively roofed by the engineers. A series of tunnels and open trenches linked the main dugouts. A small fleet of two ambulances and two jeeps was parked nearby in an open bunker to rush the treated patients to the airstrip for evacuation. A portion of the nearby GCMA dugout was earmarked for housing up to one hundred walking wounded in an emergency. A helicopter pad was located near the riverbank. The morgue was not far from the pad, a square excavation open to the sky and stocked with empty wooden coffins.

The hospital's commander and chief surgeon, Maj. Paul Grauwin, was an unflappable professional. The bald and bespectacled Grauwin had patched and repaired the torn, bloody results of the war for almost ten years. Since his arrival at Dien Bien Phu on February 17, he had been troubled by the inadequacies of the installation. His predecessor had already warned de Castries that the meager facilities would not be able to handle casualties from a major engagement. Some of the dugouts and bunkers needed additional shoring-up; the overhead protection obviously required thicker layers of steel plating, sandbags, and earth; and the open communications trenches could become death traps under artillery fire. Grauwin was particularly troubled that the success of the entire medical operation at Dien Bien Phu depended on the thin, vulnerable cord of the air-evacuation process.

This concern would deepen in early March with news of a series of Vietminh commando attacks on French airfields near Hanoi. The attack at the Gia-Lam airport alone would cost the French eleven aircraft destroyed by satchel charges. Grauwin had been promised another surgical detachment by the inspector general of the Medical Corps, General Jeansotte, during his visit to Dien Bien Phu. Jeansotte had surveyed Grauwin's facilities with a critical eye, questioned him on the thickness of his shelters, and warned him that he could well find 300 wounded on his hands.

Major Grauwin was not alone in his worries about French air force capabilities in regard to Dien Bien Phu. In early February, Gen. Henri Charles Lauzin, the chief of the French air force in Indochina, had told Ambassador Heath that he intended to urge the French government to reconsider its position in NATO and "endeavor to prevail on its allies in that coalition to permit temporary allocation of French forces now tied down by NATO commitments to active combat duty in this theater."

A few days later, at a luncheon given by Heath for General Weyland, commander of the U.S. Air Force, Far East, then on an official visit to Saigon, a terse clash occurred between General Fay, chief of staff of the French air force, and General Navarre. As Heath reported to Washington:

... GENERAL FAY WAS DEPLORING LOSSES OF FRENCH OFFICERS IN THIS
WAR. ASSERTING THAT ONE OF CAUSES OF FRENCH DEFEAT IN SECOND WORLD
WAR WAS THEIR OFFICER LOSSES IN FIRST WAR, HE SAID THAT SAME THING
WAS HAPPENING TO FRENCH ARMY IN ITS INDOCHINA OPERATIONS. HE SAID
FLATLY THAT FRANCE COULD ENDURE THESE LOSSES ONLY ONE YEAR MORE.
NAVARRE TOOK IMMEDIATE EXCEPTION TO THIS. HE SAID THAT IF THAT WERE
REALLY SPIRIT IN WHICH FRANCE WAS ENGAGED IN THIS WAR IT HAD BETTER
PULL OUT NOW.

Other American visitors complicated Ambassador Heath's diplomatic task. The gruff Lt. Gen. John "Iron Mike" O'Daniel had visited Saigon to confer with General Navarre as early as November 12, 1953. During this conference "Iron Mike" had bulled ahead with a number of suggestions that left the French seething. These had included the participation of American officers in training the Vietnamese National Army, the establishment of an Amphibious Training Center, and the fortification of the entire Tonkin Delta.

O'Daniel had also questioned Navarre on his plans for "offensive action" and recommended that Vietnamese units take a more active combat role in fighting the Communists. Navarre had tactfully responded with facts about the realities of operating in Indochina, explaining the doubtful benefits of a huge fortification project and the difficulties of finding a dependable cadre for the new Vietnamese battalions. He had cited a recent incident at the Hanoi Medical Faculty in which sixty medical students about to take their final examination had been told that those who passed would become army doctors. Forty students had immediately abandoned their medical studies to apply for a dentistry course of several years.

On January 28, 1954, another visit by General O'Daniel had threatened to exceed Navarre's tolerance level. "Iron Mike" and his entourage had arrived in Saigon on extremely short notice. Navarre had agreed to receive the American general but, after warning O'Daniel that he would speak "very frankly," had expressed his "displeasure" at "Iron Mike"'s arrival at a time when Navarre had four military operations under way and two official visitors from Paris on his hands. Apparently unperturbed by his reception, O'Daniel had proceeded to suggest that he might be able to visit Vietnam "a couple of days" each month and act as Navarre's direct link with the Joint Chiefs of Staff, thus bypassing Pentagon red tape. The hardly mollified Navarre had then remarked that "the Vietminh were fortunate in one thing: they had no Pentagon to deal with."

A few days later Ambassador Heath had sent a top secret personal letter to Philip W. Bonsal of the State Department's Bureau of Far Eastern Affairs, recommending that General O'Daniel *not* fill the role of a military counselor and "prodder" to General Navarre. In the letter Heath had described a meeting in which O'Daniel had suggested a solution to the whole problem:

> [The solution] was to build additional block-houses around the periphery of the Tonkin Delta at quarter kilometer intervals and in front of that, to have a whole wall of barbed wire. This, he said, would largely solve the whole question of pacifying the Delta, since the Vietminh could neither get in or [sic] get out. This suggestion, voiced with Iron Mike's usual positiveness, was so preposterous in view of the balance of forces between the Vietminh and Vietnamese forces that I merely stared at him and finally said mildly that the French Command didn't have the force necessary to garrison such a wall of block-houses and accomplish its other tasks.

Heath had pointed out that the O'Daniel proposals were "neither realistic or [sic] sound" and had warned that "if O'Daniel's advice were accepted and this advice proved to be faulty, the French government might seek to throw the blame on us for what in fact was the accumulation of shortcomings over past years."

Meanwhile, the real war had continued. The Vietminh 308th Division's departure from Dien Bien Phu had prompted an exchange of messages between Navarre and Cogny in which they were debating the wisdom of reducing the garrison of Dien Bien Phu now that the threat had lessened. Cogny had previously relayed to Navarre the proposal made by de Castries to temporarily withdraw a Legion battalion from Dien Bien Phu. This would have been a ruse designed to tempt the Vietminh into attacking the weakened garrison. The proviso had been that the withdrawn battalion had to be parachuted back into the valley within twenty-four hours if an attack began. Navarre had stalled in his response, citing the need to take more Vietminh prisoners for further information on Giap's intentions, and the proposal had died on the vine. Cogny had then proposed to reduce the Dien Bien Phu garrison to six battalions if the Vietminh 312th Division, which appeared to have left its positions, followed the 308th into Laos. This plan had also been rejected by Navarre. In addition to tactical objections, he had suspected Cogny of coveting any units evacuated from Dien Bien Phu for use in his precious delta. By February 28, intelligence reports had identified the 308th Division as being back in its previous positions west of Dien Bien Phu.

Although Cogny had told Consul Sturm that he believed that Giap had given up plans for a massive assault, he had now begun to change his mind. A top secret/flash telegram from Cogny to Navarre in late February had transmitted the gist of an intercepted Vietminh message.

NEW TELEGRAM FROM [VIETMINH] BASE AT TUAN GIAO INSISTS ON NEED TO RECEIVE—BEFORE MARCH 15—TWO TONS OF PHARMACEUTICAL PRODUCTS. THIS DATE COINCIDES APPROXIMATELY WITH THAT MENTIONED FOR THE SENDING OF SUPPLIES AND AMMUNITION TO DIEN BIEN PHU. IT APPEARS, THEREFORE, THAT AN ACTION IN FORCE COULD BE ATTEMPTED ON DIEN BIEN PHU IN THE SECOND HALF OF MARCH, MAYBE BETWEEN THE 20TH AND 25TH. BASE OF TUAN GIAO MENTIONS—FOR PERIOD MARCH 1–APRIL 25TH—NEED OF UP TO 2,900 TONS OF RICE, OR AN AVERAGE OF 55 TONS A DAY FOR FEED-ING OF 70,000 MEN.

Sturm had been able to report in a telegram to Washington on March 8 that "GENERAL COGNY SAYS EVIDENCE APPEARS TO BE CONVERG-ING TOWARD INDICATION THAT VIETMINH WILL ATTACK DIEN BIEN PHU, NOW THAT VIETMINH DIVISION 308 HAS WITHDRAWN FROM ADVANCED POSITION IN LAOS."

While coded messages dealing with their fate had filled the air-waves, the French garrison had been learning to live under artillery fire. The Vietminh seventy-five-millimeter guns had concentrated on the airstrip, their shells exploding on the pierced steel plates under puffs of dirty gray smoke. A number of aircraft had already been destroyed or damaged, and the air-control tower had taken several hits. Departing aircraft had behaved like runaway windup toys as their pilots swiveled through the gauntlet of flying shell fragments. On March 11 a C-119 stuck overnight at Dien Bien Phu for emer-gency engine repairs had been totally destroyed.

Giap now chose to unveil his 105-millimeter batteries. The teeth-jarring thump of their arrivals heralded a new escalation. The enemy guns walked their fire over the strip and began to search out the fighters and observation aircraft in their protected revetments. Outgoing fire from Colonel Piroth's batteries counterpointed the Vietminh barrage, but they were firing blind and had no noticeable effect. Nor was there any respite during the night. The Vietminh gunners had locked onto the range for the fighter shelters, and a flaming "Bearcat" provided a convenient aiming stake in the dark-ness. For the infantry in the strongpoints, the shells bursting on the distant strip had a mesmerizing effect. Although the riflemen real-ized the somber significance of the heavy bombardment, they had more immediate concerns. For some time now the French listening posts had reported the nightly thump and scrape of methodical dig-ging. The jagged outlines of the new, freshly dug Vietminh trenches had appeared at first light. These were not defensive positions but offensive saps, reaching out toward the French positions. Shovel-wielding patrols had been sent each morning to refill the trenches and leave antipersonnel mines behind as a lethal surprise for the Vietminh sappers. This procedure had become a risky, unpopular game, the wartime equivalent of the peacetime army's make-work proposition of digging a hole only to fill it in. But this time it was the enemy who was doing the digging. On the morning of March 12, the Legion officers at strongpoint "Béatrice" noted that the rules had changed. The Vietminh were now digging in broad daylight under the protection of lookouts. Their tunnellike trenches were snaking upward toward the French position like the tentacles of some determined, earthbound devilfish.

5

Thunder from the Hills

"Then I found myself facing the Viets, who I welcomed with shots from my Colt."

First Sergeant Bleyer,
Third Battalion of the Thirteenth demi-Brigade,
Foreign Legion

The Vietminh trenches soon formed a one hundred-kilometer network around the fortifications. Giap's sappers burrowed through the earth while French mortars and artillery hammered the freshly dug trenches. The flat report of telescope-sighted sniper rifles signaled the death or wounding of any *bo doï* careless enough to show his helmet above the trench line. But the work continued, the clods of soft earth flying up and onto the parapets. Vietminh wounded and dead were carried from the narrow trenches, and their spades passed to replacements. Junctions of two or more trenches were camouflaged, and protective dugouts were cut into the trench walls.

Before beginning the "first phase" of his attack on Dien Bien Phu, General Giap sought to reduce the enemy's air capabilities at the source. Following the successful attack on Gia-Lam, he had ordered another group of commandos to attack the military airfield of Cat-Bi, near Haiphong. The result was four B-26 bombers and six Morane observation planes destroyed on the airstrip. Aircraft losses would have been heavier if Major General Cogny had not sent Bigeard and his Sixth Parachute Battalion to reinforce the defenses. A dispute with the airfield commander, who had argued forcefully that he was adequately protected, had put Bigeard's battalion outside the defense perimeter at some distance from the airstrip.

Nevertheless, despite a painful pulled calf muscle, Bigeard had reacted quickly. A number of C-119s had been spared and several Vietminh commandos killed. On the night of March 12, another commando group slipped past Dien Bien Phu's defenses to destroy some of the steel grilling of the airstrip. The infiltrators also confirmed specific target locations for their artillery.

For several days French intelligence reports had been predicting a major enemy attack on or about March 15. There had also been indications that Vietminh attacks on the crucial Hanoi-Haiphong road and rail line would be stepped up. Meanwhile, General Navarre issued a directive from his Saigon headquarters lauding the strategy of "entrenched camps" supported by air. "When the enemy makes a massive commitment of important forces," Navarre declared, "he is obliged to engage in the long, costly and difficult operations of a veritable siege war, requiring large [numbers of] effectives that cannot go unnoticed by [our] aviation and thus offer vulnerable objectives." Field commanders recognized the fine hand of Navarre's deputy for operations, Col. Louis Berteil, in the directive's lofty prose. Berteil, who had Navarre's ear, had uncritically championed the "entrenched camp" theory in the face of all opposition. Dien Bien Phu had become known as "Du Berteil Pur" ("Pure Berteil") in the officers' messes. In light of the precarious situation in the Muong Thanh Valley, the directive only emphasized the rarefied, detached atmosphere at the High Command. But the real threat confirmed by intelligence reports could not be ignored. Navarre ordered the air force to muster enough C-47s on standby to drop three parachute battalions into Dien Bien Phu.

March 12 proved to be a busy day at "DBP Airport," the nickname that some air force crew chiefs had given the airstrip. A Curtiss "Commando" aircraft, two C-47s, and a fighter had been destroyed by a Vietminh bombardment. André Lebon, the tough, carefree cameraman who had jumped with the first wave of Operation "Castor," had returned to Dien Bien Phu, along with Jean Martinoff, a photographer. Their C-47 swiveled through the firing to land safely. The twice-wounded Lebon sensed the imminence of a major battle and did not want to miss it. Both he and Martinoff were soon putting the shelling of the airstrip on film. It was the last coverage that either of them would accomplish at Dien Bien Phu. A salvo of 105-millimeter shells bracketed the duo. Martinoff died on the spot. Within minutes Lebon was on the hospital's operating table. Major Grauwin removed what remained of Lebon's right foot, cut a bit of exposed bone, cleaned the wound, and applied a tourniquet. Lebon left for Hanoi fifteen minutes later on a medevac C-47. Major General Cogny also braved the artillery fire that day to make a lightning visit to Colonel de Castries. During a hurried conference in the CP, de

Castries's intelligence officer, with the help of intercepted radio traffic and prisoner interrogation reports, predicted a Vietminh attack for 1700 hours, March 13. Shells were falling on the airstrip when Cogny said his good-byes. It would be his last visit to Dien Bien Phu. At 1600 hours the battered airstrip control tower canceled any further landings for that day.

General Giap had chosen to concentrate his first major assaults on the northern strongpoints: Him Lan or "Béatrice"; Doc Lap, or "Gabrielle"; and Ban Kéo, or "Anne-Marie." Him Lan, or "Béatrice," was his first objective. The infantry force from the 312th Division that he had massed for the attack was more than three times the strength of the reduced Legion battalion holding "Béatrice." Additional Vietminh units were in reserve. In addition, he had moved some of his seventy-five-millimeter howitzers and heavy mortars closer to the strongpoint. Fire teams with fifty-seven-millimeter recoilless rifles only one hundred meters from the fortifications were assigned to provide direct fire support. In the forty-eight hours preceding the assault, the Vietminh infantry had pushed their trenches to the foot of the French barbed wire. The enemy implantation around "Béatrice" had become extremely tight. The strongpoint's last sortie to the Nam Yum River for drinking water had required the support of another battalion and two tanks.

Throughout the afternoon of March 13, six Vietminh assault battalions took up their positions in the trenches. They had been briefed thoroughly on the terrain and studied reduced models of their objectives. Some of the first strands of enemy wire had already been cut by Vietminh scouts. Their political cadre and officers read messages of encouragement from General Giap, the government, and the division commander. A message from President Ho Chi Minh concluded: "I am waiting for your news. I embrace you." Groups of army musicians encouraged the troops with renditions of "March to the Front."

The Legionnaires at "Béatrice" watched the enemy buildup with a mix of anticipation and foreboding. They were professional soldiers with confidence in their commanding officer, Maj. Paul Pégot, and an appreciation of their own worth. They considered the three mutually supporting positions of their defenses solid. "Béatrice" had always been on the intinerary of de Castries when he wanted to show visiting VIPs the strength of his fortifications. Many of the Legionnaires thought the Vietminh completely mad for even considering an attack on their strongpoint. But they were puzzled by the enemy's apparent assurance. Colonel Piroth's guns were still delivering interdiction fire on the approaches to "Béatrice," raising geysers of smoke-shrouded earth and occasionally pinwheeling an enemy corpse or some unrecognizable body parts into the air. Despite this fact, the Vietminh on the facing slopes remained visible, going about their preparations with a disconcerting sangfroid.

At 1700 hours on March 13, a distant thunder, like the warning of a monsoon downpour, sounded from the hills. Within seconds the thunder descended on Dien Bien Phu. The ear-splitting clap of high explosives shook the earth. The 105-millimeter and seventy-five-millimeter howitzers and 120-millimeter mortars of the Vietminh 351st "Heavy" Division were sending hundreds of shells whistling onto their preselected targets. "Béatrice" disappeared under a curtain of smoke and thick dust, pierced only by the flash and flicker of exploding shells. The barrage pinpointed "Gabrielle" and fell on "Dominique," collapsing dugouts and trenches, killing and wounding French artillerymen and mortar teams in their open pits. One battery of Giap's 105-millimeter guns opened fire on "Isabelle" to dampen the fire from its supporting artillery. Other guns pounded "Eliane," concentrating on gun positions and the CP areas. Few among the 12,000-man garrison of Dien Bien Phu had ever experienced the shock of such a sudden cataclysm.

The Legionnaires at "Béatrice" clung to their fortifications as the storm of fire and steel raged around them. The explosions rained a deluge of stones and debris into the trenches. Hot shrapnel hummed through the air and thudded into the sandbags. A strange half-light hung over the position as dust blotted out the fading sun. The bombardment ripped open bunkers and gun positions, leaving smoking heaps of smashed equipment and dislocated bodies. The field-telephone wire linking the Third Legion Battalion with its companies and other strongpoints was shredded; many of the radios were holed or smashed. The acrid smell of cordite and the stench of bowels ripped from shell-torn corpses—a battlefield odor rarely mentioned in military histories—assailed the defenders' nostrils. The Vietminh assault waves poured from their trenches, advancing through the thick haze, preceded by the "volunteers of death." These sappers carried bangalore torpedoes, long lengths of bamboo packed with explosives to open breaches in the barbed wire. Others were laden with explosive charges to be placed against the embrasures of the pillboxes and gun positions.

Captain Nicolas, commander of the Tenth Company of the Third Legion Battalion, recorded the intensity and confusion of the battle.

At 17:30 [sic] on March 13th the Vietminh artillery preparation began. The entire day had been spent trying to fill in the Vietminh approach trenches. During this extremely violent preparation, the

Vietminh reopened their trenches and pushed them up to the wire under cover of the thick dust raised by the explosions that surrounded the center of resistance with a veritable smoke screen.

During the first hour of bombardment, a 120mm shell with a delayed fuse penetrated the Command Post, simultaneously killing Major Pegot, Captain Pardi and Lieutenant Pungier and destroying all the radio installations. Lieutenant Carriere, commander of the 9th Company was killed, and Lieutenants Turpin and Lemoine of the 11th and 12th Companies were wounded and forced to abandon command of their units. . . .

As the bombardment had completely disorganized our telephone and radio network, I was only informed of Major Pégot and Captain Pardi's deaths a half hour after they occurred. I quickly went to the Battalion CP to take command. This left my Company without an officer. In the interim, enemy attacks were launched simultaneously against the 11th and 9th Companies. The 11th Company was quickly overwhelmed. Deprived of its commander, without officers, its platoon leaders decimated in the previous day's action, it could not mount a coordinated defense, each Legionnaire fighting individually and finally taken from the rear by the enemy.

Captain Nicolas reported attacks coming from different directions, further losses, and the fact that all communications with the exterior depended on a sole surviving radio. The Vietminh mounted one assault wave after another, pouring through gaps in the wire to shouted exhortations and leaving mounds of dead and wounded in their wake. The overheated machine-gun barrels of the defenders glowed in the encroaching darkness. Supporting mortar fire was cutting gaps in the attacker's ranks, and the French artillery, after a frustrating, unexplained delay, had begun to do damage. The battlefield had taken on a surreal look as a circling "Luciole" ("Firefly") C-47 illuminated the scene with the pale, flickering glow of its parachute flares.

At 2200 a temporary, informal truce was arranged to recover and tend the wounded. "The Vietminh profited from it to bring in fresh troops," Captain Nicolas explains. "On our side, we resupplied our units with ammunition." An hour and a half later a new assault erupted.

It was stopped by a particularly well-placed machine gun of the Twelfth Company that—we learned after the battle—caused enormous Vietminh casualties. The Vietminh put a recoilless rifle in place to neutralize it, and the machine gun was completely destroyed. With a breach thus opened, the enemy masses hurled themselves at the hill's summit, and the last phase of the fighting began, hand-to-hand in the trenches, while the shelters were systematically grenaded.

First Sergeant Bleyer's men had just been fed when the attack began.

> Heavy-artillery fire smashed everything, and it had barely stopped when the Viet were already in our wire. I went to get my orders, but the blockhouse of Lieutenant Carriere had collapsed under direct fire from bazookas and recoilless rifles. The lieutenant himself had been killed, and the controls of the defensive charges weren't working. I tried in vain to make contact with Lieutenant Jego. Then I found myself facing the Viets, who I welcomed with shots from my Colt. A grenade exploded between my legs.

The wounded Bleyer then tried to reach the battalion CP, rallying other Legionnaires on the way. Their own barbed wire delayed them, but they finally reached the survivors of the Tenth Company in time to help them fight off another wave of attackers before the position was finally overrun.

Gen. Tran Do describes the Vietminh view of the battle for "Béatrice" through the actions of individual *bo doï*, such as "model fighter" Nguyen Huu Oanh.

> Two white signal rockets flew up into the sky. Oanh readjusted the flag fixed to his back, rushed up, and jumped into an enemy communication trench. He crept through a line of barbed wire, dashed up again, lay flat on the ground, threw a hand grenade, and machine-gunned a blockhouse, neutralizing an enemy loophole. Then, quickly taking advantage of the uneven ground to dodge the return fire, he crept close to the blockhouse and hoisted the flag. His men followed close behind him.

Tran Do cites Deputy Platoon Commander Hoi, who, although wounded, covered Nguyen Huu Oanh with fire from his submachine gun. He also mentions Platoon Commander Tue, who "threw a ten-kilogram charge into Major Pégot's blockhouse" and "had dozens of grenade splinters, each as big as a grain of maize, burning all over his body."

The French were not the only ones suffering from faulty communications. Tran Do explains.

> No artillery cover came from the battalion. Liaison with the regiment could not be established, the radio being out of order. We had to rely

on the company's firepower. But hardly had our two machine guns been put into position when enemy artillery sighted them. The gunners were killed, the guns buried under clods of earth.

A Legion heavy-mortar platoon on "Dominique" was delivering supporting fire to "Béatrice" despite the concentrated enemy barrage falling on their exposed positions. A direct hit on the ammunition dump exploded a quarter of their 120-millimeter mortar shells and put half the Legionnaires out of action. The platoon suffered eleven dead and three seriously wounded.

Lieutenant Colonel Langlais had been taking a shower from a makeshift overhead container rigged by his men when the bombardment began. Grabbing his clothes, he sprinted for cover, dressed, and made his way to his CP. He contacted the commanders of the First BEP and the Eighth "Shock" Battalion to make sure that they were ready for action. A direct hit then collapsed Langlais's command shelter. He and his staff dug themselves out of the debris of roofing, split sandbags, and earth, miraculously unhurt. A whistling rush heralded the arrival of a second shell. It narrowly missed one of Langlais's staff officers before burying itself, unexploded, in the dirt wall of the CP.

Lieutenant Colonel Gaucher had been following the defense of "Béatrice" from his bunker, the CP of the Ninth Groupe Mobile at "Claudine." Although Gaucher had been named commander of the Central Subsector, the Thirteenth Legion demi-Brigade was his unit, his second family, his life. The sudden break in radio communications with Major Pégot's CP at "Béatrice" was both frustrating and ominous. But the uncertainty did not last. Confirmation of the deaths of Pégot and his staff filtered through from "Béatrice." Gaucher would now have to maintain contact with the individual companies of the Third Battalion and direct the defense until a replacement for Pégot was found. He called a conference in his CP to choose Pégot's successor from among the company commanders at "Béatrice," unaware that most were either killed our wounded. He was about to address the small group of officers when a direct hit on the CP turned night into day, splattering the small room with blood and bits of flesh. Lieutenant Colonel Gaucher lay amid the wreckage armless, his chest ripped open and his face disfigured. Two other officers were sprawled out dead nearby. One had been decapitated. A surviving aide bent over the lieutenant colonel to hear his last order. "Wipe my face," Gaucher demanded, "and give me something to drink." He was rushed to the hospital. After one look at Gaucher's wounds, Major Grauwin summoned Père Heinrich, the senior chaplain, to administer the last rites.

On hearing of Gaucher's death, Colonel de Castries ordered

THE BATTLE OF
DIEN BIEN PHU

Brig. Gen. Jean "Père" Gilles arrives to take command at Dien Bien Phu during Operation "Castor," November 21, 1953. The one-eyed forty-nine-year-old insisted on jumping with his men, rather than landing later by helicopter. *Képi blanc**

**Képi blanc is an official publication of the French Foreign Legion. All other photos were taken by the author as a U.S. Information Agency correspondent.

General Gilles (right, on collapsible motor scooter) greets troops disembarking from one of the first C-47s to land on the repaired airstrip. *USIA / H. R. Simpson*

Maj. Marcel "Bruno" Bigeard, Resistance hero and habitually unarmed commander of the Sixth Colonial Parachute Battalion, in contact with an artillery spotter aircraft during a patrol. The faded inscription reads "To my dear comrade Simpson—with the lasting and profound friendship of your Bigeard." *USIA / H. R. Simpson*

The Foreign Legion digs in. *USIA / H. R. Simpson*

The author (left) at lunch with noncoms of the Sixth Colonial Parachute Battalion. *USIA / H. R. Simpson*

Foreign Legion paratroop officer.
Képi blanc

The chaplain of the Sixth Colonial Parachute
Battalion. *USIA / H. R. Simpson*

Paratroopers of the Sixth Colonial Parachute Battalion prepare for a patrol outside the perimeter while T'ai tribeswomen carry water from the Nam Yum River. *USIA / H. R. Simpson*

Scouts from the Sixth enter a deserted village north of Dien Bien Phu. *USIA / H. R. Simpson*

Paras take cover on napalm-burned hills. *Képi blanc*

French paratroop officers discuss intelligence findings with Black T'ai partisans during a patrol. *USIA / H. R. Simpson*

A Foreign Legion heavy mortar in action. *Képi blanc*

Maj. Gen. René Cogny visits the garrison shortly after the airstrip's seizure by French forces. *USIA / H. R. Simpson*

Vietnamese paras on patrol near Dien Bien Phu. *Képi blanc*

Members of a newly arrived T'ai battalion. *USIA / H. R. Simpson*

A Moroccan noncom and a T'ai guide lead riflemen along the Nam Yum River. *USIA / H. R. Simpson*

Captured Vietminh carry supplies to one of Dien Bien Phu's hilltop strongpoints. *USIA / H. R. Simpson*

Unprotected French artillery in action. Crushed by the inability of his guns to counter the Vietminh fire, the French artillery commander committed suicide. *USIA / H. R. Simpson*

The aristocratic Col. Christian Marie Ferdinand de la Croix de Castries (foreground, left) arrives on December 8, 1953, to take command. He is speaking with Lt. Col. Louis Fourcade, the leader of the First Airborne Battle Group. *USIA / H. R. Simpson*

Thunder from the hills: Dien Bien Phu under Vietminh artillery fire.
Képi blanc

A helicopter bringing wounded to Dien Bien Phu during the evacuation of Lai Chau. *USIA / H. R. Simpson*

T'ai partisans arrive at Dien Bien Phu after the evacuation of Lai Chau. With Lai Chau gone, Dien Bien Phu now stood alone. *USIA / H. R. Simpson*

Reinforcements en route to Dien Bien Phu. *USIA / H. R. Simpson*

A supply drop over "DBP Airport." *USIA / H. R. Simpson*

Replacements arrive. *Képi blanc*

Maj. Paul Grauwin operating in a hospital dugout. French casualty figures vary, but all indicate extremely heavy losses. One source states that as many as a third of the 15,000-man garrison died. Fewer than a hundred were known to have escaped capture. *Képi blanc*

Wounded members of the French forces, including a Vietnamese still clutching his submachine gun, return to the hospital after an evacuation is aborted because of artillery fire. *Képi blanc*

Vietminh infantrymen entering Hanoi five months after the fall of Dien Bien Phu. Soldier in the foreground is armed with a Czech automatic rifle and Chinese stick grenades. *USIA / H. R. Simpson*

Lieutenant Colonel Langlais to assume Gaucher's command and informed him that Maj. Hubert de Séguin-Pazzis, de Castries's chief of staff, would take over the Reserve Group, including Langlais's paras. As the tight-lipped Langlais made his way through the bombardment to Gaucher's shattered dugout, a huge explosion sent a shock wave through the air. Billowing yellow and red flames pierced the night and threw distorted shadows over the shell-torn ground. The Vietminh artillery had scored a direct hit on the storage dump containing Dien Bien Phu's aviation fuel and napalm.

At his post in the hospital's operating room, Major Grauwin timed the arrival of sixty enemy shells a minute in and around the headquarters complex. But he soon had no time for counting. His telephone jangled continually with demands for ambulances and casualty reports from the battalions. Within minutes, the hospital reception area, the triage dugout, the mess, and the staff sleeping quarters were filled with groaning casualties. It was a surgeon's nightmare: stomach, head, and chest wounds, torn limbs, and extreme shock. Swamped by the wounded, Grauwin suspected the battalion surgeons of sending too many of their patients to the hospital. Some hurried telephone calls confirmed that their aid stations were also full. They had had no choice but to send the overflow to him. Before operating, Grauwin contacted de Castries's CP to demand that a surgical team be parachuted onto "Isabelle." He was already receiving wounded from that isolated strongpoint and feared that the Vietminh might soon cut the road linking "Isabelle" with the main positions.

There were now 150 wounded throughout the hospital complex. Some were on litters; some lay on the damp ground. The odor of fresh blood and urine and the acid stench of vomit hung heavy in the cramped underground spaces. Grauwin's staff applied tourniquets, administered morphine, and decided the precedence of those destined for the operating table. French, Legionnaires, Algerians, Moroccans, black Africans, and Vietnamese; officers and men; PIM and coolies—all waited their turn under the scalpel. The stolid, hairy-chested Grauwin worked stripped to the waist in a surgical apron, his rimless spectacles sometimes peppered with blood from spurting arteries. Laboring through the night, with brief pauses for a tot of rum or sip of coffee, the surgeon and his team operated on ten abdominal wounds, fifteen fractured limbs, two cranial wounds, and ten chest wounds. Grauwin fought to save limbs and avoid the onset of gangrene. For some, it was already too late, and the limbs had to come off. Before the night was over, fourteen amputations were performed by Grauwin and Lieutenant Gindrey, who had arrived in February with the Forty-Fourth Mobile Surgical Team of the Vietnamese National Army.

Major Grauwin later described the hospital's morgue on that first night of heavy bombardment.

> The square hole was full [of dead]; outside, between the hole and the barbed wire, there were a hundred corpses, pell-mell, thrown on stretchers or onto the ground, stiffened in grotesque or tragic positions. Some were wrapped and tied in their tent cloth; others were dressed in their combat uniforms, motionless in the pose where death had surprised them.

The nocturnal struggle for "Béatrice" had become a noncom's battle. All of the Third Battalion's officers were either wounded or killed, and the sergeants and corporals had taken over. The deafening, deadly bombardment, the determined successive enemy attacks, and the lack of a friendly counterattack or the arrival of reinforcements would have already broken the will of a lesser unit. But this was the Legion. A unique mix of discipline, professionalism, tradition, and camaraderie kept the majority of survivors—including many of the wounded—at their posts. An unexpected lull in the attacks and a more organized fire from Piroth's artillery had allowed some fragmented platoons to regroup, distribute more ammunition, and prepare for the next onslaught. Then the *bo doï* reappeared, climbing over their own dead to charge the remaining Legionnaires. The Vietminh corpses on the barbed wire were thick. According to one Legionnaire, "Toward the end, we were machine-gunning the dead rather than the living." Over 500 Vietminh were to die in the attacks on "Béatrice." One by one, the company's radios went silent. The last message from "Béatrice" was received at 0015 on March 14. The radio operator of the Ninth Company was calling for artillery fire on the command bunker—and himself.

March 14 dawned gray and wet. The belated attempt at an early-morning tank-supported counterattack by the paras of the First BEP and the Eighth "Shock" Battalion had been abandoned. The Viet had been waiting along Route 41, and the paras had been stopped by heavy fire. While they regrouped and awaited new orders, a wounded officer from "Béatrice" appeared on the road. Bloody and unsteady, he was carrying a message. The commander of the Vietminh 312th Division was offering a four-hour truce, beginning at 0800, that would allow the French to pick up their dead and wounded. After a brief wait, while de Castries received Major General Cogny's telephoned acceptance of the truce offer, a work detail, led by Captain Le Damany, the Third Battalion's surgeon, and including its chaplain, drove to "Béatrice" under a Red Cross flag. The jeep, truck, and ambulance moved slowly up Provincial Route 41 through an eerily silent countryside.

A Vietminh officer joined them before the vehicles reached the foot of the hill below the CP of the Third Battalion. The battered strongpoint was a lunar landscape of shell holes, ruined bunkers, and destroyed gun positions. The debris of battle—smashed weapons, empty shell casings, discarded field radios, and abandoned helmets—had turned "Béatrice" into a giant garbage dump. Bloodstained medical dressings fluttered from the barbed wire like Buddhist funeral pennants. The Vietminh had removed their own dead and wounded, their prisoners, and the captured arms and munitions. Hundreds of Legion dead were sprawled over the lacerated terrain. The disfigured, swelling corpses were already covered with humming clusters of sticky blue flies. A Vietminh litter party appeared with several seriously wounded Legionnaires, followed by a group of walking wounded. The turnover was formal and without superfluous conversation. At 1130 Captain Le Damany led his small command back to Dien Bien Phu. There was considerable speculation on the reason for the brief truce of March 14. The French High Command in Saigon told the press that it had been arranged in response to a Vietminh request. The Vietminh refused to go into detail, except to say that it had been a "humanitarian gesture." Some observers saw the truce as a psychological-warfare ploy designed to demoralize the French garrison. They argued that the Vietminh were certain that tales of the depressing spectacle at "Béatrice" would spread throughout Dien Bien Phu once the work party and the Legion wounded returned.

Whatever the truth, the entire garrison was stunned by the fall of "Béatrice" and the death of Colonel Gaucher. "Le Vieux," as the colonel had been affectionately known by his Legionnaires, had been a symbol of invincibility and a link between the Legion's recent past and its present. Moreover, the news that only two lieutenants and 192 men of the Third Battalion had survived the attacks and made their way back to Dien Bien Phu came as an added shock. The Thirteenth demi-Brigade had fought Rommel's Afrika Korps to a standstill at Bir Hakeim. Now one of its battalions had been overrun by the Viet. It was unbelievable. Dark rumors of the debacle ran through the uneasy garrison like lit fuses.

There was considerable negative speculation on the performance of Colonel de Castries during the night of March 13. Much was made of the fact that he and his immediate staff had not left the safety of the CP thoughout the action, preferring to urinate in empty cans rather than risk shellfire. Such criticism was probably unfair, considering that any commander in the same circumstances would wish to remain close to his maps and radios and in touch with Major General Cogny in Hanoi. More serious was the impression of indecision and hesitation stemming from de Castries's delay in ordering an early counterattack. It did not reassure the garrison on March 14 to learn that de Castries's secretary had been sent back to Hanoi. She had been bundled, along with some seriously wounded men, onto a "Beaver" that had defied the artillery barrage to deliver six liters of whole blood to Major Grauwin.

The fall of "Béatrice" had an immediate significance for the men of the Fifth Battalion of the Seventh Algerian Rifle Regiment holding "Gabrielle." As occupants of the northernmost strongpoint in the defense complex, they had been direct witnesses to the battle. They had heard the deluge of artillery that had fallen on "Béatrice" and watched the lethal fireworks display of the shell bursts. These riflemen from Algiers and Oran, from Blida and the Aurès Mountains, had grown up in a land where the Legion, for all its faults, had the status of a legend. There had always been a healthy professional rivalry between the Algerian rifle regiments and the Legion. They had fought side by side in Europe during World War II. Together with the Moroccans and the Legion, they had formed the hard core of the French ground forces in Indochina. The veteran Algerian noncoms had been shocked by the collapse of "Béatrice." The commander of the Fifth Battalion, Maj. Roland de Mecquenem, and his replacement, Major Kah, who was scheduled to take over the battalion, had been able to monitor some of the dramatic radio exchanges between "Béatrice" and Gaucher's CP. Now, with "Béatrice" gone, "Gabrielle" was even more isolated and vulnerable. Nevertheless, the men of the Fifth Battalion prided themselves on the teak-reinforced blockhouses, dugouts, and shelters that they had built on "Gabrielle" and considered themselves ready for any attack.

The end of the truce at noon on March 14 found Dien Bien Phu under a persistent *crachin* rain that infiltrated the trenches and dugouts, turning the earth into thick mud. The Vietminh artillery was now back in action, methodically pounding the airstrip and the headquarters complex. That afternoon, thirty C-47s broke through the rain clouds to drop the first of the reinforcements requested by de Castries. The Fifth Vietnamese Parachute Battalion, or Bawouan, now commanded by Capt. André Botella, a veteran para who still limped from a World War II wound, had returned to Dien Bien Phu. The weather and enemy artillery fire made it a particularly difficult drop. Some of the Fifth Bawouan's companies suffered casualties before reaching their designated positions at "Eliane," exhausted from a ten-kilometer hike from the DZ.

At 1500 a solitary C-47 dropped the surgical team that Major Grauwin had requested near the central CP and not, as instructed, on "Isabelle." Grauwin had watched the eight parachutes drift to earth among the shell bursts. Luckily, none of the team were hit.

They were hurriedly sent off to "Isabelle" in a truck that had arrived earlier with a cargo of wounded from that strongpoint. Later, a telephone call from "Gabrielle" informed Grauwin that Dr. Dechelotte, the Fifth Bawouan's surgeon, had been wounded. The wounded Dechelotte arrived at the hospital with word that the assault on "Gabrielle" was imminent. With no doctors available, a Legion sergeant-medic, who also happened to be an Austrian medical student, was dispatched to the Fifth Algerian Battalion as Dechelotte's replacement.

While the Algerians on "Gabrielle" braced themselves for an enemy assault, the air force mechanics in the open shelters bordering the airstrip had been working around the clock to repair the remaining "Bearcat" fighters. The enemy artillery fire had made the strip untenable. It was now a question of saving what remained of Dien Bien Phu's aircraft. Although they handled wrenches and drills rather than rifles and submachine guns, the mechanics had no lessons to learn from the infantry when it came to courage. Their workplace had become a constant target. Shell splinters sliced into the fuselages as they patched engines and repaired landing gear. With dusk fast approaching, it was time for a triple risk. The pilots of three serviceable "Bearcats" gunned their powerful engines, shot out of the shelters like bees from a hive, thundered down the airstrip, and pulled up into the low clouds. Taken by surprise, the Vietminh gunners vented their frustration by concentrating fire on the six remaining fighters. The stubby aircraft were soon reduced to flaming, twisted wreckage. All close air support would now have to come from Hanoi, Laos, or the aircraft carrier *Arromanches*. As the escaped "Bearcats" flew to safety, the garrison of "Gabrielle" was watching two Vietminh regiments massing for their attack. An unidentified officer in the Fifth Algerian Battalion CP described the scene.

> They came down hills 604 and 702 like termites. Everyone in our four Companies took their combat posts. At 1800, the artillery preparation . . . a damned deluge! This was something new . . . Giap's surprise! The 81s, the 105s, the 120s . . . truly modern warfare, no more *maquis*. Our mortars were put out of action. The men tried to leave their holes, to put their pieces in order and proper firing positions, but it [enemy fire] was falling everywhere on the red sand. At about 2000 the transmission CP took a direct hit. Two men out of four wiped out and no more radio.

The Fourth Company took the brunt of the first attack. Enemy heavy mortars collapsed the CP, killing Lieutenant Moreau, the company commander. The defensive position dominated a steep slope and was protected by a "forest" of barbed wire, but despite the heavy French fire, the *bo doï* did not hesitate.

> The Viets came straight on like Alpinists: for ten that fell, mowed down by the 4th's fire, fifty were still climbing. The messages came through to the Major, "Viets have reached the barbed wire. Viets pouring out of the barbed wire. Viets within our position." Our interdiction fire blended with that of the enemy. A pretty fire-fly display. Then, a respite. They were waiting for the moon to set.

Major de Mecquenem informed de Castries that his men were holding and waiting for the next assault.

The lull was brief. The enemy artillery fire was now even more concentrated, seeking out what remained of "Gabrielle"'s heavy weapons. The Vietminh infantry appeared to have abandoned their mass attacks for a more cautious, steady infiltration. The Fifth Battalion's intervention platoon rushed from one hard-pressed company to the next to shore up the defenses. The Algerians used automatic weapons, grenades, and bayonets to drive back the Vietminh. Flamethrowers spouted gouts of liquid fire at enemy groups trying to hold what they had taken, and the smell of burned flesh carried to the gun positions. The Algerian riflemen fought with a dogged determination, doing their best to ignore the continuing barrage and concentrate on the live targets close at hand.

At 0200 a sudden, blessed silence descended on "Gabrielle." The defenders used the time to drag more ammunition into their emplacements and eat some cold rations. Although the wish remained largely unspoken, many hoped that the Viet had abandoned their costly effort. But losses had never deterred Giap, particularly in a contest where so much was at stake. His battered 308th Division was being relieved. It had lost close to 1,200 dead, including officers and cadre, and many more wounded. A fresh regiment of the 312th Division, one that had not participated in the attack on "Béatrice," was moving up to lead the next assault.

No one had thought it possible, but the next bombardment beginning at 0330 was even worse than the last. Additional enemy batteries joined in. A direct hit wiped out the Legion mortar platoon and destroyed its weapons. At 0400 Major de Mecquenem spoke with de Castries. He was assured of more artillery support and a tank-led counterattack if the enemy pressure increased. The taciturn Algerians fought a new assault that reached the breached wire. As at "Béatrice," there had been heavy casualties among the French officers. Their places were taken by Algerian noncoms. Ironically, some of the the noncoms who fought so hard at "Gabrielle" were destined to become officers of the Algerian National Liberation Front during the coming war for independence with France.

Following his conversation with de Castries, de Mecquenem and his senior officers were grouped together briefly in his CP. At that precise moment, a delayed-fuse shell penetrated the shelter and exploded. It was a replay of the disaster at "Béatrice." Major de Mecquenem suffered shrapnel wounds and lost consciousness, one of Major Kah's legs was blown off, and a number of other officers were seriously wounded. The CP's radio contact with the Fifth Battalion's companies and de Castries's headquarters was cut off. "Gabrielle," "the destroyer," was temporarily rudderless. After a short delay, the radio of Captain Gendre's Third Company made contact with headquarters. Gendre, who had taken command, explained what had happened and asked for reinforcements. He was promised a counterattack at dawn and was asked to "hold until then."

The officers of the First BEP and the Eighth "Shock" Battalion had been expecting to participate in the counterattack to save "Gabrielle." A detailed plan for such an action had been prepared by Major Séguin-Pazzis with his usual precision. It took into account the probability of enemy moves to block the relieving force's route north along the piste Pavie. The para commanders had identified the ford of the Nam Ou River at Ban Khé Phai, where the engineers had installed a temporary floating footbridge, as a likely location for any Vietminh blocking force. But the paras, with their escort of three M-24 tanks, were confident of blasting their way through.

A last-minute change by Lieutenant Colonel Langlais then turned the planning upside down. Enemy feints against "Dominique" had made him wary of a possible full-scale attack on Dien Bien Phu's inner defenses. The First BEP was already holding positions covering "Junon" to the south and "Claudine" to the west. The Eighth "Shock" Battalion was securing the airstrip. Langlais might have to draw on them if an assault was launched against "Dominique." He thus made the fateful decision to assign the counterattact to the Fifth Bawouan.

Although Langlais had cleared this move with de Castries, his para commanders and Séguins-Pazzis argued against it. They had gone over the scenario in dry runs, they had studied the terrain, and they knew the problems. The First BEP and the Eighth "Shock" Battalion were used to working together. The Fifth Bawouan's airdrop under fire had been an ordeal. Worse, although the Vietnamese paras had been at Dien Bien Phu before, both the landscape and the tactical situation had changed, and they were now at "Eliane," the southernmost strongpoint of the inner defense perimeter. This meant that the disoriented Fifth Bawouan, exhausted after digging into their new positions, would have the largest distance to cover before reaching the jumping-off point at dawn. Colonel Langlais refused to change his plan, but he did compromise by agreeing that two companies of the First BEP would support the Vietnamese paras and act as guides. It was common knowledge that the outspoken Langlais had a low opinion of the Fifth Bawouan's capabilities. His decision to use it for the counterattack was, at best, questionable.

Captain Botella assembled the men of his Fifth Bawouan, and the first companies began their march. They crossed the Nam Yum River and struck out for the northern tip of the airstrip, where they expected to be met by guides from the First BEP. But the Legion paras had pressed on, spurred by repeated calls for help from "Gabrielle." As expected, the First BEP had run into a blocking force at the ford on the Nam Ou River. Lieutenant Desmaizieres of the First BEP's Third Company described the ensuing action.

> The fighting began brutally; the Fourth [Company] suffered serious losses. Norbert [the company commander] was wounded by a bullet in the thigh that made him howl with rage and pain. Standing under fire, he dropped his pants to apply a dressing while his orderly provided cover. He was later treated by Dr. Bondy, who was following at a short distance. Lieutenants Boisbouvier and Bertrand had crossed the ford, but they were pinned down with their Legionnaires. Maneuvering to the left of the trail, the source of the main firing, and supported by the tanks, the Third Company succeeded in breaking through and proceeded toward the objective.

Desmaizieres's company and "what was left of the Fourth" then arrived at "Gabrielle." "The scene was one of destruction. Innumerable Viet corpses hung on the barbed wire like laundry put out to dry. Some, cut down by the riflemen's bullets and still holding explosive charges of TNT-filled bamboo meant to blow holes in the barbed wire, had not completed their mission." Although their strength was now only slightly over one hundred, the Legion paras prepared to counterattack. Desmaizieres recounts what happened at that moment: "We were stupefied by what we saw: rolling down the hill in a pack, the [Algerian] riflemen were leaving the position in relative order." After witnessing the hurried arrival by jeep of Major Séguin-Pazzis, who brought the order to withdraw, Lieutenant Desmaizieres and his company took the road back to Dien Bien Phu. "'Gabrielle' was finished," he recalls. "In reality, a few entrenched [Algerian] riflemen held on till dusk before being overrun. The withdrawal of what was left of the BEP's companies was carried out under fire from the Viet cannons. They seemed to be celebrating their victory." The First BEP had had nine killed and 46 wounded. One of the three accompanying tanks had been hit, and its commander killed.

The loss of "Gabrielle" was due to a battlefield error compounded by faulty radio transmissions. Capt. Jean Lucciani of the First BEP explains what happened.

> The battle was really lost because of a mistake, a misunderstanding. Our counterattack on "Gabrielle" was meant to relieve the Algerians, to take over the strongpoint, not to receive the survivors as they left the position. The Algerians had fought well against heavy odds, but the wrong word was passed and the position was abandoned.

Maj. Maurice Guiraud of the First BEP had contacted de Castries by radio, requesting reinforcements. He had been told to "retrieve" what was left of the able-bodied survivors on "Gabrielle" as a stopgap measure. The embattled Captain Gendre, still holding the strongpoint, had heard bits and pieces of this radio conversation. Only the phrase "retrieve the companies remaining on 'Gabrielle'" had come clearly through the static. Taking this phrase to mean that the position was being abandoned, he ordered his men to break contact and fall back on the paras. This group was the "pack" that Desmaizieres witnessed "rolling down" the slope.

Delayed by the barbed-wire roadblocks at "Huguette," the lack of guides, and the ford, the Fifth Bawouan was over an hour behind the two companies of the First BEP. Enemy artillery fire slowed the column further. Some Vietnamese troopers failed to advance despite the shouted commands and threats of their officers. The Fifth Bawouan arrived below "Gabrielle" in time to see the tanks pulling out, loaded with dead and wounded, and the garrison's survivors streaming down the hill. A cursing Captain Botella had nothing left to do but order his battalion to join the withdrawal. The Algerians had lost 501 men defending "Gabrielle." From a practical standpoint, the battalion had ceased to exist. Two of Dien Bien Phu's strongpoints had now been wiped from the map.

During the battle for "Gabrielle," Colonel Piroth had wandered through the headquarters complex like a sleepwalker. Although Colonel de Castries had noted the strange behavior of his artillery commander and asked a chaplain to keep an eye on him, most officers had been too occupied to worry about Piroth's state of mind. Piroth had been in the CP, repeating some of the arguments that he had used earlier on the eventual success of his counterbattery fire as if he were carrying on an internal monologue. He had been seen apologizing, with tears in his eyes, to survivors of "Gabrielle" for the failure of his guns to provide adequate artillery support. He had then faded from sight. The colonel's shattered corpse was later found on a cot in his dugout. He had apparently pulled the pin from a grenade with his teeth, clasped it to his chest with his remaining arm, and released the lever. Colonel de Castries attempted to keep the incident quiet, officially reporting Piroth's death "on the field of honor," but news of the suicide soon spread from one unit to the next. March 15 had been another dark day for the defenders of Dien Bien Phu.

6

The Cauldron Bubbles

"Under the enemy napalm bombs, even stone and earth took fire."

General Tran Do

On March 14, Major Bigeard's Sixth Parachute Battalion received an urgent message to leave its security task at Cat-Bi airfield and return to Hanoi. At 0800 on March 15, Bigeard reported to Major General Cogny at his headquarters in the Citadel and was ordered to take his paras back to Dien Bien Phu. As he relates in his book *Pour une parcelle de gloire,* Bigeard found the atmosphere at headquarters understandably gloomy following the fall of the two strongpoints. "It's going badly," Cogny told him. "The Viet surprised us with his attack. Strongpoints 'Béatrice' and 'Gabrielle' have fallen. We've lost two battalions. Our artillery is ineffective. Seen from Hanoi, the battle appears badly led. We have not yet had one success. Our counterattacks are ineffective."

Bigeard accepted his orders, but he did make the point that his battalion was badly in need of rest. The Sixth Battalion had participated in all the difficult operations of the past twenty months, he explained, and needed some time to catch its breath. Cogny was understanding but firm. Bigeard's "wonderful battalion" was "indispensable" to the survival of Dien Bien Phu, and the C-47s would be waiting.

In the short time left for preparations, Bigeard was able to further gauge the attitude at headquarters. His visit to the Operations Section left him with the impression that the staff there considered the fall of the fortress imminent. "We put in our little finger," he was

81

told. "Having done that, we're now obliged to insert our entire arm." The pulled muscle in Bigeard's calf was still swollen and causing a great deal of pain. Despite medical advice to remain in Hanoi for treatment, he was determined to jump. It was inconceivable that the Sixth Parachute Battalion would go into action without Bigeard.

The gloom at Hanoi headquarters was echoed at Dien Bien Phu. The decimation of the Legion and Algerian battalions and the suicide of Colonel Piroth had jolted the morale of the garrison. The fact that de Castries's chief of staff, Lieutenant Colonel Keller, was succumbing to combat fatigue was another ominous portent. It was a period of internal tensions and taut tempers. Colonel de Castries appeared to be adopting a singular remoteness, a curious detachment that would affect his command role in the days to come. The gaunt Lieutenant Colonel Langlais's normal bad temper had become particularly spiky as he endeavored to contain the Vietminh attacks and juggle his limited reserves to plug gaps in the defenses. Teamwork and interunit coordination were suffering as key officers became casualties, and de Castries's headquarters failed to provide rapid and effective leadership.

The riflemen and gunners who were bearing the brunt of the attacks may not have been privy to the inside information available to their superiors, but they knew that the air bridge to Hanoi would soon be a thing of the past. The strip was under constant bombardment, and the only aircraft still landing were the medevac C-47s and the occasional "Beaver" liaison flights. The pilots were having to brave increasingly dense and accurate antiaircraft fire. The thought that parachute drops would keep the garrison supplied and fighting was slight reassurance. Like all combat soldiers, the men in the strongpoints pondered what would happen if they were wounded. Up to now, those suffering serious wounds had been evacuated promptly. But it was clear the medevac aircraft might soon have to abandon their heroic efforts. The only alternative was Dien Bien Phu's fetid, bloody, and overcrowded field hospital.

Pierre Schoendoerffer, the young army cameraman who had been lightly wounded on Hill 781 with the First BEP during the fighting of March 5, was recuperating in Saigon. He received an urgent telegram from Hanoi sent by his colleague, photographer Jean Péraud, informing him that they were both badly needed at Dien Bien Phu. The death of Jean Martinoff and the evacuation of the wounded André Lebon had left photographer Daniel Camus to cover the battle alone. Schoendoerffer packed his gear and rushed to procure space on a flight to Hanoi. It was not easy. Staff officers and reinforcements were filling most available flights. Under the circumstances, a rifleman had a higher priority than a cameraman. On March 16 Péraud jumped with Bigeard's battalion. Two days later, after a scramble in Hanoi to find an aircraft willing to drop him over Dien Bien Phu, Schoendoerffer rejoined his comrades. Camus, Péraud, and Schoendoerffer were to remain at Dien Bien Phu throughout the entire battle.

On March 16 the garrison received major airdrops on two DZs. The drop near the main airstrip included ammunition, a replacement VHF radio beacon, and medical supplies. The drop on the DZ "Octavie," south of the main position near the strongpoint "Isabelle," delivered gunners to replace the eight crews killed or wounded by enemy fire, disassembled 105-millimeter howitzers to replace the six guns destroyed, replacements for the First BEP and Eighth "Shock" Battalion, and the 600-plus men of Major Bigeard's Sixth Battalion.

Steady rain and a mantle of fog had delayed the drops until after 1100. Finally, the familiar steady thrumming of engines and the crack of antiaircraft weapons announced the arrival of the lead flight. Enemy shells were bursting on DZ "Octavie" as the French and Vietnamese troopers of the Sixth Battalion plunged into the void. Bigeard hit the ground hard and had to be helped to his feet. He now had a sprained ankle in addition to his painful calf. Making radio contact with his company commanders, he asked for casualty reports and ordered his men to spread out while moving toward Dien Bien Phu. He then hobbled his way to "Isabelle," where Col. André Lalande, the strongpoint commander, telephoned headquarters for a jeep to take Bigeard to the main position.

"Bigeard is back!" The news of his arrival spread through Dien Bien Phu like a fortifying tonic. The Sixth Battalion and its commander, with his hawklike appearance and coolness under fire, were symbols of what was best in the French Expeditionary Corps. If "Bruno" had returned to share their lot, the garrison reasoned, there was still hope. For his part, Bigeard quickly sensed the depression and low morale around him. Although forewarned, he was shocked by what he found. Captain Botella's tale of how he had banished a number of his Vietnamese paras from the Fifth Bawouan for their bad showing during the counterattack on "Gabrielle" impressed Bigeard with the urgent need to reinvigorate the garrison. To make matters worse, he and Lieutenant Colonel Langlais clashed the day after his return. Langlais had ordered one of the Sixth Battalion's companies on a reconnaissance patrol without checking with Bigeard. Limping into Langlais's CP, supported by a thick walking stick, a furious Bigeard confronted his superior to tell him that any orders to the Sixth Battalion were to go through him. He even went so far as to repeat Major General Cogny's comment that nothing seemed to be going well at Dien Bien Phu and added that he—Bigeard—had the intention of changing things. The seconds ticked by as the two tough para commanders hovered on the brink of a physical confrontation. Bigeard later described how Langlais broke the impasse. "He told me, 'You're a *lorrain;* I'm a *breton.* We both have hard heads. Let's bang them against this post, and we'll soon see whose is the hardest!'" At this point the two men broke out laughing. From that moment on, Langlais and Bigeard understood each other. They were to form a close team, with a partnership of shared objectives and tactics that provided some cohesion and purpose to the French effort at Dien Bien Phu.

On March 17, the habitual early-morning fog was slow to dissipate. It hung over the valley positions like a screen allowing the defenders enough time to wolf down some rations, reheat the dregs of remaining coffee or tea, and relieve themselves in the stinking, maggot-infested latrine pits. The fog also provided cover for the men in two companies of the Third T'ai Battalion at "Anne-Marie" who had decided to make their own separate peace. Out of their element in the fortress environment and worried about the families that they had had to abandon to the Vietminh, the normally loyal T'ai had been thoroughly shaken by the fall of "Béatrice" and "Gabrielle." If the tall, stolid Legionnaires and the fierce, bearded Algerians could not stand up to the hail of steel and enemy assaults, how could they be expected to fight on? The T'ai had long been the target of an effective enemy psychological-warfare campaign carried out by pro-Vietminh T'ai infiltrated into their ranks and local villagers working for the Communists. Vietminh propaganda leaflets in the tribal languages had been found in positions held by the T'ai battalions. But it was primarily the enemy artillery bombardments that had been the deciding factor in their defection. Warfare in the tribal territories had its own age-old rules. You attacked when you were strong and withdrew quickly into the jungle if the enemy had the advantage. To the T'ai, it seemed the height of stupidity to remain motionless in a trench on a treeless knoll while hot shards of jagged metal peppered the ground. Quietly and carefully, the diminutive T'ai had laid down their arms and slipped through the wire, leaving the two northernmost positions of "Anne-Marie" open to the enemy. Their French officers and the few T'ai noncoms and troops who had not fled fell back on the one T'ai company still holding. Later, a company from Bigeard's battalion attempted to retake the lost positions, but the Vietminh fire proved too heavy, and the attack was abandoned. The two remaining posts of "Anne-Marie" were then incorporated as part of "Huguette"'s defenses.

A total of 254 T'ai would be listed as deserters by March 31. Nor were the T'ai alone in leaving their posts. An article published by the New China News Agency trumpeting desertions among the Dien Bien Phu garrison prompted a query to Navarre from the Ministry of

Defense in Paris. Navarre was to report the desertion of two Legionnaires on March 17 and twelve Legionnaires later in April. Some Vietnamese and North African soldiers would also risk surrender to escape the cauldron of Dien Bien Phu. Throughout the Indochina War, a small number of deserters had become turncoats and served in the Vietminh ranks. For some, Dien Bien Phu proved to be their last battle. One top secret/flash telegram from Dien Bien Phu informed Hanoi headquarters:

SERVICE PRESS/INFORMATION FILM SHOT BY REPORTER CAMUS CONTAINS PHOTOS 6 AND 7 EUROPEAN CORPSE FOUND TODAY AMONG VM LOSSES STOP DISTINCTIVE SIGNS: TATTOO: HEAD OF WOMAN ON RIGHT FOREARM STOP BRIDGE ON RIGHT SIDE OF MOUTH STOP REQUEST IDENTIFICATION IF POSSIBLE STOP.

Another telegram stated: "AFRICAN SERVING IN VM WAS KILLED 200 METERS NORTHWEST ISABELLE STOP IDENTIFICATION IMPOSSIBLE STOP." Some Soviet thirty-seven-millimeter antiaircraft guns had now been moved closer to the airstrip, and the accuracy of their fire made medical evacuation increasingly difficult. Vietminh heavy machine guns and artillery on the captured positions of "Gabrielle" and "Anne-Marie" were an added threat. The C-47s, marked with a Red Cross, thumped down on the shell-pocked strip and were followed by an ambulance filled with wounded. As the aircraft swung around, engines still running, the medical personnel had five minutes to load the litters and walking wounded. Several seconds later, a warning bell announced the imminent takeoff. The aircraft were often forced to depart with only a few of the wounded aboard. The ambulance would then return those left behind to the hell of the hospital. In the rush and confusion of loading, a number of unwounded men had attempted to leave Dien Bien Phu by elbowing their way aboard the C-47s. A section of tough military police from the Legion had to be assigned to monitor the evacuation process.

The more deadly the antiaircraft fire, the more urgent the need for fire-suppression missions by French aircraft. It was here that the pilots and crews of the naval air force (aéro-navale) distinguished themselves. From the first heavy bombardments of March 13, the "Helldivers" and "Hellcats" from the aircraft carrier Arromanches had been put ashore to operate from the airfields of Cat-Bi and Bach-Mai. This allowed the dive-bombers and fighters to cut their flight time to Dien Bien Phu and carry out dawn attacks on the enemy gun positions. The fighters were also called on to protect the C-119s during their dropping runs over the valley. When the weather closed in over Dien Bien Phu, the aircraft from the Arromanches turned their attention to Vietminh lines of communication, strafing supply centers and truck convoys on Provincial Route 41.

Six navy "Privateer" bombers based at Cat-Bi were now flying day and night missions against Vietminh positions in and around Dien Bien Phu. Like the fighters and dive-bombers, the heavy "Privateers" were being pushed to their limit. Normal mechanical rehauls and testing had been set aside for stopgap measures to keep the aircraft flying and on target. One "Privateer" crew flew four missions, including two in darkness, for a total of thirteen flying hours in a period of twenty-four hours.

As the battle intensified, the daring and effectiveness of the naval pilots became legendary among the Dien Bien Phu garrison. A special relationship was forged between the naval aircrews and the parachute battalions. Although the French air force was sharing the same risks, the paras recognized a similarity, a unique daredevil élan among the navy pilots resembling their own philosophy of combat. Any navy pilot downed at Dien Bien Phu could expect a warm welcome from the paras and a generous jolt of long-hoarded pastis or cognac to celebrate his survival.

The urgency of providing more security to the supply effort had brought ranking French air force officers together with their American counterparts to plan the use of C-119 "Flying Boxcars" for massive napalm bombing of the Vietminh gun positions. This effort entailed considerable American involvement, including procuring additional napalm supplies from U.S. stocks in the Far East, working out the details of such operations, training aircrews in an entirely new technique, and dry-run test flights. The project first had to be approved at a high level by both the French and the Americans. This approval raised a delicate question in Washington since the majority of the twenty-nine C-119s flying missions over Dien Bien Phu now had American crews. These civilian aircrews had been supplied by the Civil Air Transport Corporation (CAT) of Taiwan, a postwar offshoot of Gen. Claire L. Chennault's "Flying Tigers," under a contract arranged by the CIA. The decision to provide the American pilots had been made in Washington earlier, on January 29, during a meeting of President Eisenhower's Special Committee on Indochina. Agreement had also been reached at the same meeting to send the 200 U.S. Air Force mechanics now working at French air bases in North Vietnam and eventually assign General O'Daniel as the new chief of an upgraded U.S. MAAG Mission in Saigon. A bizarre note in the meeting transcript records the committee's refusal to provide "a small dirigible" to the French for reconnaissance purposes. With French "Privateers" being brought down by Vietminh antiaircraft fire at a height of 3000 meters, the request was definitely unrealistic—a curious echo from the 1914–1918 war—and the refusal justified.

With French air force crews flying only five of the 29 C-119s available, Washington was uneasy about the contract pilots' involvement in anything beyond supply flights, particularly since the Pentagon had detached some U.S. Air Force pilots in mufti to the CAT team in Hanoi. General Trapnell, the outgoing chief of the U.S. MAAG Mission, had already expressed his concern for the safety of the U.S. Air Force mechanics working at French bases attacked by Vietminh commandos. Finally, reassured that French aircrews would handle the napalm drops, the Americans gave their approval.

On March 24, 1954, Ambassador Heath informed the State Department that Maurice Dejean, the French high commissioner, had found General Navarre "pleased" that permission had been granted to begin the napalm operation. Dejean said the general expected it to destroy the forest cover around the Vietminh positions, result in heavy personnel losses, and destroy or damage Vietminh artillery positions. But developments at Dien Bien Phu had obviously taught Navarre not to be too optimistic. He had also told Dejean that, since the enemy guns were "emplaced in fairly deep tunnels on the mountainside," they would be difficult to reach "by bombing or direct fire."

With the interruption of normal evacuation flights, Major Grauwin's hospital looked more and more like a Hieronymus Bosch painting of purgatory. On March 17, the Vietminh had returned eighty-six wounded to the remaining French positions on "Anne-Marie," further straining the hospital's capacity. Close to 500 wounded were now shoehorned into the available shelters. Blood, vomit, urine, pus, and solid excreta mixed underfoot with the mud to formed a sticky, fly-covered paste. Maggots moved in undulating clusters over the damp mud walls and pullulated under dirty casts and soiled dressings. Normal cleanup tasks had to be abandoned as Grauwin's exhausted team fought to save lives, removed the dead, and prepared the seriously wounded for evacuation.

An excerpt from a telegram to Hanoi reporting casualties in one Foreign Legion unit provides an insight into the routine of death and wounds faced by the garrison.

LEGIONNAIRE ALBUS JEAN KILLED BY SHELL TO HEAD STOP POUALIN PIERRE WOUNDED ABDOMEN STOP VAUCHER GEORGES KILLED STOP SWEIBERT STANISLAS WOUNDED THORAX STOP ECHEVARRY JOUE WOUNDED THORAX STOP COLLIN HUBERT WOUNDED LEGS AND LEFT SIDE STOP GRAVENBROUCK JOSEPH WOUNDED RIGHT TESTICLE STOP SCHULZ HEINZ WOUNDED LEFT CALF STOP MULTIPLE GASOLINE BURNS STOP PUTTERS JEAN WOUNDED NECK STOP ZIRKEL KARL WOUNDED LEFT SHOULDER LEFT PECTORAL RIGHT THIGH STOP BRESSAN ANDRE WOUNDED RIGHT CALF.

By March 19, the artillery bombardment was almost constant. A grim race against death was repeated under heavy fire as the ambulances and open trucks bumped over the cratered road to rendezvous with evacuation flights. Enemy shells battered the hospital zone, exploding among the corpses lying in the open morgue, causing fragments of decomposing flesh to rain onto the trenches and ground outside the dugouts.

An additional surgical team commanded by Lieutenant Vidal parachuted into the valley and set up shop across the Nam Yum River from the main hospital installation. During a rare lull in firing, an airdrop of blood, penicillin, morphine, and plaster for casts arrived undamaged. Delayed-fuse shells from the Vietminh 105-millimeter howitzers fell on the hospital installations. A 120-millimeter mortar round scored a direct hit on the crowded triage dugout and its fifty wounded. Fourteen were killed outright, and most of the survivors suffered horrible secondary wounds.

The plight of the wounded had become a major concern of the French High Command. On March 20, Consul Paul Sturm in Hanoi sent a secret telegram to Washington describing the situation:

SPOKESMAN FOR [MAJOR] GENERAL COGNY SAID THIS MORNING THAT AFTER BROADCASTING CLEAR RADIO MESSAGE TO THE VIETMINH STATING THAT RED CROSS MARKED PLANES WERE COMING INTO DIEN BIEN PHU TO EVACUATE WOUNDED, FRENCH YESTERDAY LANDED 1 C–47. THIS PLANE CAME UNDER FIRE AFTER BEING LOADED, BUT MANAGED TO TAKE OFF WITH ABOUT 30 WOUNDED. TWO OTHER RED CROSS PLANES, WHICH WERE CIRCLING, DID NOT LAND. VIETMINH DID NOT ACKNOWLEDGE FRENCH RADIO MESSAGE, AND IT IS NOT CERTAIN THEY RECEIVED IT. THROUGHOUT THE DAY, 5 HELICOPTERS BASED IN LAOS AT MUONG SAI EVACUATED SUCH WOUNDED AS THEIR CAPACITY PERMITTED: INFORMANT DOES NOT HAVE FIGURES ON NUMBERS SO EVACUATED. ONE OF THESE HELICOPTERS WAS HIT BY ENEMY FIRE, BUT SUCCEEDED IN TAKING OFF. LAST NIGHT AFTER DARK 5 C-47S WERE LANDED AT DIEN BIEN PHU AND SAFELY EVACUATED ABOUT 100 WOUNDED TO HANOI. SPEAKING PERSONALLY, INFORMANT, WHO IS COGNY'S CABINET CHIEF, SAID THAT ADVANCE PLANNING HAD NOT TAKEN ADEQUATE ACCOUNT OF PROBLEM OF EVACUATING WOUNDED, AND HE FEARS THAT PROBLEM WILL BECOME MORE SERIOUS STILL WHEN ATTACKS ARE RESUMED.

Army briefing officers in Hanoi and Saigon underlined the Vietminh's callous disregard of the Geneva Convention in firing on aircraft marked with the Red Cross. But Vietminh officers watching the activity on the airstrip through binoculars or artillery scopes had a different opinion. They had been able to observe the departure of French aircrews from the Dien Bien Phu fighter squadron aboard medevac helicopters and the arrival of staff officer replacements in Red Cross aircraft. These practices, too, were in violation of the Geneva Convention. Radio Hanoi also claimed that the French were bringing in ammunition aboard the medical flights. Whatever the claims and counterclaims, the situation of the wounded was desperate.

The air force pilots then came up with a ruse to fool the Vietminh gunners. Two medevac C-47s would approach the strip at midnight. One would fly over the strip at 200 meters, its engines roaring, as if it were parachuting supplies. The second, engines cut, would glide through the darkness following masked beacons to a landing. This procedure proved effective for several nights at the rate of forty wounded per flight. An ambitious plan to land six aircraft began well . . . until the fourth landing. At that point an illumination flare from a French position at "Huguette" popped into the air, bathing the strip in light and revealing the subterfuge. Shells began to pound the runway near the C-47. The wounded were hurriedly loaded, the pilot gunned his engines, and the aircraft lifted off into the dark sky. No one was certain whether the Vietminh had seen through the French tactic or whether the bombardment had been a blind reaction to the flare. It was decided to try again the following night. This time, there was no doubt. A C-47 glided into an ambush set by an infiltrated Vietminh patrol. Automatic weapons raked the aircraft, killing the radio operator and seriously wounding the copilot. From now on, all landings—Red Cross or not—were certain to draw fire.

Despite their successes, the Vietminh were having troubles of their own. Illness and a shortage of a medicines remained a constant problem. Ensuring that ammunition and food arrived from their depot areas at the right time and place could prove both costly and exhausting. The feeder roads built through the jungle in December and January, deteriorating rapidly under heavy use and the tropical rains, required constant maintenance. French bombing and strafing may not have cut the Vietminh supply lines, but they were taking a heavy toll on sappers, truck drivers, and laborers. The latest American-supplied antipersonnel bombs had now been added to the French arsenal with deadly effect.

The heavy losses suffered by the some of Giap's best units had also had an effect on the Vietminh troops. The role of the Communist political officers had become vital to maintaining morale and the offensive spirit. Harangues, discussions, and patriotic speeches kept the *bo doï* focused on their task with "victory" as the key word. Two days after the successful assault on "Béatrice," Giap's special message to his troops warned: "His [enemy] morale is affected, his difficulties are numerous, but don't underestimate him. If we underestimate him, we'll lose the battle. . . . " Later in the same month, Giap cautioned: "The first difficulty comes because certain comrades, unaware of the actual situation and the forces involved, show subjectivity and underestimate our adversaries, from which comes a weakening of our combat organization that can easily lead to defeat."

The problem of resupplying the French units at Dien Bien Phu did not end when the parachutes hit the ground. As the Vietminh pushed closer to the main fortifications, some of the air-dropped supplies were already falling onto ground held by the enemy, thus supplying the Vietminh directly with everything from ammunition to camouflaged parachute jackets. Although the majority of airdrops fell within the defense perimeter, it took a major, dangerous effort to retrieve the canisters and cases and deliver them to the proper recipients. Airdrops at night might avoid accurate daylight antiaircraft fire, but the heavy supply packets were hard to locate in the dark, and Vietminh artillery fire made the task of the work details even more difficult. This was particularly true of the heavily loaded, multichuted pallets dropped from the C-119s. An exchange of telegrams between de Castries's and Hanoi headquarters finally resulted in the C-119 loads being broken up into smaller, more manageable packets.

While the battle for Dien Bien Phu was drawing world attention, there had been a gradual buildup of a siege mentality in Hanoi. Following the Vietminh commando raids on the airfields at Bach-Mai, Gia-Lam, Cat-Bi, and Do-Son, Navarre had ordered the surrounding villages forcibly evacuated. This had been done despite a strong protest from Governor Tri of North Vietnam, who predicted that such an unjustified move would provide the Vietminh with a propaganda windfall. At the same time, an uneasy Major General Cogny had been watching the buildup of enemy strength close to Hanoi and Haiphong. Intelligence reports had situated thirty-six Vietminh regular battalions in the Red River Delta, supported by battle-tested regional forces and hamlet and village militias. On March 17, Consul Sturm had sent a secret, priority telegram from Hanoi to Ambassador Heath, explaining that his decision to evacuate female American staff and dependents to Saigon was directly linked with French reverses at Dien Bien Phu and the worsening security in the north. Pointing out that the situation for the moment remained unchanged, Sturm had stated:

HOWEVER, BOTH CIVIL AND MILITARY AUTHORITIES ADVISE AGAINST USING ANY ROADS LEADING OUT OF CITY, ALL OF WHICH ARE NOW UNDER SPORADIC ATTACK OR SUBJECT INTENSIVE MINING. HANOI–HAIPHONG HIGHWAY IS OPEN TO TRAFFIC ONLY IN AFTERNOONS. RAILWAY, BADLY SABOTAGED TWELFTH, WAS RESTORED TO SERVICE YESTERDAY ONLY TO HAVE FIRST THREE TRAINS SENT OVER LINE BLOWN UP. VIETMINH INFILTRATION BOTH OF REGULARS AND WELL ARMED PROVINCIAL TROOPS HAS NEVER BEFORE REACHED SUCH PROPORTIONS NEAR MAJOR POPULATION CENTERS.

Informing the ambassador that the French were considering the evacuation of women and children from Tonkin if Dien Bien Phu fell, Sturm had warned of a possible all-out campaign of terrorism and promised to keep the ambassador advised. His telegram had concluded: "MEANWHILE PLEASE KEEP ALL WOMEN AND ALL VISITORS EXCEPT YOURSELF AWAY FROM HANOI."

On March 24, the first attempt was made at the saturation napalm bombing of Vietminh positions one kilometer west of Dien Bien Phu's defenses. Three C-119s with French crews dropped sticks of twenty-liter cylinders of napalm with ten-second delayed fuses over an area three kilometers long and one kilometer wide. A second target zone was covered by C-47s, with the napalm launched by hand from the cargo doors. These wing tip–to–wing tip napalm drops did eventually destroy a number of Vietminh positions and cause limited but horrendous casualties. But bad weather, antiaircraft fire, inexperience with a new technique, and the natural cushion of damp jungle foliage combined to cut the operation's effectiveness. Vietminh Gen. Tran Do later wrote a somewhat romanticized description of the attacks from the viewpoint of those on the receiving end.

> Under the enemy napalm bombs, even stone and earth took fire; but despite the burning splashes on their bodies our fighters held on, our guns continued to fire at the enemy who were taking advantage of the smoke to make assaults. Covered with blisters, our men were still able to smash their attacks.

While the defenders of Dien Bien Phu hunkered down in their bunkers and husbanded their ammunition supplies, the relief of the beleaguered garrison was being discussed on a high level halfway around the world. Gen. Paul Ely, chairman of the French Joint Chiefs of Staff, had come to Washington on March 22, 1954, to discuss an increase in American military aid and a guarantee of U.S. intervention if China entered the conflict. The French had already linked the outcome of the upcoming Geneva Conference on Indochina to their defeat or victory at Dien Bien Phu and were convinced that Ho Chi Minh and Giap shared the same view.

Adm. Arthur B. Radford, chairman of the U.S. Joint Chiefs of Staff, presented Ely with a plan to save Dien Bien Phu with a massive American air strike code-named Operation "Vulture." The plan called for sixty B-29s, from the U.S. bases at Clark Field in the Philippines and in Okinawa, to carry out nighttime carpet bombing of Vietminh positions around Dien Bien Phu. The heavy bombers would be protected against possible Chinese air force intervention by 150 fighters from U.S. Seventh Fleet aircraft carriers. Ely took

Radford's plan back to Paris, where it received a generally favorable government reception. General Navarre, however, had his doubts about Operation "Vulture." The specter of Chinese intervention in the war had taken on more form with the advent of Dien Bien Phu. French intelligence had reported an increase in the number of MIG fighters stationed at airfields in southern China, and Chinese on-the-ground support for the Vietminh had increased. A massive U.S. raid might wipe out much of Giap's battle force, but it could trigger the movement of Chinese divisions into Tonkin and the annihilation of the French Expeditionary Corps.

While its possible salvation was being discussed in Washington, the garrison of Dien Bien Phu was surviving, waiting for Giap's next move. Like most veteran campaigners, the troops were taking each day as it came and learning to live with death. In order to keep death at a respectful distance, every lull was used to improve and strengthen their battered positions. The unique situation at Dien Bien Phu had rolled back the clock thirty-eight years. The candle-lit dugouts, the sandbagged trenches, the shellfire, and the barbed wire brought to mind fuzzy photos of World War I trench warfare. French officers and men and the Germans in the Legion were reminded of the western front and Verdun—with one troubling difference. At Dien Bien Phu, the front line was everywhere, and there was no rear area or hope of relief.

Keeping the road linking "Isabelle" to the main positions open had become a nightmare. Vietminh troops had succeeded in digging trenches at the small, deserted village of Ban Kho Lai, effectively blocking the road at its halfway point. On March 22, a combat team from the First BEP, supported by a tank platoon, tried to fight its way through to "Isabelle" without success. Algerian and T'ai riflemen from "Isabelle," accompanied by tanks from the strongpoint, were ordered to move north up the road to assist the First BEP. What had promised to be a short, stiff firefight now developed into a pitched battle. The Legionnaires of the First BEP fought hard for every yard of ground, maneuvering through the paddies and among the bullet-raked huts of the village, laying down a hail of fire from their automatic weapons and light mortars. But despite their efforts, air strikes, and the sustained fire from tank cannon, the Vietminh refused to be driven from their trenches. Colonel de Castries's headquarters had to authorize the commitment of Dien Bien Phu's remaining tank platoon before the enemy position could be taken. After almost five hours of combat, two companies of the Vietminh Fifty-Seventh Regiment of the 304th Division had been all but wiped out. The French had suffered 151 dead and seventy-two wounded. The price of maintaining the perilous lifeline between Dien Bien Phu and "Isabelle" was becoming too high.

The deterioration of the situation at Dien Bien Phu was reflected in the atmosphere at the Hanoi Press Camp, where correspondents gathered each day for briefings on the course of the battle. The "camp" was in reality a chalet-type building in the French residential section of the old colonial city. It had sleeping quarters for a limited number of accredited journalists, a bar, a lounge–cum–briefing room, and a dining area. It also housed the office of the military censor. Press cables passing through the censor received a clearance stamp after offending passages were deleted. Some dispatches were rejected entirely. In periods of military success, this office was relatively quiet. When things were going badly, it was the scene of acrimonious disputes between representatives of the international press and the harried censor.

The long struggle in Indochina had taught the army the political importance of the media in influencing French and international public opinion. The military censors were often caught in a vise between their superiors, who wanted to present a favorable view of the war for outside consumption, and the crusty correspondents who had good nonofficial sources and did not hesitate to question the credibility of the briefing officers. Events at Dien Bien Phu were straining the already shaky relationship between the media and the press officers. Newsmen checking the officially supplied data against firsthand accounts and leaks that they had received from returning pilots, wounded personnel, and talkative staff officers often found the official version wanting. For example, the First BEP's opening of the road to "Isabelle" had been presented as a considerable success, while the reporters concentrated more on the cost of the operation and the fact that "Isabelle" had become so isolated. American and British correspondents were particularly vociferous about the trickle of valid official information from Dien Bien Phu.

Senior French officers were often prevailed on to appear at informal briefings. One such meeting found Brigadier General Dechaux, commander of the Northern Tactical Air Group, denying that a C-119 destroyed on the ground at Dien Bien Phu had been crewed by Americans. The attendant rumor was that this crew was now stranded within the fortress. Dechaux categorically denied the story. Despite his denial, a number of correspondents rushed from the briefing to draft stories stating that Americans were now under fire on the ground at Dien Bien Phu. Their cables never left the censor's office.

The battle was causing further strains in Hanoi. Major General Cogny, who had the reputation of talking too much in the presence of journalists, appeared to be distancing himself from what could well become a catastrophe. Correspondents were quick to note a marked difference between the outlook of General Navarre's staff and that of Major General Cogny. While Navarre's officers radiated continued optimism, those working for Cogny made no effort to hide their pessimism. American Consul Sturm reported: "COGNY'S PAST AND PRESENT CABINET CHIEFS HAVE TOLD ME WITHIN PAST WEEK THAT COGNY NEVER APPROVED CONCEPT OF DIEN BIEN PHU BUT ACCEPTED IT AS 'SPORTING PROPOSITION' WHEN NAVARRE DECREED ITS EXECUTION." In addition, Cogny's messages to de Castries had become almost unreal in their interpretation of the actual situation. Colonel de Castries's demands for reinforcements and worries about an escape plan if the fortress was overrun were brushed aside in a directive with vague promises of "activating an airborne group" and the study of an "eventual plan for the rescue of the breakout force." Cogny began the same directive by urging de Castries to "keep in view the success of the battle." He added a paragraph emphasizing that any strong-point taken by the enemy should be retaken immediately, as if de Castries had unlimited reserve forces at his disposal. Even a neutral observer would have no difficulty in scenting a strong whiff of future self-justification in such a text.

What happened next at Dien Bien Phu was something that few veterans of the battle like to discuss. The event reflected on the per-formance of a senior officer and challenged the French army's his-toric code of discipline. Early in the morning of March 24, Lieutenant Colonel Keller, de Castries's chief of staff, who had been huddled in the command bunker, wearing his steel helmet, over a period of days, was evacuated to Hanoi. The brusque Lieutenant Colonel Langlais then assumed unofficial command of Dien Bien Phu on his own initiative and gave Major Bigeard the responsibility for planning and carrying out all counterattacks. Although the details of this impromptu change of command remain sketchy, it appears to have been inevitable under the circumstances. By March 24, de Castries's withdrawal from active and effective participation in the battle was no longer a secret. He had remained isolated in his protected CP, concentrating on his daily radio contacts with Cogny, signing off on messages and rarely venturing outside.

Langlais and his para commanders had already taken de facto command of the battle, shifting units, directing counterattacks, and coordinating air and artillery support. In reality, Langlais's move, later termed a "putsch" by some nonpara officers, only formalized the existing situation. Strangely enough, de Castries apparently accepted the new arrangement without protest, retained his official title of overall commander, tempered Langlais's impetuousness with advice, and continued to act as Dien Bien Phu's contact with Cogny's headquarters. As Bernard Fall points out in his book *Hell in a Very Small Place*, the forces at Dien Bien Phu "were finally led by a French lieutenant colonel [Langlais] who, in effect, commanded a whole division, and by a Vietnamese history professor [Giap] who, in effect, commanded a whole army."

7

The Meat Grinder

"EVEN IF I HAD 3,000 WOUNDED AT DIEN BIEN PHU, THAT FACT WOULD NOT CAUSE ME TO YIELD."

General Henri Navarre
to U.S. Consul Sturm in Hanoi

A deadly lattice of tracers crisscrossed the airstrip, counterpointed by the thump of exploding howitzer shells. Antiaircraft fire cracked over the valley, piercing fuselages and aborting drop runs. Three C-47s had been destroyed within forty-eight hours, their crews cremated within the twisted fuselages. By late March, the medevac flights and supply drops had become a turkey shoot for the Vietminh gunners. The garrison had been elated earlier to learn that an entire battery of enemy seventy-five-millimeter guns had been smashed by Dien Bien Phu's artillery. Now that elation faded as yellow flames from the burning transports lit the sky. On the evening of March 27, Colonel Nicot, the air force officer responsible for the evacuation and resupply effort, informed French Far Eastern air force headquarters that he had ordered the cessation of low-level parachute drops. His message cited the "carnage" taking place and underlined the "psychological shock" that the aircrews were suffering in addition to their physical fatigue.

Nicot's order meant that the drop altitude for parachuted supplies, previously set at just over 2,000 feet, would now be raised to a minimum of 8,000 feet. It had been difficult enough to drop parachuted supplies accurately within the shrinking defense perimeter. From now on, it would be a true gamble. The air force had been experimenting with fused, delayed-opening devices for the supply parachutes. These small explosive charges that allowed parachutes to pop open at a preselected altitude had suddenly become essential to Dien Bien Phu's survival.

Navarre's response to Cogny's urgent request for 50,000 delayed-opening devices marked a further deterioration in relations between the two generals. "I am amazed," Navarre replied, "that you, responsible for the conduct and support of the battle of Dien Bien Phu, have waited until March 26 to face the problem of high-altitude parachute resupply and alert me to your difficulties regarding this subject." Despite Navarre's testy response, an immediate effort was made to locate a source of supply. The American Air Force in Japan, already scouring its stock to provide the French with replacement parachutes, was asked to airlift whatever delayed-opening devices could be spared to Hanoi. Meanwhile, French air force technicians in North Vietnam began to work around the clock to manufacture their own. Unfortunately, the performance of the final product was often defective, the chutes opening prematurely or sometimes not at all.

In late March, Consul Sturm cabled Washington to report a conversation with General Navarre in Hanoi. The general had told Sturm that he did not expect Giap to answer his request for a cease-fire on medevac aircraft. But Navarre did hope that the publication of his message would force the enemy to face up to his responsibilities to the French wounded at Dien Bien Phu. Sturm reported:

NAVARRE SAID THAT VIETMINH APPEARED [TO] BELIEVE THAT PRESENCE AT DIEN BIEN PHU OF CERTAIN NUMBER OF FRENCH UNION WOUNDED FOR WHOM ADEQUATE MEDICAL FACILITIES WERE NOT AVAILABLE MIGHT CAUSE HIM, NAVARRE, TO BREAK OFF ENGAGEMENT FOR HUMANITARIAN REASONS. GENERAL SAID, HOWEVER, "EVEN IF I HAD 3,000 WOUNDED AT DIEN BIEN PHU, THAT FACT WOULD NOT CAUSE ME TO YIELD."

There was no time for such verbal bravado at Dien Bien Phu. It had become painfully obvious that something had to be done to reduce the antiaircraft fire that was disrupting the supply drops and having such a deadly effect on the medevac flights. Although the Vietminh were obviously preparing for another major attack, Major Bigeard had noted a renewal of hope among the defenders. The First BEP had managed to fight through to "Isabelle" once again, leaving one hundred enemy dead in its path. Bigeard's battalion had put another fifty Vietminh out of action. He had ordered his eighty-one-millimeter-mortar and recoilless-cannon crews to move from position to position, delivering fire on enemy concentrations to give the impression that "Eliane" was packed with heavy weapons.

On the evening of March 25, Bigeard was summoned to de Castries's dugout. Despite Langlais's takeover, de Castries was still nominal commander of the fortress, and his agreement was sought on important operational decisions. The aristocratic colonel and the up-from-the-ranks major were a study in contrasts and a mirror of the post–World War II French army. In Napoleonic times, de Castries would probably have been riding beside Marshal Ney, while Bigeard would have risen to the rank of sergeant as a campaigner in the Old Guard. But times, and the army, had changed. As Bigeard described it, the meeting was cordial and businesslike.

"*Salut*, Bruno, you'll accept a small whiskey?" de Castries asked, as if Bigeard were a guest in his chateau.

"Okay, *mon colonel.*"

"How are things going on 'Eliane'?"

"The morale is 5/5 [radio code for 'clear reception,' i.e., everything is fine], *mon colonel.*"

De Castries then explained the reasons for summoning Bigeard. He had received orders from Hanoi to neutralize all the Vietminh antiaircraft positions to the west of the fortress that were making airdrops next to impossible.

"Go get them for me tomorrow," Bigeard was told. "You have carte blanche. Take whatever you need to orchestrate the affair."

"Agreed, *mon colonel.* It'll be done." But Bigeard did not leave the CP before ensuring that his superior officer understood two unpleasant truths. He told de Castries to be prepared for serious casualties among the "two or three battalions capable of carrying out such an offensive action with any chance of success." He also explained that he was being given little time to organize an operation that had to be precise, delicate, and rapid and in which everyone had to fully understand his part in the mission.

"I know, Bruno," de Castries responded, "but I have confidence in you."

Bigeard then embarked on a marathon planning session, working steadily for six hours on a makeshift table in a dugout adjacent to Langlais's CP. He took de Castries at his word and commandeered the best that was available. The final, roughly typed orders were simple and direct. They outlined the mission of the task force, provided an intelligence summary that situated a regiment of the Vietminh 308th Division in the zone of operation with two of its battalions protecting the antiaircraft units and their tasks. Two para battalions—the Eighth "Shock," thrusting toward the village of Ban Ban, and Bigeard's Sixth, moving on the Ban Ong Pet—would act as the principal assault force. The First BEP would serve as a reserve, ready to intervene on five minutes' notice, while a battalion of Legion infantry would act as a backup force. Artillery support would be provided, according to the original orders, by "twelve 105mm cannon, twelve 155mm cannon, and twelve 120mm mortars."

Eventually, although Bigeard got his 105-millimeter howitzers and mortars, only two 155-millimeter howitzers would be available for the task. The mission orders called for the maximum available air support. This, as always, would depend on the weather. A tank platoon was to provide close fire support. Capt. Yves Hervouët, the senior tank commander, was leading his squadron with both arms encased in plaster casts, and Maj. Jacques Guérin, the air force liaison officer, was suffering from a debilitating case of amebic dysentery. Both men attended Bigeard's 0200 briefing. Their presence symbolized the unwritten rule of Dien Bien Phu: An officer remained on his feet until it was absolutely impossible to continue.

Bigeard knew that surprise and speed were essential to the operation's success. He arranged for a heavy, rolling artillery barrage to open the attack at 0600 and insisted that the assault battalions be within 300 meters of their objectives by that time. He also instructed any unit encountering the enemy during its nighttime approach march to give the impression that it was carrying out a simple night patrol. Above all, to avoid a long, costly battle and the arrival of Vietminh reinforcements, he emphasized the need for a rapid withdrawal once the job was done.

The night was moonless and eerily quiet as the components of the task force moved toward their jumping-off points: the Sixth Battalion crossing the Nam Yum River from "Eliane," the Eighth "Shock" Battalion moving out from the central redoubt, the First Battalion of the Second Legion Infantry Regiment moving out from "Huguette," and the First BEP moving out from its positions at "Claudine" and "Junon." Bigeard had ordered complete radio silence, authorizing his units to come on air only at 0530 to report their arrival in position. A platoon of three tanks led by M. Sgt. Aristide Carette moved up as quietly as possible, the drivers nursing the growling engines and avoiding abrupt gear changes. Bigeard was in his element. It was not often that a mere major had the opportunity to plan and command a major operation involving four battalions and a tank squadron, plus artillery and air support, without someone looking over his shoulder or questioning his decisions.

The bombardment started on time, rending the dawn with explosions, blasting fresh furrows in the soft, red earth, and sending the surprised Vietminh scrambling for cover. At 0630, as the rolling barrage moved on, scouts preceded the assault force into the curtain of smoke and dust hanging over the enemy positions and the shattered villages. The paras knew that it would not be easy. It was not. The Vietminh had been jolted by the heavy shelling and the appearance of the paras so close to their positions. But the *bo doï* of the 308th Division were no strangers to battle. Vietminh artillery and mortars were soon ranging in on the attackers, and the barrels of the heavy antiaircraft machine guns were lowered to target the oncoming paras. The lead para platoons reached the Vietminh trenches and gun emplacements amid a din of exploding grenades and the staccato chopping of automatic weapons.

Bigeard was flat on his belly, directing the attack from a shallow hole near the action, shouting into his radios to be heard over the blast of incoming shells. Bad weather had delayed his air support for one hour. Once arrived, the aircraft attacked like angry hornets, buzzing low on their strafing and bombing runs to suppress enemy fire and frustrate the arrival of Vietminh reinforcements. The determined paras fought from one gun emplacement to the next, destroying the twenty-millimeter guns and fifty-caliber machine guns with explosive charges. Casualties mounted as the battle continued. A well-aimed shot to the head killed one para lieutenant as he was reporting the successful capture of an enemy trench. Another young officer, motioning his men forward, had his hand blown off at the wrist.

Accounts of combat tend to become technical and detached as they outline the movement of battalions, companies, and platoons. For those involved, be they French and Vietnamese paras, Foreign Legionnaires, or Vietminh *bo doï*, the fight before Ban Ban and Ban Ong Pet was exceedingly personal. Each cracking bullet or humming shell fragment threatened the survival of the individual combatants, the tension drying the saliva in their throats, knotting their stomachs, and increasing their heartbeat. Motivation, esprit de corps, and training contributed to the success or failure of each small action. The loss or capture of fifty yards of trench was often the result of individual behavior. The troops of both armies fought within a close-knit grouping of comrades at the platoon and squad level. The final outcome often depended on the strengths or weaknesses of that relationship in an environment where death could be the penalty for failure.

As the battle progressed, one of Bigeard's companies suffered heavy losses from an enemy mortar barrage that killed its commander. Vietminh infantry moved quickly along an approach trench to attack the stunned survivors. Despite doubts that it would arrive in time, another company was dispatched as reinforcement. The real-life scenario suddenly took on the appearance of a Hollywood script. The tank platoon at "Isabelle," summoned as the battle commenced, had covered the six kilometers from the distant strongpoint in record time. The three M-24s had broken through an enemy battalion on the road to Dien Bien Phu and sped across the open plain in a rocking charge worthy of the French cavalry. They arrived at the crucial moment, their cannons firing directly into the oncoming Vietminh, their machine guns stitching a pattern of death along the trenches, their heavy tank treads grinding fleeing enemy troops into the mud. Two of the tanks were hit by bazooka fire but not disabled. By 1530, the Vietminh were withdrawing, and the battle for the batteries was over. It was time for the task force to withdraw before the enemy reorganized and brought up reinforcements.

Operation "Bigeard" had been a success and an immediate morale booster. The final results were impressive. The Vietminh had suffered 350 dead and an undisclosed number of wounded, and ten prisoners had been taken. Five twenty-millimeter guns, twelve heavy machine guns, two bazookas, and twenty-four automatic rifles had been destroyed. Over one hundred individual arms had been captured. The French losses were twenty dead, including two officers, and seventy wounded. Looking back on the action in September 1954, Bigeard wrote in his special report: "I knew it was only a flash in the pan because such an effort would require rest and reorganization of the units involved. Seven officers, including three Company commanders, and twenty elite non-coms were out of action. With our units broken and exhausted we [now] had to 'bluff' the Viet."

In his book *Dien Bien Phu*, General Giap makes no mention of this attack on his antiaircraft positions. In 1991, while interviewing the general in Ho Chi Minh City, I mentioned Bigeard. "Ah, Bigeard!" Giap murmured with a knowing nod and a brief shadow of a smile. The name was not mentioned again.

March 28 marked a new low for Major Grauwin and the wounded in his charge. A medevac C-47 had run the gauntlet of antiaircraft fire and glided onto the strip in the early morning hours, to be met with the usual reception from the Vietminh artillery. It was piloted by Maj. Maurice Blanchet, the second in command of the Transport Group "Béarn," on his first night flight into Dien Bien Phu. Blanchet's C-47 was to have the dubious distinction of being the last medevac aircraft to land at Dien Bien Phu, as well as the last to be destroyed on the ground by enemy artillery fire. The pilot and crew, including the twenty-eight-year-old air force nurse Lt. Geneviève de Galard-Terraube, escaped injury and joined the garrison.

Like other stranded pilots, Blanchet soon found his niche on the ground. A section of airmen was fighting as infantry with the First BEP. Others were ensuring the supply of ammunition to the French positions. Blanchet was soon manning the headquarters VHF radio, guiding pilots in for their airdrops. Lieutenant Galard-Terraube took her place in Major Grauwin's hospital, sharing the dangers, the sleepless nights, and the horrors of the rat-infested dugouts. Her calm, professional presence throughout the battle was to have a soothing effect on the wounded and dying. At first, Grauwin's patients addressed her as "Mademoiselle," but she was soon known as "Geneviève." Not only was she tending the seriously wounded and seeing to their nourishment, but she took additional risks by visiting the medical installations at the other strongpoints. Although the legend of the "Angel of Dien Bien Phu" was a product of propaganda hype and a natural peg for romantic flights of journalistic fancy, the self-effacing "Geneviève" would never be forgotten by the men who passed through the hospital.

The monsoon hit Dien Bien Phu on March 29. By the next day, the rain was falling in solid sheets, drumming on the shelters and turning the trenches into ankle-deep canals. The softened red mud slid from the trench walls and parapets like slow-moving lava, invading the dugouts and gun pits. It formed a putrid ocher soup, enriched by human waste and the decomposing bodies of the unburied dead. The steady downpour loosened the logs bracing the dugouts and threatened to collapse the roofs. Work details struggled to move ammunition and supplies above water level. On March 13, the preparation of warm meals had become "difficult." Now such a luxury was increasingly rare. Water gurgled down the walls of the hospital, detaching the plaited lantana panels and rising to litter level among the wounded on the odiferous mud floor.

An ambitious contingency plan had been elaborated earlier to deal with the advent of the monsoon season. It entailed the shifting of units and supplies to higher ground and major changes in the camp's defensive posture. The planners had envisioned an orderly process that included an adequate labor force assisted by the engineers, the necessary trucks, and full participation by the units involved. The plan had not taken into account constant enemy artillery fire, the dwindling motor pool, the state of the wounded, the shrinking of the perimeter, and the need for every ablebodied man to participate in combat operations. Under the endless rain, the orderly redisposition of the strongpoints became another faded dream.

Since mid-March, General Giap had been formulating the plans for the "2nd phase of the offensive." His objectives would be

> to occupy the defending hills to the east of the central sub-sector, to push our approach trenches to rapidly encircle the enemy, to enclose him in a network of our attack lines, to neutralize, then occupy, the main airfield, to block and then completely cut the enemy's route of reinforcement and supply, to wear down and annihilate his forces, [and] to restrict his zone of occupation and his air space, creating the conditions for launching a general assault.

This ambitious program called for approaching the French fortifications of "Dominique" and "Eliane" over open ground and fighting day and night, without respite, under artillery fire, tank attacks, and air strikes until the strongpoints were taken. Giap realized the difficulties and dangers of such a plan. Up to now, his attacks had usually taken place at night. This factor had allowed his troops the cover of darkness to approach their objective, engage the enemy, and withdraw before dawn. It had also meant a reduction in the effectiveness of French air support.

To reduce the hazards of sustained daylight combat, Giap ordered the construction of a new trench network around "Dominique" and "Eliane." This network would include communications trenches running from the eastern hill crests to the outer wire of the French positions and lateral support trenches to assist movement and obstruct enemy counterattacks. These earthworks were to include casemates for automatic weapons and recoilless rifles, ammunition dumps, and dugouts for aid stations and sleeping areas. The slogan was "Dig Now—Fight Later." Over one hundred kilometers of trenches were dug over a ten-day period in late March. Gen. Tran Do wrote:

> The men could sleep for only three hours or so a day. At 7 or 8 a.m. they came from the battlefield; after a meal they attended a meeting to review the work, slept from 9 a.m. to 12 o'clock, then went to cut and carry wood. From 3 p.m. onwards they had a social, took their meal, then went away with pickaxes and shovels on their shoulders until the next morning.

Although French artillery and air strikes were a constant threat, Tran Do's description underlines the comparative freedom of movement and leisure moments enjoyed by the besieging force, in contrast to the molelike existence of Dien Bien Phu's defenders. But digging the trench network remained a costly business. Tran Do relates:

> Though they had finished preparing an assault base against an eastern post, Phung's company still continued digging about ten meters from the enemy position in order to consolidate their shelters, cover them with wood and build galleries to protect them from enemy [shell] splinters and mortars. This work cost the lives of many fighters and stirred further the seething hatred of hundreds of others.

The preattack preparation of "Bald Mountain" and "Phony Mountain" as fire bases was a major project for Giap's combat engineers. Since the beginning of the French occupation of Dien Bien Phu, Colonel Piroth and his artillerymen had assured de Castries that Giap's guns would never be installed on these exposed hills east and southeast of "Eliane" 2, one of the positions of the strongpoint. In a sense, they had been correct. No Vietminh commander in his right mind would have risked his guns in such exposed positions. But the French had not taken into account the enemy's ability to dig tunnels and galleries through the center of an innocent-looking hill. As Giap moved his assault force into position, he could now be sure of fire support from a daunting number of recoilless rifles and heavy machine guns firing from the camouflaged, newly dug caves of "Phony Mountain." Both hills were to provide invaluable cover to the Vietminh's movements as well as act as fire bases.

For Lieutenant Colonel Langlais, all signs pointed toward a major Vietminh attack on the eastern hill positions. Quick visits to "Dominique" and "Eliane" convinced him of the necessity of rein-forcing both strongpoints with paras from his dwindling reserves. He was particularly worried about the condition of the below-strength Algerian rifle battalion holding "Dominique." His practiced eye had noted the telltale signs of fatigue and low morale. To make matters worse, Capt. Jean Garandeau, the battalion's commander, was incapacitated with a severe case of flu, and many of its officers and noncoms had been evacuated with malaria, dysentery, or wounds. The need to occupy the various hill positions within "Dominique" had fragmented Garandeau's command. If Langlais had been disturbed at finding these emplacements occupied by such meager manpower, he was shocked to learn that one of the positions on "Dominique" 2 was defended by a ragtag company of native levies armed with obsolete .303 Enfield rifles and apparently without officers. He was slightly reassured by the apparent readiness of a Legion mortar company in support of the Algerians. Although the Moroccan rifle battalion holding "Eliane" appeared to be in better condition than the Algerians, Langlais doubted the staying power of the T'ai battalion on "Eliane." He ordered a company of the Fifth Bawouan to relieve the Algerian company on "Dominique" 1 and a company of the First BEP to reinforce the Moroccans on "Eliane" 2. In addition to two companies and the headquarters section of Captain Botella's Fifth Bawouan on "Eliane" 4, a company of the Eighth "Shock" Colonial Parachute Battalion occupied "Eliane" 10. Elements of Major Bigeard's Sixth Colonial Parachute Battalion were in place as a reserve force, and a tank platoon was standing by.

The relief of a front-line position under battle conditions is never an easy operation, particularly when the enemy is observing every move. By 1800 on March 30, a company from the Fifth Bawouan was climbing up through openings in the wire to relieve the Algerian rifle company on "Dominique" 1. The Algerians had removed their automatic weapons from the emplacements and gathered their packs and equipment. Forming up in the trenches, the North Africans were smoking and talking in low voices. Not unhappy to leave the exposed position, they watched the bobbing helmets of the approaching Vietnamese paras with contained impatience. Suddenly, all hell broke loose. The sky seemed to split open. Giap's massed guns had begun an orchestrated pounding of "Dominique" and "Eliane" and were reaching out to stifle movement and create havoc in the central headquarters redoubt. The exploding howitzer and heavy-mortar shells left bloody, misshapen bundles of dead sprawled in the trenches and sent the surviving defenders scrabbling for cover. What would become known as the "Battle for the Five Hills" had begun. The hills "Dominique" 1 and 2 and "Eliane" 1, 2, and 4 disappeared behind a dense curtain of smoke and flying debris.

The relief process of "Dominique" 1 became a disorderly shambles as the para officers urged their heavily laden troopers toward the position and the cadre of the Algerian rifle company tried to bring some order out of chaos and hold their men in place. Normally, the defenders would have endured the bombardment under whatever cover was available, waiting to meet the expected enemy attack with withering machine-gun and small-arms fire once the barrage had lifted. This time, it was different. The first waves of *bo doï* seemed to rise from the ground within the barbed-wire defenses. They came forward *through their own artillery barrage*, uprooting the wire pickets that they had already weakened by nocturnal digging. The lead elements carried woven mats filled with earth that were unrolled in their path to neutralize the standing wire and take the first shock of exploding mines and booby traps. The Vietminh broke through the defense line so quickly that the Legion mortar company did not have time to readjust its sights and supporting French artillery fire fell behind the attackers. Determined to win and counting on a massive numerical superiority, Giap had committed the Vietminh 312th and 316th Divisions and two regiments of the 308th "Iron" Division to the assault. A bird's-eye view of the attack seen through the shell bursts and smoke would have revealed waves of green-clad attackers pouring from their trenches and rushing for the French positions as if drawn by some gigantic magnet.

It was too much for the Algerians on "Dominique" 1. The men in the company broke and ran, every man for himself, as they fled downhill past the cursing Vietnamese paras. The commander of the para company ordered his men to open fire on the fugitives. This action managed to stop some, but the majority continued to run and stumble down the slope toward the relative safety of the central redoubt. Outnumbered ten to one, the Vietnamese paras, the survivors of the Legion mortar company, and a handful of Algerian noncoms held the position for a miraculous three hours before finally being overrun.

It was much the same on "Dominique" 2, the main position. Most of Captain Garandeau's riflemen fled to the rear, and the CP was overrun in an hour's time. The Moroccans on "Eliane" 1 joined the flight, and Major Nicolas, the battalion commander on "Eliane" 2, was barely hanging on with the hard core of his battalion.

This was infantry warfare at its worst, a vicious, uncompromising, nighttime contest fought by the intermittent light of flares in a continual din of artillery and automatic-weapons fire. The participants struggled through mud, wire, and corpses, taking or giving ground, seeking to inflict as much damage as possible on their opponents. Small pockets of defenders grouped around a chattering automatic rifle would halt an enemy attack yards from their trench only to find Vietminh troops rushing toward them from their flank. Radio contact was often cut, and confusion reigned. Shouted orders died in the cacophony, and urgent commands had to be mimed.

On "Eliane" 4, Bigeard maintained radio liaison with Langlais, monitoring the messages from the hard-pressed Major Nicolas. At one point, Langlais, losing radio contact with Nicolas and presuming the position lost, ordered artillery to fire on "Eliane" 2. Fortunately, Bigeard intervened to cancel the order, explaining that he was still in contact with Nicolas and suggesting that Langlais adjust his radio frequency. Bigeard, his neck grazed by a shell fragment, had watched the rout of the Algerians and Moroccans and braced himself to receive the full force of the assault on his position. To the west, the Vietminh 308th Division had begun an attack on "Huguette."

A battery of 105-millimeter guns manned by black African gunners was in position near Provincial Route 41 on comparatively flat land between "Dominique" and "Eliane." Lieutenant Brunbrouck, a 1952 graduate of Saint-Cyr and the battery commander, had watched the disintegration on the strongpoints. Retreating riflemen were flowing around his position as they fled toward the Nam Yum River. It was clear to Brunbrouck that his guns and the less than one hundred men of his battery would soon be the only sure force blocking the draw between the two strongpoints, a direct route to Dien Bien Phu's inner defenses. One company of Algerian riflemen was dug in around his battery, and mines had been laid in a dry stream that formed a shallow trench beyond the sandbagged gun positions. Considering what had happened on "Dominique," Brunbrouck was not sure that the Algerians would hold. He had ordered every available automatic weapon to cover the draw to his front. The howitzers were loaded with short-fused shells, their barrels lowered for direct fire.

Brunbrouck and his gunners were spared the ordeal of a long wait. Two overconfident regiments of the Vietminh 312th Division, encouraged by their success on "Dominique" and advancing without artillery support, soon surged from the draw along Provincial Route 41. They were heading for the bridge over the Nam Yum River that led to "Claudine" and de Castries's CP. The four 105-millimeter cannons roared, their shells exploding so soon after leaving the guns that there seemed to be a continual barrage. The concentrated shrapnel cut bloody swaths through the surprised Vietminh. The firing continued, empty shell cases clanging to the ground, acrid smoke rising from the overheated cannons. At the same time, two quad-.50s opened up from "Épervier" ("Sparrow Hawk"), a newly established strongpoint manned by the Eighth "Shock" Battalion. Their eight barrels delivered a withering direct fire, scything the enemy like blades of a thresher. The attack slowed, wavered, and broke as the *bo doï* went to ground below "Dominique." In desperation, close to 200 Vietminh sought cover in the dry stream bed. Most of them died there when the Algerians—who had held their ground—electronically detonated the minefield. During the subsequent lull, the battery bombarded the lost positions on "Dominique" and "Eliane" now occupied by the enemy and dropped shells on Provincial Route 41.

The lieutenant's request for replacements for his wounded and dead gunners was refused, and he was twice ordered to destroy his guns and fall back. But Brunbrouck remained in place, knowing that his battery was the only obstacle between the 312th Division and the central redoubt. The battle continued through the night. Mortar fire fell among the stoic, sweating gunners, and the regrouped enemy tried repeatedly to break through to the Nam Yum River. But no troops, no matter how motivated, could stand up to the direct-fire butchery of the 105-millimeter cannons. By dawn, the assault force had vacated the draw, leaving windrows of its mutilated dead. A company of paras appeared through the mist to form a defensive screen in front of the battery. They were followed by tractors to haul Brunbrouck's guns back toward the main redoubt. Once again, the key to the outcome of a crucial battle had been decided by fate, chance, and the behavior of a few individuals.

It was no different on the besieged hill positions. Lieutenant Colonel Langlais had pulled companies of Legionnaires from the First BEP and the Thirteenth demi-Brigade and thrown them into the battle for "Eliane" 2. From his position on "Eliane" 4, Bigeard could hear the "marvelous Legionnaires" bellowing a German marching song as they climbed toward their objective. Lieutenant Lucciani had led a mixed force of his paras and Moroccans in a successful counterattack toward the heights of "Eliane" 2. It had been a hand-to-hand struggle fought with bayonets, knives, rifle butts, and entrenching tools. When it ended, Lucciani's men had joined the remnants of Major Nicolas's Moroccans still hanging on to a portion of the strongpoint.

The torn ground around "Eliane" 2 was littered with bodies. Legion, Moroccan, and Vietminh dead lay grouped together where they had fallen. The defenders had dragged and pushed some enemy dead into place to form protective parapets, the incoming bullets and shrapnel thudding into the lifeless corpses. By now the exhausted survivors of Lucciani's company were supported by reinforcements from the First BEP and Bigeard's Sixth Battalion. They met the last Vietminh assault with a head-on counterattack that stopped the *bo doï* in their tracks.

Both de Castries's staff, relatively secure in the dank CP dugout, and the exhausted paras on "Eliane" 2 knew that the embattled hill positions were the key to the survival of Dien Bien Phu. Langlais and Bigeard now planned to retake "Dominique" 2 and "Eliane" 1 with a strong, tank-supported counterattack by the best battalions available. These were the Eighth "Shock" Battalion, Bigeard's Sixth Battalion, and elements of the Sixth Bawouan, with the Third Battalion of the Legion Infantry from "Isabelle" in support. In reality, the usual designation of "battalion" was no longer numerically applicable. Losses had reduced the manpower of the fighting units, and some companies could more aptly be described as reinforced platoons. Officer casualties had been so high that junior officers had taken over command responsibilities and senior noncoms had moved in to fill the gaps. Some of the officers still at their posts would have been classed as walking wounded and sent to the rear in a normal battle situation. The artillery's losses in men and guns had cut its effectiveness by half. The surviving gunners were suffering from fatigue and psychological trauma. Manning their guns around the clock and under heavy fire in poorly protected emplacements had been a harrowing ordeal. The knowledge that much of their fire had failed to knock out the enemy's guns and that the ammunition supply was dangerously low was an added sap to their morale.

Langlais and Bigeard completed their planning with the expectation that help was on its way. The reinforcements repeatedly requested by de Castries had now arrived in Hanoi. Cogny's headquarters had sent a cable to Dien Bien Phu promising that "if you hold the next heavy attack a battle group of paras (two or three Bns.) will arrive immediately as reinforcements." This tentative relief force included Major Bréchignac's Second Battalion of Parachute Chasseurs, Maj. Hubert Liesenfelt's Second BEP, and the First Colonial Parachute Battalion, commanded by Capt. Guy de Bazin de Bezon. All of these crack units were ready and waiting for the green light to fly to the aid of their fellow paras at Dien Bien Phu.

Bigeard launched the counterattack at 1330 on March 31, with Major Tourret's Eighth "Shock" Battalion heading for "Dominique" 2 and Bigeard's Sixth Battalion and elements of Botella's Fifth Bawouan targeting "Eliane" 1. The supporting Legion battalion and a platoon of tanks expected from "Isabelle" were fated not to take part in the operation. Their six-kilometer trek from the distant strongpoint had been stopped by a Vietminh regiment barring their route at Ban Kho Lai. The Legionnaires then had to fight their way back to the security of "Isabelle" at a cost of fifteen dead and fifty wounded.

The French assault force pushed up the hills in the face of heavy fire through a nightmare scene of twisted wire and pulverized trenches. The noxious stench of rotting flesh rose from the battered emplacements. The advancing paras grimaced and cursed as they inadvertently trod on dismembered limbs and fly-covered hunks of flesh. The rain had stopped, and fighter aircraft had joined the artillery to pound the Vietminh positions. By 1500, Bigeard was able to report that "Dominique" 2 and "Eliane" 1 were again in French hands. But there was no untoward elation at the success of the counterattack. The price had been too heavy. As the paras dug in to await the expected enemy reaction, they searched the clear sky, hoping for the arrival of the promised reinforcements. Bigeard, writing in his postaction report, described that crucial period with ill-disguised bitterness.

> The men's morale was fantastic, it's beautiful, good weather. We wait. Alas, at 1600 hours—nothing. The Viet then counterattacked in force and retook Eliane 1 and Dominique 2. Morale is low—one dreads nightfall. It is likely that the arrival of two para battalions that day would have had a serious repercussion on the future.

At 1800 hours on March 31, at about the same time that Tourret's Eighth "Shock" Battalion was abandoning its hard-won positions on "Dominique" 2, a code clerk in the communications room of the American Embassy in Saigon was transmitting a secret NIACT (night action) telegram to Washington. The message from Ambassador Heath, drafted with information from French sources and the assistance of his military attachés, was a succinct analysis of the situation at Dien Bien Phu.

UNFORTUNATELY, WEATHER THIS MORNING HAS BEEN BAD AND FRENCH HAVE BEEN UNABLE UP TO 1100 HOURS TO TAKE OFF FROM HANOI EITHER IN HEAVY BOMBERS OR DROP MISSIONS ALTHOUGH FIGHTER BOMBERS HAVE BEEN ABLE TO OPERATE OVER BATTLE FIELD AND LAST NIGHT BOTH B–26's AND PRIVA-

TEERS WERE ENGAGED. INABILITY THUS FAR TO DROP IS OF CRITICAL IMPOR-
TANCE AS IT IS NAVARRE'S APPARENT INTENT TO DROP ONE OR TWO PARA-
CHUTE BATTALIONS AND ONE ADDITIONAL BATTERY OF 105'S OR 75'S TODAY.
IN LAST NIGHT'S BATTLE FRENCH LOST 7 GUNS AT CENTRAL REDOUBT AND 6
OUT OF 12 GUNS AT "ISABELLE". IF BY NIGHTFALL TODAY THESE REINFORCE-
MENTS HAVE NOT BEEN MADE AVAILABLE TO DE CASTRIES OUR MILITARY FEEL
THAT VIETMINH MAY BE ABLE THIS NIGHT TO OVERPOWER "ELIANE" WHICH IS
A HILL POSITION, AND THUS BE IN POSTURE FOR A FINAL ASSAULT. NAVARRE
WILL THEN BE FACED WITH CRUCIAL DECISION WHETHER TO ENGAGE MORE
FORCES OR FIGHT IT OUT TO LAST MAN WITH WHAT IS LEFT AT DIEN BIEN PHU.
WEATHER IS STILL THE VITAL ELEMENT IN THIS EQUATION. HEATH

Other classified telegrams from Saigon reporting on the potentially disastrous situation at Dien Bien Phu and sent through military
and intelligence channels clattered into message centers at the
Pentagon and CIA headquarters. The urgency of the situation created a crisis atmosphere in Washington. Admiral Radford, with the
support of Vice President Richard M. Nixon, continued to push for
the adoption of Operation "Vulture." But President Eisenhower, who
had recently ended U.S. involvement in the Korean conflict and
promised to reduce both the defense budget and taxes, was unenthusiastic about any new military adventure in Asia. Gen. Matthew B.
Ridgway, the Army chief of staff, who had replaced Gen. Douglas
MacArthur in Korea, was opposed to Operation "Vulture." Like
many veteran infantrymen, he doubted the effectivess of such air
strikes. He predicted that U.S. participation would eventually mean
involvement on the ground. Remembering his firsthand experience
fighting Chinese "volunteers" in Korea, Ridgway predicted that at
least seven U.S. divisions would be needed to bolster the French and
more if the Chinese entered the conflict. He forcefully argued that
the United States should never again become involved in an Asian
land war.

On March 29, Secretary of State John Foster Dulles had publicly
called for "unified action" to stop Communist expansion in
Southeast Asia. Such action would be based on the cooperation of
the United States, France, Great Britain, Australia, New Zealand,
Thailand, the Philippines, and the three Associated States of
Indochina (Vietnam, Cambodia, and Laos). Dulles's proposal
demonstrated America's continued involvement in Southeast Asia
and provided the Communists with food for thought as they prepared for the upcoming Geneva Conference, but the initiative was
weakened by a lack of detail on military commitments.

The high-level conferences, redrafted contingency plans, and
heated disagreements in peaceful, springtime Washington were far

removed from the realities of the "Five Hills." The night of March 31 on "Eliane" was lit up by star shells and the searing passage of tracers. Hunkered down on "Eliane" 4, an exhausted Major Bigeard listened intently to a sputtering radio message from Lieutenant Colonel Langlais.

"Bruno," Langlais told him, "if you estimate you can't hold, join us in the main redoubt."

"Out of the question, *gars Pierre* [Langlais's code name]," Bigeard responded. "As long as I've got one man alive, I'm not going to let go. Otherwise, Dien Bien Phu is finished!" Gen. Tran Do later summed up the Vietminh view of the battle in one short sentence: "The enemy suffered heavy losses, but did not admit themselves beaten."

8

Calls for Help

*"Armed intervention of U.S. aircraft carrier at Dien Bien Phu
is now necessary to save the situation."*

George Bidault,
French Foreign Minister

The first strong assault by elements of the Vietminh 308th
Division on a key position at "Huguette" had been contained by a
platoon from the First Company of the Fifth Bawouan, commanded
by Captain Bizard. Since their questionable performance during the
counterattack on "Gabrielle" and the purging of hesitant troopers
from their ranks, the wiry Vietnamese had fought well. The
Vietnamese paras on "Huguette" equaled their counterparts on the
"Five Hills," throwing back the shouting Vietminh with a fury common to civil wars when countrymen fight countrymen. Following the
death of its commander, Lieutenant Thélot, the platoon that had
borne the brunt of the attack was commanded by Sergeant
Tournayre. On the night of March 31, the Vietminh tried again, the
bo doï pouring through the wire to cries of *"Mau lên!"* (hurry!) as
their officers urged them forward. This time Tournayre had been
ordered to abandon the position and pull the platoon back, leaving
the bunker and trenches empty. In that vulnerable moment of surprise and indecision, while the attackers swarmed over the abandoned position, Bizard called in a deluge of bracketing artillery fire.
Once the guns had done their work, the outnumbered paras counterattacked, and all of "Huguette" was once more in French hands.

The morning of March 31 had been marked by hostilities of
another kind in Hanoi. General Navarre, troubled by reports of the

Vietminh successes, had flown to Hanoi from Saigon. On his arrival
at 0115, he was met by Colonel Bastiani, who made excuses for the
absence of Major General Cogny, explaining that Cogny had been
very tired and had gone to bed. Cogny's absence at the airfield only
added to the existing tension between the two commanders. Later,
according to military historian Jules Roy, Navarre put a call through
to Cogny's quarters only to be informed that the general had left
word not to be disturbed. Cogny, spending long hours under pressure as the senior officer responsible for Dien Bien Phu, had doubtless been *fatigué*. But, whatever his fatigue, it could not possibly
have matched the exhaustion of the men fighting for "Dominique,"
"Eliane," and "Huguette."

In Cogny's absence, General Navarre, assisted by Colonel
Bastiani, set to work drafting a special order. Addressed to Cogny, it
envisioned a worst-case scenario and detailed the orders to be sent
to de Castries. The two-page, *très secret* document called for the
preparation of the central redoubt of "Claudine" and the strongpoint
of "Isabelle" so that they should hold as long as possible under difficult conditions. Insisting that the garrison be informed of the situation, Navarre then sugarcoated the pill. "It should be explained that,
as long as the resistance lasts, all hope is not lost and the moment
will come, with the arrival of the rainy season, that the V.M. will
have to loosen his encirclement." Here again Navarre revealed the
cloudy, unjustified optimism that had plagued the whole campaign.
The order emphasized the need to boost morale by underlining that
the garrison is "defending the honor of France and Vietnam, that the
whole world has its eyes fixed on it." The point to be stressed was
that "by its [the garrison's] resistance, pushed to the limit, and the
losses it inflicts on the V.M. it delays to the maximum the moment
when the 30 battalions and numerous artillery groups and heavy
battalions it is now immobilizing will again be available." After rul-
ing out any idea of surrender, Navarre then arrived at practicalities.
"All measures must be taken, nevertheless," he ordered, "that no
cannon and, above all, no tank, fall into the hands of the enemy
without having been thoroughly destroyed and that the maximum of
provisions (particularly munitions) be destroyed before seizure by
the enemy."

The second half of the order provided cold comfort to the
besieged garrison. Navarre stated:

Colonel de Castries should be informed that everything will be done
to evacuate his wounded and drop replacements for his parachute
battalions, and reinforcements limited to one parachute battalion and
one battery of 75mm recoil-less rifles, but he should be warned that
the general situation forbids me from going over that limit merely to

obtain a prolongation of the resistance. I cannot provide him with supplementary resources—and particularly some or all of my 1st Airborne Group—unless I am convinced that their intervention will provide us with victory.

Navarre then reiterated his confidence in Colonel de Castries and his certainty that the troops under his command would follow his example. The concluding sentence above Navarre's signature was less than reassuring. "The commander of strongpoint Isabelle should be informed of these instructions in the event that, at a particular moment, he alone remains capable of resisting."

Major General Cogny arrived at his headquarters just before 0800 to find General Navarre hard at work and as impeccable and detached as ever. Reports vary on whether their argument took place there and then or at a later conference. Whatever the timing, all the stored-up resentment of the past weeks surfaced. "I exploded," Navarre later told Jules Roy. "I chewed him out. And he, in turn, told me to my face all that he had been telling others for some time." The clash might have been avoided if Cogny had met his superior officer at the airport. As it was, the knowledge that, prior to retiring, Cogny had been absent from his headquarters attending a social event the previous evening undoubtedly fueled Navarre's anger.

Following their open disagreement, the two senior officers maintained a public facade of sociability, but any student of body language would have had little difficulty deciphering their true feelings. Any hope of a truce between them was obliterated by the delayed arrival of a letter from Navarre to Cogny dated March 29. In this letter the commander in chief denied Cogny's latest request for more men and matériel, stating, "the forces at your disposition are entirely adequate to fulfill your present mission." In a tone more suitable for lecturing a junior officer, Navarre warned Cogny, in regard to the possibility that any of the dire situations that he had cited in arguing for more support might come about, ". . . you will be entirely responsible for such a situation because it will have resulted from the improper use of your resources." The most stinging language appeared in the closing paragraphs. Navarre accused Cogny of not providing a more vigorous impetus to the "preparation and conduct" of the battle. The accusatory litany continued: The attention of Cogny's staff had never risen above the routine of the delta to concentrate on Dien Bien Phu; there had been a lack of liaison between Cogny's headquarters and the air force staff responsible for air support, a lack of preparation for the use of artillery, and an absence of directives regarding organization of the terrain at Dien Bien Phu.

Cogny's official reply was not long in coming. He disputed

Navarre's letter point by point and refused to accept the "entire responsibility" for the possible fall of Dien Bien Phu. Citing Navarre's "lack of confidence" in his ability, Cogny stated that he no longer wished to serve under Navarre's orders. Since he did not want to abandon his command in the middle of a battle, Cogny left the decision and timing of his departure to Navarre. French army archives also contain a second letter from Cogny to Navarre (unsigned and unsent) going into greater detail in support of his views. While the two generals exchanged recriminations and filed written records of their arguments for the future, the bloody, seesaw contest continued at Dien Bien Phu.

Major Bréchignac's battalion arrived over Dien Bien Phu at 2030 on April 1. This was the battalion of reinforcements that Navarre had mentioned in his special order to de Castries. As feared, the Vietminh antiaircraft fire was heavy, clawing the sky in search of the buffeted transports as the pilots tried to keep on course for the DZ. The DZ at the south end of the airstrip was so reduced and the drop time so short that the paras had to jump in small groups. This requirement meant that aircraft had to pass over the valley more than once, adding risk from ground fire and inevitable delays.

Claude Sibille, a young *caporal chef*, was one of those standing by the open door of a lurching C-47. A Parisian, he had joined the army at 18 years of age, drawn by the "mystique of North Africa." Finding no assignment available in the Moroccan *goumiers*, he had volunteered for the paras. After five years' service in Madagascar, Sibille had participated in six operational jumps in Indochina.

"It was like a fireworks display," Sibille recalls, "with tracers passing on each side of us. We were heavily laden with leg bags, supply sacks, machine guns, and sixty-millimeter mortars. It was daunting, but we knew we had to go." On signal he jumped into the dark with the rest of his stick. On the way down, he could see the tracers arcing upward toward the canopies of the oscillating parachutes. He landed hard. "I found myself on my back, caught on the barbed wire. Then I was hit in the leg by a shell fragment. There was a first-aid bag nearby. I could see the Red Cross in the flash of firing. A wounded Vietminh soldier and I reached it at the same time . . . we shared its contents."

Only one company of the battalion, a command section, and a seventy-five-millimeter gun crew reached the ground that night. The dropping process had been so slow that the C-47s, with the remainder of the battalion, were forced to return to Hanoi, ceding the DZ to higher-priority drops of ammunition and supplies. It took two more night drops to complete delivery of the Second Battalion, the First Chasseurs Parachute Regiment. Each drop was marked by casualties, many suffered while in the air. The piecemeal nature of this

meager reinforcement was hardly a morale booster. Bréchignac and
his men were welcomed in a situation where the redeployment of a
squad or the arrival in a bunker of an additional automatic-rifle
team was considered an event. But from the garrison's point of view,
the battalion should have been dropped earlier. Bigeard later
summed up the prevalent feeling at Dien Bien Phu.

> What a pity they hadn't been sent on March 31 at the moment we
> were counter attacking on Eliane and Dominique. What an error by
> Hanoi! . . . the unnecessary losses [could have been] avoided if they'd
> been dropped that day! We vaguely sense that nothing is working in
> Hanoi. Fortunately, we are unaware that Navarre and Cogny are
> tearing each other apart at the same time we're there, nose in the
> shit. . . .

Bréchignac arrived at the CP, bruised and with his uniform
ripped by a rough landing in the wire. He, too, was a legend in
Indochina and a leader worshiped by his men. His battalion, like
Bigeard's, could always be counted on to accomplish the impossible.
The two battalions had often fought side by side, seizing Dien Bien
Phu and blocking Giap's push into central Laos. Now, forgetting
their long-standing professional rivalry, Bigeard greeted "Bréch"
with open arms.

Despite Bigeard's disappointment at the late arrival of
Bréchignac's battalion, he was pleased with his new responsibilities.
His role in direct command of all counterattacks—in sum, the
hands-on defense of Dien Bien Phu—had been officially confirmed.
He now presided over a daily briefing at 0900 in the para CP. "This
meeting was a valuable morale builder," he wrote in his report on
the battle. "Camaraderie excellent . . . we were fighting for our
skins! We discussed orders, intelligence on the enemy, air support
expected. The sharing of artillery resources was decided for everyone . . . 20 to 30 shells per sector." This last sentence reflects the
serious shortage of artillery ammunition at Dien Bien Phu. From
March 30 to March 31, the French 105-millimeter guns alone had
fired 9,500 rounds. By April 1, only 10,500 105-millimeter rounds
remained.

The hazards of antiaircraft fire and the short DZs meant that
much of the ammunition dropped was falling into enemy hands. A
curt secret/personal telegram from de Castries to Cogny on April 13
revealed that not everything falling on Dien Bien Phu was welcome:
"IN 24 HOURS WE HAVE SUSTAINED THREE [FRIENDLY] BOMBING ATTACKS
WITHIN OUR DEFENSIVE PERIMETER—STOP—ON THE OTHER HAND THE
CARGO OF FIVE C–119S, OR A MINIMUM OF 800 ARTILLERY ROUNDS, HAS
BEEN DELIVERED TO THE ENEMY—STOP—NO COMMENT. DE CASTRIES."

These misdropped cargoes had become a welcome supplement to Giap's supply system. One Vietminh regiment alone had recuperated over fifty tons of cargo, including artillery shells and rations. The *bo doï* were enjoying the luxury of tinned sardines, Gitane and Bastos cigarettes, vinogel, and the occasional bottles of rum, cognac, or eau-de-vie courtesy of the French army. At one point the loss of 105-millimeter ammunition had become so serious that Langlais suggested that Hanoi booby-trap some shells dropped within enemy lines to explode on use in the Vietminh guns.

On April 3, Navarre sent a highly classified, limited-distribution telegram to Paris. It contained intelligence information on the increase of Chinese support for the Vietminh effort at Dien Bien Phu. The message informed the French government that fourteen Chinese technical advisers were at Giap's headquarters and numerous others, including logistic specialists, at division and regimental levels. The advisers were using a special telephone net installed and maintained by the Chinese. All advisors were "under the command of general Ly Chen-Hou who is stationed at operational CP beside General Giap." The Chinese had provided forty thirty-seven-millimeter antiaircraft guns, each served by twenty Chinese, and 1,000 trucks manned by Chinese drivers—500 of the trucks had arrived since March 1. The delivery of forty "Bofors" guns and super-"Molotova" trucks was expected.

Other military supplies included 395 machine guns, 1,200 automatic rifles, 4,000 submachine guns, 4,000 rifles, 44,000 thirty-seven-millimeter rounds, 15,000 105-millimeter rounds, 10,000 seventy-five-millimeter rounds, 60,000 mortar rounds, and 5,000,000 cartridges, including 1,500,000 for heavy machine guns, as well as 4,000 cubic meters of gasoline and 4,300 tons of rice. The report stated that twenty-four of the 105-millimeter guns in action at Dien Bien Phu had arrived from China via the border town of Lao Cai in April 1953. It concluded with the notation that the bulk of this intelligence information was gleaned from material of class-A value (the best) and that care should be taken to ensure that its utilization would in no way compromise the source.

On April 5, the American ambassador in Paris, Douglas Dillon, sent an urgent secret cable to Secretary of State John Foster Dulles describing an emergency meeting with Georges Bidault, France's foreign minister, and Joseph Laniel, the French prime minister. Dillon had been summoned to the prime minister's residence late on a Sunday night to be told that "ARMED INTERVENTION OF U.S. AIRCRAFT CARRIER AT DIEN BIEN PHU IS NOW NECESSARY TO SAVE THE SITUATION." Navarre's report on the scope of Chinese involvement at Dien Bien Phu was provided to Dillon, who included it in his message. Dillon also passed on Bidault's warning that the French chief of air staff had stated that U.S. intervention at Dien Bien Phu could lead to Chinese air attacks on French airfields in the Tonkin Delta. Regardless, the French government was making its request for aid. Dillon quoted the French foreign minister's conclusion that "FOR GOOD OR EVIL THE FATE OF SOUTHEAST ASIA NOW RESTED ON DIEN BIEN PHU" and that "GENEVA [CONFERENCE] COULD BE WON OR LOST DEPENDING ON OUTCOME AT DIEN BIEN PHU." Dillon commented that "THIS WAS REASON FOR FRENCH REQUEST FOR THIS VERY SERIOUS ACTION ON OUR PART." He also informed Dulles that according to Bidault, Admiral Radford had given General Ely his personal assurance that if the French required U.S. naval air support at Dien Bien Phu, he would do his best to obtain such help from the U.S. government.

The Dillon cable arrived in Washington two days after Secretary Dulles and Admiral Radford had presented the outline of Operation "Vulture" to a restricted meeting of congressional leaders. The congressmen, whose general reaction had been negative, insisted that no unilateral action be taken but let it be known that they might rethink their position if the British agreed to participate. There is a cruel irony in the fact that then-Senator Lyndon B. Johnson of Texas was one of those most opposed to any U.S. intervention in Vietnam. The desperation of the latest French request impressed the Eisenhower administration with the urgency of the situation and the need to make a decision. It also hardened the internal dispute within the government. The detailed report on Chinese involvement provided ammunition for both arguments. Admiral Radford saw it as practical proof of China's intention to extend Communist rule throughout Southeast Asia. General Ridgway considered Chinese presence on the ground at Dien Bien Phu an indication that any U.S. involvement would provide an excuse for massive Chinese intervention on the Korean model, inevitably escalating into an unwanted ground war in Asia.

Black sedans ferried briefcase-carrying State Department officials to the White House, Pentagon representatives lobbied Congress, and the National Security Council amassed the facts needed to supply President Eisenhower with a pragmatic recommendation. Meanwhile, the U.S. military had already gone to work on Operation "Vulture." The Korean War had awakened the American armed forces from their post–World War II doldrums. The tragic lack of readiness at the beginning of the Korean conflict had meant heavy casualties, poor performances, and lost ground. The subsequent Chinese intervention that had sent UN forces reeling south in retreat was still a fresh memory. Readiness and advance planning were now two of the Pentagon's highest priorities.

In early April, Lt. Gen. Earle E. Partridge, commander of the U.S.

Air Force in the Far East, and his bomber command chief, Brig. Gen. Joseph D. Caldera, arrived in Saigon for a series of conferences with Navarre and his air force staff. From the beginning, it became obvious that the French were unprepared for such a large undertaking as Operation "Vulture" and did not understand the extent of destruction involved in the use of B-29s. The U.S. commanders were shocked at the seeming indifference of their French counterparts to the danger of friendly casualties from such an operation. Brigadier General Caldera insisted on a firsthand look at the situation. The tough, outspoken Caldera overflew the embattled valley twice in his own B-17 and once in a French air force C-47. Although the Americans had misgivings about the inadequate navigational and guidance systems available, they decided that Operation "Vulture" would be possible as a daylight raid. All that Caldera needed now was the go-ahead from Washington.

A persistant official haze still hangs over the proposed use of tactical nuclear weapons to save Dien Bien Phu. The relevant documents remain classified, but enough has seeped out through personal comments and written memoirs to suggest that such a proposal was seriously considered. Fortunately for the garrison of Dien Bien Phu, the project was abandoned. The comparatively crude nuclear weapons of 1954 risked wiping out the defenders as well as the attackers, and the second use of U.S. nuclear weapons in Asia would have had disastrous and long-lasting political consequences.

While America hesitated to pull France's chestnuts out of the fire, an in-house dispute over the delivery of parachute reinforcements had developed between Hanoi and Dien Bien Phu. Colonel Sauvagnac, Brigadier General Gilles's replacement as commander of airborne forces, had been insisting on the usual training period for troops without parachute qualification. Since many urgently needed specialists—the artillerymen, tankers, and radio operators who had volunteered to jump into Dien Bien Phu—were nonparas, such a by-the-book approach had threatened to slow the reinforcement trickle to a drip. Sauvagnac had also been insisting that the drops be made over established, relatively safe DZs. This condition had now become a practical impossibility. Colonel Langlais had argued without success that troops dropped over Dien Bien Phu were simply arriving at their combat posts by other means. Although it had not attained the proportions of the Navarre-Cogny confrontations, the Langlais-Sauvagnac row had come to a head during the night drops of Bréchignac's battalion. As the C-47s had circled overhead waiting for a lull in the firing near the DZ, Langlais, aware that time was running out, had told the air force to drop the paras on the

main position. When the air force officer responsible for the operation had hesitated, Langlais had ordered him to do as he had been
told and had taken full responsibility for the action. Sauvagnac's
protest had drawn a scorching reply from the feisty Langlais.

> HAVE RECEIVED YOUR MESSAGE. IT PROVES TO ME THAT YOU STILL
> HAVEN'T UNDERSTOOD THE SITUATION AT DIEN BIEN PHU—STOP—I REPEAT
> THAT THERE IS NOTHING LEFT HERE, NEITHER GONO, NOR AIRBORNE GROUP,
> NOR LEGIONNAIRES, NOR MOROCCANS, BUT ONLY 3000 FIGHTING MEN OF
> WHICH THE PARAS ARE THE PILLARS. WHO, [sic] AT THE PRICE OF EXTRAORDI-
> NARY COURAGE AND SACRIFICE, ARE HOLDING FAST AGAINST FOUR OF GIAP'S
> DIVISIONS. THE FATE OF HANOI AND THE INDOCHINA WAR IS BEING DECIDED
> AT DIEN BIEN PHU—STOP—YOU MUST UNDERSTAND THAT THE BATTLE CAN
> ONLY BE MAINTAINED BY PARACHUTED REINFORCEMENTS QUALIFIED OR
> NOT.—STOP—COLONEL DE CASTRIES TO WHOM I SHOWED YOUR MESSAGE
> WILL ASK FOR AND OBTAIN FROM THE COMMANDER–IN–CHIEF ALL THAT YOU
> REFUSE ME.—STOP—SIGNED: LANGLAIS AND HIS SIX BATTALION COMMAN-
> DERS.—STOP AND END.

Several days later, Major General Cogny had joined the dispute
with a secret note to General Navarre. Explaining the urgent need
for reinforcements and the shortage of jump-qualified paras, Cogny
had pointed out that 200 nonparachutists had recently volunteered
to be dropped at Dien Bien Phu and had suggested that para training be reduced to ten or twelve days. He then had asked Navarre to
direct Colonel Sauvagnac to arrange for such training as soon as
possible, adding that those who completed the brief training could
be awarded a special jump bonus.

The Muong Thanh Valley had become a moonscape of shell
craters and debris: shell casings, ration boxes, twisted airfield stripping, rolls of unused barbed wire, and the blackened skeletons of
destroyed aircraft. Collapsed, abandoned parachutes dotted the
ground like huge, deflated mushrooms. The defenders of Dien Bien
Phu moved hesitantly from trench to dugout, ever ready to dive for
cover. Like ants from an overturned nest, the Vietminh seemed
continually on the move. The artillery fire was almost constant, a
thudding din that shook the ground and sent geysers of mud into the
air. What had remained of the village was now gone, swept away by
high explosives. The strongpoints, identifiable by their shattered
wire and trench networks, were ringed by scattered clumps of
motionless corpses. Close to 1,500 Vietminh and 300 French dead
were sprawled in and around "Eliane" alone. Those recently killed
were swollen within their uniforms like overfilled sausages, their
stiff arms extended by rigor mortis. Others, exposed to the elements

over a period of time, had lost their body fat and were shrunken and wrinkled. Clouds of slow-moving blue flies vied with seething clusters of maggots for their share of the feast. Depending on wind direction, the stench could be unbearable, reminding the living on both sides of their mortality. The orderly use of latrines was a thing of the past. Shell bursts had demolished the fetid pits, scattering their contents over the trenches. The defenders, taking advantage of momentary lulls in the bombardment, relieved themselves when and where they could.

The stretch of flatland southeast of "Eliane" 2, baptized "Champs-Élysées," had become a killing ground, a scene of attack and counterattack. The 174th Regiment of the Vietminh 316th Division had thrown itself repeatedly and without success at the resolute paras, Moroccans, and remaining T'ai. Early on the morning of April 4, the *bo doï* were on the move again, their flat, camouflaged helmets bobbing along the approach trenches. But this time, like a receding tide, they were moving away from "Eliane" 2.

The French hoped that the enemy would pause to lick his wounds after the horrendous losses suffered in fighting for the "Five Hills." But Giap, like a boxer seeking his opponent's weak spot, chose "Huguette" for his next effort. The night of April 4, he sent four battalions of his 312th Division and a heavy-weapons company against "Huguette" 6 after a heavy-artillery bombardment. This strongpoint at the northern tip of the airstrip was defended by only eighty-six Legionnaires and two officers. Many of the these men were survivors of the Thirteenth demi-Brigade from "Béatrice." First Sergeant Bleyer, who had blasted a path through the Viet on "Béatrice" with his Colt .45, was the senior noncom in charge. The experience and rock-hard solidity of this veteran of the Russian front would prove invaluable in the struggle for "Huguette."

By 2200 hours the diminished force of Legionnaires had given ground but were still holding. The same sickening scenario of massed attacks was filling the barbed wire with Vietminh dead. The surviving Legionnaires slowed the assaults, firing at point-blank range at the oncoming enemy while many of their comrades slumped lifeless in their firing positions. Mindful of "Huguette"'s importance as the northwestern anchor of Dien Bien Phu's defenses, Langlais sent a company of paras from the Eighth "Shock" Battalion and two tanks to the assistance of the hard-pressed Legionnaires. Advancing along the drainage ditch on the east side of the airstrip, the paras were stopped cold by a Vietminh blocking force, and the tanks were stalled by artillery and bazooka fire.

Early on the morning of April 5, an understrength company from Bréchignac's battalion made a hell-for-leather dash across the exposed airstrip to take the attackers from the rear and shoot their way to "Huguette" 6, now held by only twenty men. Langlais then ordered Bigeard to stabilize the situation. As Bréchignac's men drove back the Vietminh within the position, Bigeard pulled together a task force of two companies from his own battalion on "Eliane," totaling 160 men, with the First BEP in reserve. He arranged artillery and air support and told the Legionnaires, "Hang on—we're coming." The counterattack was launched at 0600. The paras drove the Vietminh from their blocking positions around the drain and slammed into the enemy surrounding "Huguette" 6. Once again, it was a bloody hand-to-hand struggle as the outnumbered paras shot, stabbed, and clubbed their way forward. Although the Vietminh had committed their reserve battalion to the attack, the fury of the unexpected French reaction came as a shock. First individual *bo doï*, then squads, platoons, and companies began to waver, give way, and pull back.

The timing could not have been worse for the withdrawing Vietminh. French artillery and heavy mortars caught them threading their way out of the wire and chopped them down like a hashing cleaver. As the dawn spread from the east, the fighter-bombers responded to Bigeard's call. Giap's worries about attacking over flat, open ground without the benefit of jungle or hill cover now proved fully justified. The aircraft zoomed in low over the withdrawing battalions, decimating their ranks with chattering machine guns and antipersonnel bombs. Slow-moving lozenges of napalm bounced and skipped over the ground before exploding in bursts of liquid flame and tar-black smoke. The four para companies and what remained of the Legionnaires on "Huguette" 6 cleaned out the enemy stragglers and reoccupied the entire position. It was a damp, dismal vista. Over 500 enemy dead were found within the defense perimeter. Using binoculars, the French officers were able to count another 300 dead *bo doï* hanging on the barbed wire or scattered on the approaches to the strongpoint.

The heavy losses suffered on "Dominique," "Eliane," and "Huguette" brought Giap's total of dead and wounded close to 10,000 men. Frustrated by the bitter French resistance, Giap called for more reinforcements and decided to abandon mass assaults. He ordered his commanders to concentrate on the *grignotage*, or "nibbling away," of the French positions by the less costly tactic of pushing assault trenches even closer to the fortifications. This practice, Giap explained, would allow his men to "completely intercept reinforcements and supplies." The heavy losses also affected Vietminh morale. Fiery, doctrinaire Communist dialectic about duty, sacrifice, and the struggle against imperialism worked best on fresh troops counting on quick victories. It tended to lose its appeal among battle-weary men who had seen so many of their comrades die in repeated and inconclusive frontal attacks.

The retaking of "Huguette" 6 had cost the already depleted French units dearly. Over 200 men had been lost in the battle, and this figure included four indispensable officers. As always, the balance of forces played against the defenders. Whereas Giap could summon fresh troops from his rear areas, the battle had already eaten into the meager French reinforcements that had just arrived by parachute. Artillery ammunition had reached a new low; there were only three tanks in working order in the central position; and the closer Giap pushed his trenches, the more reduced were the DZs. There had also been an ominous increase in Vietminh pressure to the south on isolated "Isabelle," where the monsoon rains had made a morass of the swampy ground. April 6 saw both antagonists on the ropes. The comparative calm, however, was to be short-lived.

While the paras buried some of their dead in disused trenches on "Huguette" and brought up more ammunition and rations, General Navarre received a specially coded *très secret* telegram from Paris signed by Marc Jacquet, secretary of state for the Associated States of Indochina. Jacquet informed Navarre:

THE TWO PARACHUTE BATTALIONS THAT THE FRENCH GOVERNMENT HAS DECIDED TO SEND AS REINFORCEMENTS ARE THE 7TH COLONIAL PARACHUTE BN. AND THE 3RD B.E.P. THE FIRST WILL BE TRANSPORTED BY AIRCRAFT OF THE U.S. AIR FORCE AND WILL ARRIVE TOWARD THE 25TH OF APRIL. THE SECOND WILL EMBARK ON THE PASTEUR AND ARRIVE TOWARD THE 22ND OF MAY. A SECOND FLIGHT OF U.S. AIRCRAFT WILL BRING ABOUT 400 VOLUNTEER CONSCRIPTS. THE U.S. PLANES TRANSPORTING THE BATTALION AND THE CONSCRIPTS CAN BE USED ON THEIR RETURN FLIGHT FOR TROOP TRANSPORT OR FREIGHT. . . .

This should have been good news, but, under the circumstances, the dates mentioned were more appropriate for a normal troop rotation than an urgent need for combat replacements. Navarre now decided to commit a second battalion from his parachute reserves to the battle. On the night of April 9, the first companies of the Second BEP, commanded by Maj. Hubert Liesenfelt, dropped into the central redoubt of Dien Bien Phu. The arrival of Liesenfelt's tough German, Spanish, Eastern European, and Vietnamese paras was proof that Dien Bien Phu had not been forgotten. The thought that decisive outside help would eventually arrive had the garrison grasping at straws. Pierre Schoendoerffer recalls:

We wanted and hoped for a strategic air strike by the U.S. When a B-26 dropped a bomb on the Eighth "Shock" [Battalion], we thought it was the Chinese air force attacking . . . and that would mean U.S. intervention. This rumor was killed by de Castries, but we still hoped for a UN-arranged cease-fire. A part of us knew it was all over, but, you know, youth always says no. The air force pilots were pessimistic, but even Bigeard thought we could hold.

For a few days there were no major attacks or counterattacks. The Vietminh continued their harassing fire, patrols clashed, grenades thumped, booby traps exploded, and litter bearers struggled toward the hospital with bloodstained, shocked casualties. The Vietminh dug more trenches under cover of darkness, and the French launched dawn forays to fill them in. But not all the excavation work was done by the Viet. Bigeard had decided to retake "Eliane" 1. The lost position dominated the remaining French posts at "Eliane" and constituted a constant threat. The slightest movement of Bigeard's men could draw enemy sniper fire or a rain of rifle grenades and mortar shells. One of the officers under Bigeard had been killed at Bigeard's side by a Vietminh sniper while they were observing enemy positions from a trench.

Langlais and de Castries approved the plan by Bigeard, and he set to work. Throughout his service in Indochina, Bigeard had made a point of studying and adapting the enemy's successful tactics for his own purposes. Now he put his men to work with picks and shovels, emulating the Vietminh sappers, burrowing their way through the night toward the enemy battalion holding "Eliane" 1. The assault was choreographed with precision: Four companies of Bigeard's Sixth Colonial Battalion, their total strength down to 320 men, would form the attacking force; Bréchignac's battalion would stand by as a ready reserve; the First BEP and the Eighth "Shock" Battalion would concentrate their infantry weapons on the objective. Twelve 105-millimeter guns from Dien Bien Phu, eight 105-millimeter guns from "Isabelle," twelve 120-millimeter mortars from Dien Bien Phu, and the three remaining tanks would provide the artillery support. The Sixth Colonial Battalion's 81-millimeter mortars were zeroed in on the route used to supply and reinforce the Vietminh on "Eliane" 1.

At 0600 hours on April 10, 1,800 rounds of artillery fire began to fall on "Eliane" 1 like blows from a giant hammer. The tanks joined in with direct fire from their seventy-five-millimeter guns, each shot rocking their shrapnel-scarred hulls on their treads. At 0610 Bigeard raised the artillery barrage and ordered one of his companies forward. Smoke shells burst on the slopes to screen their movement, and ripping bursts of automatic fire marked their progress. French navy "Helldivers" roared out of the sky to block further enemy access to "Eliane" 1. With his first company pinned down by heavy fire, Bigeard committed a second company. It was accompanied by a flamethrower team. The click of the flamethrower's hand trigger was followed by a swooshing jet of flame that billowed over the Vietminh bunkers, carbonizing the defenders at their posts. Those attempting to flee were turned into human torches that slowed, fell, and shriveled, like insects touched by an open flame. Waves of heat shimmered in the air; scrub brush, trench supports, and abandoned ammunition boxes cracked and snapped as they burned. Although one-third of the enemy battalion had been wiped out by the barrage, the Vietminh held, fighting to the last man. "Not one withdrew," Bigeard would later write. "What marvelous combatants, those men trained by Giap!"

When the ten-hour action ended, this tenacity had cost the Vietminh 600 dead. Bigeard's battalion had lost one hundred men. He pulled back the two companies that had spearheaded the attack and replaced them with men from Bréchignac's battalion. At dusk a heavy enemy bombardment signaled Giap's determination to recapture "Eliane" 1. Giap now raised the ante by committing a full infantry regiment to the assault. Langlais, dipping into his meager reserves, responded to Bigeard's call for reinforcements by ordering two understrength companies of the First BEP into action.

At this point one of those rare events occurred that remain in men's minds long after the blurred memories of horror, victory, or defeat. The recollection still causes a catch in the voices of Dien Bien Phu veterans. Lieutenant (now Colonel) Lucciani of the First BEP, speaking of the move up the slope of "Eliane" 1, recalls without dramatics, "Our Legionnaires sang the song of the First BEP." In the midst of a night battle, the flying tracers, yellow explosions, and the hellish roaring of the flamethrower, the deep resonance of the slow-paced, cadenced marching song "Contre les Viets" ("Against the Vietminh") could be heard. The chant broke through the din in disjointed waves of sound and died as the Legion paras closed with the enemy.

Aware that his best troops were fighting for their lives, Bigeard sent in the last units available, two companies from Botella's Sixth Bawouan. One of the companies was led by Lt. Pham Van Phu, the only parachute officer of the Vietnamese National Army at Dien Bien Phu. The Vietnamese paras—hardened noncoms of the old colonial units; Tonkinese troopers from Hanoi or Haiphong, Ninh Binh, and Phu Ly; some recruits from central and South Vietnam; and a sprinkling of tough Cambodians—began their trek toward the holocaust of "Eliane" 1. Not to be outdone by the Legion, they searched for a song of their own. Vietnamese culture does not lend itself to rousing marching airs. Even the doctrinaire Vietminh relied more on songs carrying a political message or legends of heroism adapted to music in a poetic style. Finally, if hesitantly, the Vietnamese paras reached back to their school days in the French

education system and began the only fitting song that they remembered. The higher register of their voices could not match the resonance of the Legionnaires, but they sang it at the top of their lungs.
For the first time in many years, "La Marseillaise" was being sung in
battle.

By 0200 the battered Vietminh regiment was withdrawing from
"Eliane" 1. Later, a monitored enemy radio message would reveal
that Giap had summarily relieved the colonel who had failed to
retake the position.

If General Giap was disappointed in the battle performance of
one of his senior officers, General Navarre was displeased with air
force support at Dien Bien Phu. Col. Jean-Louis Nicot, the commander of the air transport effort, had been attempting to guarantee fifty
supply flights a day to the battle zone. But the weather, antiaircraft
fire, mechanical wear and tear, and crew exhaustion made this goal
almost impossible to meet. Constant reports of misdropped cargo
and de Castries's pleas for increased supply flights added to
Navarre's frustration. At about the same time that the Vietminh
proudly announced downing their fiftieth French aircraft, Navarre,
irritated by an air force response to one of his messages, sent a gruff
telegram to Maj. Gen. Henri Charles Lauzin, the air force commander in Indochina. Reading that Navarre was threatening disciplinary
action against members of his staff, Lauzin put full responsibility on
himself and demanded to know what errors his officers had committed. He also told Navarre that he thought it necessary to inform him
of the "intolerable mistrust and hostility" that his staff had encountered from Navarre's headquarters. He revealed that Colonel Nicot
had requested to be relieved of his command because of the unac-
ceptable treatment that he had received in contacts with Navarre's
inner circle. This brisk defense appeared to take some of the steam
out of Navarre's complaint. In a subsequent personal note to Lauzin,
Navarre stated that he would not punish anyone but said, "I think,
nevertheless, that there is something about your organization that is
not working [properly] because, after investigation, it has been
impossible to determine where the responsibilities lie." Navarre
went on to deny the existence of any "mistrust" or "hostility" but
accused Lauzin's staff, up to the past few weeks, of not having "lived
the battle" as they should. This dispute was hardly needed in the
already tense atmosphere of Hanoi. It is puzzling that the French
commander in chief did not choose to thrash out the problem face to
face while in Hanoi. In fact, events were only proving the wisdom of
Brigadier General Dechaux's remarks of November 17, 1953, during
the planning for Operation "Castor," when he stated his objection to

the operation and warned Navarre of the difficulties inherent in supplying Dien Bien Phu by air.

Most of Colonel Nicot's aircrews were unaware of this additional high-level feud. They were relying on their own stamina and courage to endure the daily pressure. Above all, they put their faith in the stolid, U.S.-supplied "Dakotas" (C-47s) that they were flying. Few, if any, aircraft rivaled the performance of these twin-engined workhorses. They dropped paras and supplies, acted as flare ships, transported the wounded, attacked enemy formations with napalm bombs, scattered psychological-warfare leaflets over Vietminh territory, served as airborne CPs, and performed intelligence missions, including the resupply of the GCMA (GMI) commandos operating behind enemy lines. Although all attention was now focused on Dien Bien Phu, the "Dakota" squadrons in central Vietnam, the Mekong Delta, Laos, and Cambodia were fully operational, ensuring the survival of isolated French posts and handling everything from mail deliveries to the evacuation of wounded villagers.

The defenders of Dien Bien Phu had little time or inclination to worry about the plight of the airmen or understand their problems. Major Grauwin was having difficulty operating his overcrowded hospital, in addition to supplying the battalion surgeons with medical supplies received through airdrops. The DZ had become so reduced that he was receiving ten crates out of every thirty dropped, and these had been recovered under fire and only at great risk. In need of 1,000 bottles of streptomycin, he was lucky to recuperate a box of one hundred. Fifty liters of medical alcohol were recovered when 500 were needed. On April 13, Colonel de Castries informed Hanoi that the preparation of air-dropped supplies was faulty. He complained: "THE ELECTRIC GENERATOR REQUESTED WAS NOT PROPERLY PACKED. IT ARRIVED BROKEN AND UNUSEABLE. THE GASOLINE WAS PARACHUTED TO US IN FILLED JERRICANS. THEY BURST ON HITTING THE GROUND. AS IT IS, WE DON'T HAVE ENOUGH GAS TO FILL THE RESERVOIRS OF OUR TANKS."

Two days earlier, the gray bulks of the U.S. aircraft carriers *Boxer* and *Essex* had cut through the oily swells of the Gulf of Tonkin to take up position within strike range of Dien Bien Phu.

9

A Jump into Hell

"The strange thing about the battle, there were not many screams or cries."

Pierre Schoendoerffer, cameraman,
French Army Information Service

Colonel Langlais's clash with Hanoi over parachute replacements continued with an exchange of sharp radio messages and more formal telegrams. Advised that an untried Vietnamese parachute unit was being considered, the dyspeptic Langlais threatened to disarm the entire battalion once they arrived at Dien Bien Phu and put them to work as coolies. A more temperate top secret message to General Cogny bearing de Castries's signature made clear the urgent need for dependable, elite forces. It cited the flight of some Vietnamese paras from one battalion under artillery fire and stated that the incident "once again demonstrated their ineptitude for the hard fighting going on here." The telegram added that the incident had occurred despite "the most definitively convincing arguments employed by their energetic chiefs." The message continued:

IN ATTACK AS WELL AS DEFENSE I CAN ONLY COUNT ON EUROPEAN PARAS AND LEGIONNAIRES AND SOME RARE NORTH AFRICANS. ONLY THE PARA BATTALIONS HAVE RECEIVED REINFORCEMENT PERSONNEL. I INSIST THAT LEGION VOLUNTEERS BE PARACHUTED WITHOUT BEING QUALIFIED. SUGGEST JUMP WITHOUT ARMS OR EQUIPMENT [WILL BE] LESS DANGEROUS. RESULT WILL HAVE IMPORTANT EFFECT ON MORALE AND SHARING OF DIFFICULT MISSIONS, NOW THE LOT OF THE PARAS.

The intense wrangling over parachute training for nonpara volunteers was soon muted by the urgency of the situation. At first, the volunteers underwent a minimum of training, and some actually performed practice jumps. But time was running out, and all available aircraft were needed for operational purposes. Colonel Langlais and his commanders would have preferred to receive qualified paras as replacements, but it was now a question of plugging the gaps with anyone who could handle a weapon and take orders.

A call was issued for volunteers on a larger scale. Notices were tacked on the bulletin boards of units throughout Indochina and read aloud to the troops. Although the rank and file of the French Expeditionary Corps knew that the loss of Dien Bien Phu was a definite possibility, the positive response was surprising. It was also oddly touching. Veteran parachutists in administrative positions, or limping from previous wounds, elected to join their comrades at Dien Bien Phu. Clerks in supply units, drivers, cooks, newly arrived conscripts, headquarters personnel, and line infantrymen raised their hands and stepped forward to put their names on the list. The final count on volunteers varies. General Navarre, in his book *Agonie de l'Indochine 1953–1954*, lists 800 French, 450 Legionnaires, 400 North Africans and Africans, and 150 Vietnamese as volunteering to jump as reinforcements. Of this number, following the usual weeding-out process and the inevitable last-minute jump refusals, only 681 would actually hit the ground at Dien Bien Phu.

The nonpara volunteers left their units, traveled to Hanoi, and reported to the skeptical parachute officers and noncoms assigned to prepare them for their risky venture. Some arrived fully equipped and armed. Their rifles were soon replaced with the collapsible-stock para issue or a MAT-49 submachine gun. Their fatigues were exchanged for baggy jump jackets and large-pocketed trousers. Jump boots were issued if available. Some volunteers endured eight or ten days' training with the para cadre snapping at their heels, trying to produce a rough facsimile of the real thing. Others had time for only a brief familiarization course in a wingless carcass of a C-47 or "Junker" transport. They learned the general configuration of the aircraft, the function of the static line, the para ritual of "Stand up! Hook up! Go!," the proper launch stance, and the regulation bent-knee roll.

The motivation of these volunteers would have provided abundant material for a doctoral thesis in psychology. Few other modern conflicts record as many men volunteering to participate in what most realized was essentially a lost battle. In addition, they were agreeing to jump from an aircraft for the first time, under fire, with the possibility that they might not reach the ground alive. If they did, there was a good chance of landing inside enemy lines. Were the Dien Bien Phu volunteers reacting to what de Gaulle often referred to as a "certain idea of France"? That is hardly likely, particularly for the Legionnaires, North Africans, and Vietnamese. Could it have been a search for glory linked to a form of machismo? That is doubtful. Most of the volunteers had been in Indochina long enough to have no illusions about the grim nature of the war. Even for the comparatively naive newcomers, the gray skies and sifting rains of Tonkin were more conducive to pessimism than dreams of glory.

Perhaps, for many, it was simple, unadorned camaraderie and a certain esprit de corps common to all fighting men in varying degrees. Their comrades-in-arms were *dans la merde* and needed their help. Some, without fully realizing it, were acting to prevent the end of the world as they knew it and the collapse of a proud colonial army, with its traditions and codes. Others, volunteers from noncombat units, may have been proving something to themselves, and a few firebrands may simply have been seeking action. Whatever the final analysis, each individual had his own reason for volunteering for what would later be described as a "jump into hell."

An eyewitness account of a nighttime takeoff from Gia-Lam in the French Expeditionary Corps's magazine *Caravelle* describes the jumpmasters' handling of the volunteers as paternal. Many nonparas were still wearing regulation hobnailed footwear rather than parachutist's boots. To keep them from skidding on the metal floor of the transport and tumbling out the open door in a badly regulated fall, the jumpmasters carefully fitted wool socks over the hobnails.

The command C-47, designated to act as the "traffic cop" for the drop, took off early. It would remain over the Muong Thanh Valley for seven or eight hours at an altitude of 10,000 to 12,000 feet. While the command aircraft circled the valley, the aircrew and staff shared a snack of garlic sausage and crusty bread washed down with *gros rouge*, the army-issue red wine.

In the troop carriers, the carefree, forced singing and rough jokes faded as the lights of Hanoi twinkled briefly and disappeared from sight. Bottles of rum were passed from hand to hand. The first air pockets and turbulence had a foreseeable effect on the neophyte paras, particularly those with no flight experience who had eaten too heartily or filled their bellies with beer before departure. The noise of their retching was lost in the engine drone. Nearing Dien Bien Phu, the C-47s began their descent. "A mass darker than the sky blocks the windows," the *Caravelle* writer recalled. "These are the mountains. They completely surround the Dakota cutting its visibility. Now only the radio guides the pilot in this descent into hell that seems to last an eternity. A two minute error and he'll smash against the peaks." The actual drop was a nightmare of hissing tracers, exploding thirty-seven-millimeter shells, chunks of metal flying off the wing, and the solid thunk of bullets or shrapnel piercing the fuselage.

The C-47s usually returned empty except for the flight crew. On other occasions, one, two, or three volunteers remained slumped in their bucket seats, pulled from their stick by the jumpmaster after having frozen at the windswept door or simply refused to take the first step toward the void. The majority had jumped one after the other. They hoped to land near the flickering cross marking the DZ, but it often slid from sight as capricious currents carried them downwind at a surprising speed. Those drifting toward the darkness of the enemy lines or the flashing antiaircraft batteries knew that fate had dealt them a bad hand. For many, their first and last jump would end in death or captivity. Others landed in a tangle of defensive wire, to be dragged through the lacerating barbs by their undoused chutes. Some crashed onto blockhouse roofs and mortar positions or found themselves in no-man's-land between the lines. One unlucky jumper dropped into the stinking confines of the open-air morgue and had to scramble to safety over the putrescent corpses. White-faced, he made his way to the hospital, where Major Grauwin restored his color with a generous jolt of rum. In his book *J'étais medécin à Dien Bien Phu*, Grauwin describes the battlefield humor that can emerge in the midst of chaos. Seeing a religious medal on the chest of a newly arrived Vietnamese para, Grauwin asked in pidgin French, "You Catholic?" "Me, no, not Catholic," the Vietnamese trooper responded. "Me colonial!," meaning that he belonged to a colonial parachute battalion.

Once on the ground, the old para rule of marching upwind to the DZ no longer applied. "Here is the DZ," the briefing officer had told them. "Move toward the lights. The Viets are on the other side . . . be careful not to move in that direction." This rule proved easier said than done as the firing, explosions, and unknown terrain combined to confuse the new arrivals. Search parties armed with flashlights watched the nocturnal jumpers land and guided them toward safety. In some cases, when the paras had fallen between the lines, there was a race between French patrols and the Vietminh to reach them first.

Not all the nonparas volunteered as individuals. On April 20, Major General Cogny informed Colonel Sauvagnac that the entire Second Battalion of the Third Legion Infantry Regiment had volunteered for parachute training. He asked for an estimate of how long it would take to prepare the battalion to be dropped by companies onto a secure DZ and requested a date for the training to begin. Sauvagnac, still going by the book, pointed out that the volunteer battalion making their first jump could expect "20 percent jump casualties from a drop in good weather and 30–40 percent in a 4 or 5 meter per second wind." As an example, he cited a recent training jump of sixty men resulting in "12 accidents, including 8 hospitalizations." The following day, an urgent/top secret telegram from Major General Cogny to General Navarre dramatically canceled the training project and illustrated the continued intensity of the war in locations other than Dien Bien Phu.

FOR THE PERSONAL ATTENTION OF THE COMMANDER IN CHIEF
SUBJECT: EVENTUAL PARACHUTING OF THE 2/3RD FOREIGN LEGION INFANTRY
2/3 FOREIGN LEGION INFANTRY WAS ATTACKED TODAY ON NATIONAL ROUTE 5
BY TWO BATTALIONS OF VIETMINH REGIMENT 42 STOP—PROVISIONAL COUNT
OF LOSSES STOP—23 DEAD INCLUDING 3 OFFICERS STOP—MAJOR CARA-
BIERE—STOP—CAPTAIN PERNET—STOP—LIEUTENANT RIGNEBAULT—STOP—
50 WOUNDED INCLUDING THREE OFFICERS—STOP—BECAUSE OF LOSSES SUF-
FERED AND DEATH OF BATTALION COMMANDER UPON WHOM RESTED THE WILL
OF THE 2/3 TO BE PARACHUTED I BELIEVE THIS PROJECT SHOULD BE ABAN-
DONED—STOP—SIGNED COGNY STOP.

Even experienced paras found their arrival at Dien Bien Phu harrowing. First Sergeant Robert Mallet, who jumped with one of the companies of the Second BEP, recalled:

Even though I'd been in the Far East since 1951 I'd never found myself under such a deluge [of shellfire]. The following night Sergeant Braun and his section were entirely annihilated by a single shell while regrouping in an old mortar emplacement. A few days later stray bombs from one of our aircraft fell on us, and some red berets of the 8th shock, causing serious damage. A wounded man on a litter, the bearers, and a medic accompanying them were totally obliterated before my eyes. In the trench beside me I recovered some human debris, all that remained of those poor unfortunates.

The saga of the volunteers and replacements dropped into Dien Bien Phu in small packets underlined the French High Command's continued uncertainty and lack of decision in its approach to the battle. To ask the garrison to fight to the end, inflicting heavy casualties on the enemy and buying time, was an understandable military procedure. To feed volunteers into a battle in numbers so small that they could not affect the outcome bordered on the criminal.

An understandable preoccupation with the infantry-artillery contests for the strongpoints of Dien Bien Phu often slights the service units—the supply, signal, repair, and medical detachments whose job it was to keep the fortress functioning and the wounded treated.

Already these "rear-echelon" soldiers were enduring more hardship and running more risks than some combat troops had experienced in other wars. The French military engineers, true to their motto "Build—Sometimes Destroy," were performing their task under fire and in steadily worsening conditions. Continually on call and suffering from a lack of matériel and mounting casualties, they reinforced dugouts, dug new trenches, laid more mines and booby traps, repaired fields of barbed wire, and shored up damaged gun positions. They were also filling the traditional role of combat engineers, defending positions and participating in counterattacks as infantry.

The army photographers Camus and Péraud and cameraman Schoendoerffer continued to cover the cutting edge of the battle. They accompanied the Eighth "Shock" Battalion and Bigeard's battalion during counterattacks, struggling through the mud with their Rolleiflex, Leica, and Arriflex. When they were not with the battalions, they slept in the intelligence bunker near the hospital, occupied by Meo tribesmen of the GMI. Schoendoerffer recalls the hand-to-hand fighting for "Eliane" and "Huguette" and describes the period with considerable understatement as a time of permanent stress. "The artillery positions," he explains, "were filled with dead gunners who had been blown apart." On a visit to "Elaine" 1, he noted the horrible odor from the corpses and the "intolerable" buzzing of the flies. "It was hot and we were thirsty," he states. "A work detail of P.I.M., sent for water, had been killed by a mortar burst. I saw their bodies when I came down the hill, six mangled corpses in the red mud that their blood reddened even more." As the perimeter narrowed, Schoendoerffer and his colleagues were asked to help defend the intelligence bunker beside the taciturn Meo tribesmen. "The Meo were good shots," he recalls, "and helped break the Vietminh assaults." Pausing to gaze out a window at the Paris dusk many years later, Schoendoerffer adds, "The strange thing about the battle, there were not many screams or cries."

In Washington, Pentagon planners were discussing the technicalities of Operation "Vulture." It had been suggested that the U.S. B-29s be painted with the red, white, and blue cockade of the French air force and that the American pilots be put on temporary leave status and assigned to the Foreign Legion. In the elusive search for "cover," it was decided that the American airmen would carry no identification papers or other indications of their nationality or rank. But the military preparations to save Dien Bien Phu now depended on a diplomatic decision that was slow in coming. Secretary of State Dulles had flown off to London and Paris on April 10 to put his unified action plan before America's leading allies. By

April 14 both Great Britain and France had agreed to "examine" the principles of the plan. However, there was a fateful gap between examining a broad plan for future unified action and actually putting U.S. bombers in the sky to save Dien Bien Phu. Dulles, his brief for Operation "Vulture" weakened by the misgivings of influential congressmen and certain high-ranking military leaders and the lukewarm attitude of President Eisenhower, ran into a stone wall in London. Prime Minister Winston Churchill and his foreign secretary, Sir Anthony Eden, struggling to hold the postwar British Commonwealth together, were in no hurry to become embroiled in a colonial war with such serious political overtones. They were also busy with preparations for the imminent Geneva Conference on Indochina. Churchill was adamant that the British government would not become involved in any action before the results of the conference were known. Although the diplomatic waltz would continue for weeks and new tactical plans would be presented, Operation "Vulture," for all intents and purposes, was now dead.

General Giap continued to concentrate his effort on the French positions at "Huguette," the key to control of the airstrip. Although the airstrip was totally unusable, the loss of its terrain would mean that Vietminh artillery and heavy weapons could move even closer to the heart of Dien Bien Phu's defenses. More important, the thirty-seven-millimeter antiaircraft guns could be placed in new positions that would close the range between them and the supply transports as they flew over the shrinking DZ. The Vietminh were well aware of the difficulties that their enemy was facing in receiving reinforcements and supplies. Giap wrote of the limited area now occupied by the French, the transports not daring to fly low because of the antiaircraft fire, and the parachuted crates of food and ammunition falling within his lines. "We thus," Giap reported, "bombarded the enemy with his own shells." He also refers to the "so-called volunteers" of whom "a certain number fell into our lines and were captured on reaching the ground." The rations that the garrison was now involuntarily sharing with the besiegers included cases of fresh onions, other vegetables, and fruit. These drops were designed to augment the tinned fare that provided the mainstay of the garrison's diet and fight the onset of beriberi and other diseases caused by vitamin deficiency.

On April 16, while de Castries was pleading with Hanoi for more artillerymen to keep his guns firing, word reached him that he had been promoted to brigadier general. Nor was he alone. Langlais was now a full colonel, Bigeard and de Séguin-Pazzis were lieutenant colonels, and many captains had become majors. A number of decorations, the Legion of Honor and the Croix de Guerre, were to be dropped to the garrison. At the moment when the hard-pressed defenders needed more experienced parachute battalions to survive, Hanoi was showering them with promotions and long-overdue decorations. Major General Cogny announced that he was parachuting the stars that he had worn as a brigadier general to de Castries, along with bottles of celebratory cognac and some cigarettes. Cogny's stars would never reach de Castries. The packet was said to have dropped among the Vietminh. According to the writer Erwan Bergot, who was serving with the First BEP, the Fourth Company of his battalion on "Huguette" 5 recuperated the packet and found the bottles smashed. Reasoning that de Castries would never believe that they had not emptied the smashed bottles before risking the long trek under fire to his CP, the Legionnaires smoked the cigarettes and buried the stars. Eventually, some makeshift stars for de Castries were fashioned from metal. Shortly thereafter, the Vietminh radio triumphantly announced that a box containing a number of French decorations had landed among their troops.

The day before the stars fell on Dien Bien Phu, U.S. Consul Paul Sturm had made a farewell call on Major General Cogny at his Citadel headquarters in Hanoi. Sturm was departing his post on a normal rotation and reported on the meeting in a long, secret telegram to Washington. Sturm cabled: "[MAJOR] GENERAL COGNY REVIEWED ONCE MORE, BUT WITH UNWONTED BLUNTNESS, HIS DIFFERENCES WITH GENERAL NAVARRE, PARTICULARLY REGARDING CONDUCT OF BATTLE OF DIEN BIEN PHU." Cogny had lauded the Vietminh planning for the Dien Bien Phu campaign, pointing out their concentration on the strategic aspects of the operation. He mentioned that enemy operations in Laos, the "battle of the Hanoi-Haiphong road and railway," and the upsurge of guerrilla activity throughout the delta had a direct or indirect bearing on the battle at Dien Bien Phu. Cogny then characterized the French response to Dien Bien Phu as "purely tactical." Among other things, Cogny criticized the negligence in supplying adequate air support. Cogny told Sturm, "WHEN THEY BESEECH U.S. TO MAKE MORE PLANES AVAILABLE, AND RECEIVE SATISFACTION, THEY FIND THEMSELVES SHORT OF PILOTS AND HAMPERED BY AN INADEQUATE INFRASTRUCTURE." The last sentence of the telegram sets out the general's position on Dien Bien Phu, one that he would maintain later during the official hearings on the battle in France. "COGNY REMAINS CONVINCED THAT FRENCH HIGH COMMAND SHOULD NEVER HAVE ACCEPTED BATTLE IN REMOTE JUNGLE OF THAI [T'AI] COUNTRY, FOR AT DIEN BIEN PHU THE SEVEN-YEAR BATTLE FOR THE RED RIVER DELTA MIGHT VERY WELL BE LOST."

Sturm had also sent a telegram in clear requesting that the State Department relay the following message from Colonel Langlais to his sister, Mrs. Jim Corbett, at the University of Notre Dame.

We are receiving at Dien Bien Phu many messages of sympathy from U.S., especially from Americans of French origin in Louisiana. Would it be possible for you to talk over the radio to your compatriots and to tell them that you are the sister of the paratroop Colonel at Dien Bien Phu and to say that he and his chief Colonel de Castries are deeply touched by these messages? All is well. Love to Mother and yourself. Signed Langlais.

Easter Sunday, April 18, was an unusual day at Dien Bien Phu. The sky was blue, the sun warm, when a flight of fighter-bombers appeared overhead to clear the way for a unique airdrop. The C-47s and C-119s came in low to loose their cargoes. Most of the multicolored parachutes remained within the perimeter. Despite the enemy's harassing fire, the defenders soon retrieved the crates and canisters. In addition to supplies and ammunition, they found a treasure trove of tinned meat, chocolate, fruit, and cigarettes. Parachuted bottles of rum and cognac added to the joy of this very special Easter.

The perilous situation of Captain Bizard and his men at "Huguette" 6 did not allow time for any celebration. The Vietminh trench network surrounding the position had tightened into a garotte. Not only did the enemy trenches face "Huguette" 6, but some had even been dug to face the central redoubt and block French counterattacks or relief attempts. One Vietminh trench now bisected the airstrip. Already the task force carrying water to the position each night had to fight its way past enemy roadblocks and machine-gun positions at a heavy cost. On the night of April 17, Bigeard had attempted a breakthrough to "Huguette" 6 with a mixed force of parachutists and Legionnaires supported by two tanks. After six hours of heavy fighting and the commitment of some meager reinforcements, Bigeard's men had secured the second line of Vietminh trenches. The attack had run out of steam only 500 meters from its objective. By dawn it had become painfully obvious that a further effort to reach "Huguette" 6 would be too costly.

Major Clémençon, whose Legionnaires had participated in the battle, had made radio contact with Bizard. Speaking in English to confuse enemy eavesdroppers, Clémençon had told the young captain that he and his 200 men were now on their own. Bizard's courage and his cool performance on "Huguette" 6 had impressed everyone at Dien Bien Phu. An Officer's Cross of the Legion of Honor meant for him had been among the decorations parachuted behind enemy lines. It was now decision time for Bizard, and he did not hesitate. Rather than fight to the end for a lost position or surrender, he chose to attempt a breakout. He set the time at 0800 on Easter Sunday and spread his men along the southernmost trench of

"Huguette" 6, facing the nearest Vietminh positions thirty meters away. After making the wounded as comfortable as possible and destroying all his heavy weapons, Bizard ordered his men to arm themselves with grenades and had them sling half-filled sandbags over their chests and backs to protect them from grenade fragments. A wounded Legion sergeant armed with an automatic rifle positioned himself to provide covering fire. He was to die at his post.

At the chosen moment, and under a providential mantle of fog, Bizard ordered his men over the parapet. The desperate sprint began. The element of surprise was in their favor. The majority of the *bo doï* had been turned toward the south, concentrating on blocking the breakthrough force about 300 meters distant. Now, under a rain of grenades, they turned to find the exhausted paras and Legionnaires of "Huguette" 6 vaulting over their trenches and running in a ragged line toward the relief force. Illness, short rations, wounds, and general fatigue slowed the escaping men and accounted for more casualties. The first roll call after Bizard's men reached safety showed sixty men missing, killed, wounded, or captured. Of the strongpoint's original garrison of 300 men, 106 had been killed, forty-nine had been wounded, and 79 were missing. Of the sixteen officers who had seen duty on "Huguette" 6, only five survived.

On April 20 Langlais and his para commanders made a sober assessment of their combat strength. Bigeard recalls that of the 13,000 men available at the start of the battle, approximately 2,400, not counting the isolated garrison of "Isabelle," could be counted on to perform well in combat. Bigeard's Sixth Battalion numbered 150; Bréchignac's Second Battalion could muster 200; Tourret's Eighth "Shock" Battalion, 250; Botella's Fifth Bawouan, 200; the First and Second BEP together, 550; the Legion infantry, 400; and the Moroccan riflemen, the artillery, some T'ai units, and the engineers, about 650. Bigeard would later write that "only an elite" were still fighting. The others had collapsed. "At night, they went to pillage the air-dropped supplies. At the time, Langlais was considering a punitive expedition against these slackers. But there were already so many dead, so many wounded. What good would it do? We'd take care of it later if we got out."

The night of April 20, a group of one hundred volunteers jumped over Dien Bien Phu. Each succeeding dribble of air-dropped volunteers was listed in a secret telegram from Hanoi to de Castries's headquarters.

FROM MOROCCAN UNITS 4 NON-COMS 18 TROOPS—STOP—ALGERIAN UNITS 1 OFFICER 2 TROOPS—STOP—COLONIAL UNITS 2 NON-COMS 9 TROOPS—STOP— ARTILLERY 1 OFFICER—STOP—REMAINING EFFECTIVES TO BE DROPPED—

STOP—LEGION 95—STOP—NON LEGION EUROPEANS 45—STOP—NORTH AFRICANS—STOP—MOROCCANS 170—STOP—ALGERIANS 170—STOP.

Hanoi would then request to be informed of the assignments given the troopers in an attempt to keep their personnel records current.

The continued, desperate search for replacements was underlined by another telegram from Hanoi. "CAN SEND YOU A HUNDRED FRENCH, LEGION, AND NORTH AFRICAN SOLDIERS ACCUSED OR SENTENCED BY MILITARY COURT AND VOLUNTEERING TO BE PARACHUTED IN EXCHANGE FOR PARDON—STOP—KINDLY TELEGRAPH IF YOU WILL ACCEPT THESE CANDIDATES—STOP." Dien Bien Phu responded:

PRESENCE OF PERSONNEL OBJECT OF YOUR 81/31 NOT DESIRABLE AT DIEN BIEN PHU—STOP—ON OTHER HAND ISABELLE WISHES RECEIVE THESE REINFORCEMENTS AFTER CAREFUL SELECTION IN ORDER TO RETAIN ONLY THOSE ELEMENTS HAVING PROVEN REAL QUALITIES AS COMBATANTS—STOP—PARACHUTING OF PERSONNEL TACTICALLY AND TECHNICALLY POSSIBLE—STOP.

The situation in the hospital had worsened. Major Grauwin was now facing what he described as "an invasion of maggots." The sticky flies were everywhere, buzzing in from the corruption of the morgue, laying their eggs in hospital waste, under bloody bandages and plaster casts. "At night," Grauwin later wrote, "it was a shocking sight to watch those repugnant, little white worms moving over the hands, the faces and in the ears of the sleeping wounded." To reassure his patients, Grauwin explained that the maggots, by eating infected and dead tissue, were keeping their wounds clean.

Strangely enough, the hospital was to become a previously untapped source of reinforcements. During a hurried lunch of tinned sardines, peas, and vinogel with Langlais and Bigeard, Langlais had suggested that Grauwin check to see if any laggards might be loitering in the hospital. Hesitating to begin a witch hunt among the wounded, Grauwin casually mentioned to some patients from Bigeard's battalion that their colonel was seeking men to form a new company. The words "volunteers" . . . "Sixth Battalion" . . . "Bigeard" spread through the fetid dugouts like wildfire. In his book Grauwin describes the dramatic scene as he was suddenly faced with an assembly of wounded volunteers. "I saw my one-legged supported by their comrades who still had two legs; my one-armed with their chests still wrapped in bandages; my blind who told me they could see very well; my casts of the upper and lower limbs; my panting chest wounds with feverish eyes. . . ." Impressed with such a show of solidarity but professionally shocked at the risk involved to his wounded, Grauwin reacted angrily. "No," he told them, "not everyone!" Their response was simple and direct. "Our buddies are waiting for us; now, we know it, it's certain. If they must die, we want to die with them." Beyond the central redoubt, some of the wounded in the battalion aid stations had already limped or dragged themselves back to their posts.

The enemy had now shifted his attention to "Huguette" 1, south of the fallen "Huguette" 6 and just west of the airstrip. It was not far from the tilted, bullet-holed wreck of a Curtiss "Commando" aircraft that had long been a reference point for the French in planning patrols and counterattacks. Its fuselage housed a dogged Vietminh machine-gun crew that was to play a deadly role in the fight for the airstrip. Before the fall of "Huguette" 6, the Vietminh had pushed two intersecting trenches close to "Huguette" 1. Now that network had been expanded and refined. Seen from the air, the trenches around the strongpoint divided the earth like sections of a crazy quilt.

Under cover of darkness on April 18, a fresh company from the First Battalion of the Thirteenth Legion demi-Brigade, under the command of Captain Chevalier, was ordered to move from "Claudine" to relieve a company of exhausted Legionnaires of the First Battalion of the Second Legion Infantry Regiment on "Huguette" 1. Shortly after midnight, Chevalier's company was stopped by heavy resistance from the Vietminh trenches and pillboxes surrounding the strongpoint. The Legionnaires were facing a battalion and a half of *bo doï* determined to block their progress. Chevalier called for artillery and air support while his men fought from trench to trench. By 1000 hours on April 19, Chevalier's company had reached "Huguette" 1. It had taken the Legionnaires fourteen hours to cover 1,500 yards. Chevalier had lost one-third of his company, and its strength had been reduced to eighty men. The Vietminh were waiting for the relieved company as it attempted to make its way to safety, and they, too, suffered irreplaceable losses.

The distant, isolated strongpoint of "Isabelle" was being pounded steadily by Vietminh artillery, and the fingers of the enemy trenches had extended close to the outer defenses. Of its eleven 105-millimeter howitzers, only eight were still in action, and only two out of its three tanks were serviceable. The swampy, flat topography of "Isabelle" offered no real cover or concealment, and its perimeter, measuring only one-fourth of a square mile, provided a difficult and fleeting target for airdrops. Colonel Lalande, the strongpoint commander and a Legion veteran of World War II, had a mixed garrison at his disposal. Legionnaires, Algerian riflemen, T'ai riflemen, and irregulars were holding the positions of "Isabelle." Although the strongpoint's prime function had been to provide artillery support for Dien Bien Phu, it, too, was now plunged into an infantry and artillery battle for survival.

Earlier, before its road link to the main position had been cut, "Isabelle" had received reinforcements from Dien Bien Phu. These had included T'ai riflemen who had fled from the battle on "Anne-Marie" and Algerians still shocked by their experience on "Gabrielle." By April 20 a bitter contest had begun for the strongpoint "Wieme," held by Lieutenant Wieme and a force of 219 T'ai. This position extended to the northeast off "Isabelle" like a fat finger. The small auxiliary airstrip stretching north from "Wieme" was now totally under Vietminh control and useless to the French. The strongpoint was a morass of mud and shallow trenches connected to the main position by a tiny bridge over the Nam Yum River. "Wieme"'s small force and the entire garrison of "Isabelle" were now suffering from a shortage of rations. The Vietminh committed the Fifty-Seventh Regiment of the 304th Division and the 888th Battalion of the 316th Division, a total of 3,800 bo doï, to the battle for "Isabelle." Colonel Lalande's total strength on April 20 numbered 1,400 men. The pattern of attacks and counterattacks that had drained French units at the "Five Hills" and at "Huguette" had now begun at "Isabelle."

Captain Chevalier's men on "Huguette" 1 were now under continual attack. The enemy artillery fire was so heavy that the strongpoint resembled an erupting volcano. Vietminh gunners delivering direct fire with seventy-five-millimeter recoilless rifles from the captured fortifications of "Dominique" 2 made movement impossible. During the turnover of the position, Chevalier had been warned that the sound of digging had been heard under the French positions, but there was not much that he could do about it. On April 22, Chevalier gathered the sixty survivors of his company in the trenches around his CP for a last stand. That night the Vietminh assault troops emerged from the earth within the position like menacing specters. In desperation, Chevalier ordered the French 120-millimeter mortars to lay fire on "Huguette" 1. As the Legionnaires crouched under cover, the heavy-mortar shells decimated the exposed bo doï. At dawn the Legionnaires cleared their position of enemy dead by swinging them up and over the battered trench parapets.

The Vietminh returned the next night. Erwan Bergot, in his book *Les 170 Jours de Dien Bien Phu*, describes the system employed by Chevalier's Legionnaires to cope with the enemy's underground saps. "They killed the first enemy to emerge, filled the hole with plastic [explosive], and tamped it with the dead body." But, for each excavation plugged by an explosive charge, a new one appeared. The last message from "Huguette" 1, a plea for reinforcements, was recorded at 0230 hours. It was followed by a consistent radio silence. A Legionnaire who had escaped from the lost position described his last glimpse of Chevalier. Formed in a ragged square, the captain and a few of his men were being submerged by a mass of attacking *bo doï*. If Dien Bien Phu, with its bare, wire-strewn terrain and muddy trenches, now resembled Verdun, the fall of "Huguette" 1 recalled a scene from the nineteenth-century battles that had made the Legion famous.

Brigadier General de Castries then decided to retake the position. Both Colonel Langlais and Lieutenant Colonel Bigeard were against the operation. Bigeard cited the reduced strength of his remaining troops and their general exhaustion as indications that the effort might fail. He also expressed doubt that the strongpoint could be held once it was recaptured. But de Castries, knowing that the enemy presence at "Huguette" 1 would mean the loss of the remaining DZ, insisted that the attack go ahead. He ordered that the position should be retaken by 1600 hours and turned his attention to a telegram that he had drafted in response to a message from Hanoi.

Cogny's headquarters wanted to know what would be needed to move various units and supplies out of the areas of Dien Bien Phu flooded by the monsoon rains. The query was phrased as if de Castries commanded a normal garrison with adequate manpower and equipment to carry out such a major redeployment. Hanoi's suggestion that the troops on "Isabelle" might be brought in to reinforce the main center of resistance underlined the existing lack of understanding at headquarters. The desk-bound tacticians seemed to ignore the fact that isolated "Isabelle" was already fighting for its life.

De Castries explained that moving the garrison out of the flooded areas would involve retaking "Dominique" 1 as well as "Dominique" 2 and its approaches. He then listed the inundated positions, said that it was impossible to recapture "the Dominiques" with the reduced force at his disposal, and made it clear that he wished to maintain "Isabelle" as a supporting fire base. He explained that evacuation of "Isabelle" would "stuff" the shrinking central position with infantry. There would also be a major operation required to open the road to "Isabelle" and protect it long enough to evacuate the wounded and all its equipment, ammunition, artillery, and personnel. The general cited the lack of vehicles available and predicted heavy losses in men and matériel during any pullback from "Isabelle." He concluded that only the dropping of three parachute battalions near Ban Nong Cong on or about April 30 would permit him to retake "the Dominiques" and possibly "Anne-Marie" 1 and 2, ensure a secure drop zone, and move the garrison to high ground.

Meanwhile, Bigeard proceeded, if reluctantly, with his preparations for the counterattack. He selected Major Liesenfelt's relatively fresh Second BEP for the task and arranged for the preattack hammering of "Huguette" 1 by B-26s and fighter-bombers. The French artillery stood by to deliver 1,200 rounds of artillery fire on the enemy-held position and enough smoke shells to temporarily blind the Vietminh artillery observers at "Dominique" and "Anne-Marie." Bigeard had faith in the Legionnaires of the Second BEP and considered them among the best of the para units in Indochina. Once he had finished his planning and presided over the detailed briefing, he was confident that Liesenfelt's battalion could complete its mission. By now Bigeard was dead on his feet. The constant lack of sleep, insufficient nourishment, and the strain of battle had taken their toll. He decided to rest, walked to his sagging cot, and fell immediately into a deep slumber.

Bigeard's rest period did not last. He was awakened to hear de Castries's concerned voice describing the counterattack on "Huguette" 1 as lacking "punch." The brigadier general then directed Bigeard to go have a look at "what is going on." The well-planned action had become a fiasco. After a brief, initial success, Liesenfelt's companies had been pinned down and had suffered heavy casualties. The flat, open approach to "Huguette" 1 was a machine gunner's dream, and the Vietminh were taking full advantage of it. The heavy machine gun hidden in the nose of the Curtiss "Commando" had caught two companies in the open as they crossed the unprotected expanse of the airstrip. Despite the smoke barrage, the enemy artillery was showering the blocked paras with shrapnel.

Bigeard jumped into a jeep and sped to Liesenfelt's CP dugout at "Huguette" 2 to find the commander of the Second BEP sitting by his radio. Bigeard asked how things were going. Liesenfelt responded that things must be going well since he had not heard from his companies. Bigeard then discovered that Liesenfelt's radio was not on the proper wavelength. The desperate radio messages from the Second BEP's pinned-down units that had alerted de Castries had not been reaching Liesenfelt's CP. Furious, Bigeard took command of the operation on the spot. Some Legion officers maintain that the metal stripping of the airfield had been responsible for the radio malfunction. To this day, they feel that Bigeard was too hard on Liesenfelt both during and after the battle. Others argue that the commander of the Second BEP could have observed the plight of his men if he had been above ground in a position that gave him a view of the operation. Such arguments, however, would surface later.

Sizing up the situation, Bigeard decided that the counterattack had failed. His goal now was to salvage what was left from the disaster. He ordered the Second BEP to withdraw and called in artillery and air to cover its retreat. The two companies that pulled back over the exposed airstrip had lost 80 percent of their strength. One officer, his two legs almost severed from his body, fired a shot into his head to spare his Legionnaires the added risk of carrying him to safety. The once-fresh Second BEP had lost 154 dead in its abortive attempt to retake "Huguette" 1. It had ceased to exist as a unit, and the survivors were amalgamated with the tattered First BEP to become the "Battaillon de Marche Étranger de Parachutistes."

Many years later Bigeard cut through the fog of dispute surrounding what had happened that day. He wrote:

> Despite my weariness, I should have simply taken personal command of the operation. The wonderful officers of the Second BEP were as good as mine, those of Bréchignac or of Tourret, but that day the orchestra conductor to animate and back up those exceptional combatants was missing. I therefore consider myself responsible for this defeat.

Another of General Giap's messages to his troops was circulating as his battered *bo doï* consolidated their hold on "Huguette" 1 and continued the pressure on "Isabelle." "Huguette" 1 had cost the Vietminh 300 dead and many more wounded. Giap exhorted his men to compete in "hunting the enemy." In order that the French garrison live in continual "anguish and fear of dying at any moment," he called on "all marksmen, machine gunners, mortarmen and artillerymen to kill the enemy at Dien Bien Phu one by one." Like most of Giap's orders, it focused on a simple, easily remembered slogan: "For each bullet fired—an enemy killed." His troops were urged to aim accurately and make each shot count. Giap then asked: "Who will be the best shot on the Dien Bien Phu front? Who will be the best machine gunner, the best mortarman, the best artilleryman on the Dien Bien Phu front? The [Vietminh] High Command awaits your exploits in order to bestow awards on you and your units."

10

Living with Death

"It was 3,000 of them against eighty of us."
Captain Jean Lucciani, First BEP,
describing the assault on "Huguette" 4

While General Giap was calling for their annihilation, the troops defending Dien Bien Phu shared the hope that someone was at work on a plan that would get them out of the valley alive. That often unspoken hope nourished morale on a day-to-day basis. Positive rumors were savored almost as much as the rare packet of cigarettes or bottle of hoarded wine. Even the wildest flights of fancy were accepted as possibilities and discussed soberly by unshaven, bandaged men huddled in flooded trenches: Cogny was sending a task force to cut Giap off from his supplies; the Americans had finally decided to intervene; an air armada loaded with paras fresh from France would soon appear overhead; a strong relief column from Laos was within a day's march of the valley. Only the last of these rumors came anywhere close to the truth.

General Navarre and his staff had developed a contingency plan to send a column from Laos to Dien Bien Phu. On paper the original Operation "Condor" had called for an ambitious mopping-up operation to clear the northwestern border area of battered Vietminh forces reeling back from a defeat at Dien Bien Phu. It had been formulated during the heady, hopeful days of December 1953 and constructed along the lines of Operations "Ardèche" and "Régate," the abortive operations that had proven that the jungle could be as formidable an enemy as the Vietminh. The original plan had called for four battalions from Laos to clear Muong Khoua and the zone west of the Nam Ou River. They would then have marched northeast to meet a four-battalion force of parachutists at Ngha Na Son and move on to capture Limestone Pass (Col des Calcaires), the mountain pass leading to the Muong Thanh Valley and the southern approaches to "Isabelle." The passage of time and events at Dien Bien Phu had changed the scenario. The air transport and parachute battalions needed for such a large-scale effort were no longer available.

On April 13, General Navarre ordered Col. Boucher de Crèvecoeur, the commander of French forces in Laos, to launch a reduced version of Operation "Condor." Three Laotian battalions (including one airborne), a Legion battalion, and Commando Group "Mollat," composed of Meo and Laotian tribesmen under the command of Lieutenant Colonel Mollat, began the long march toward Dien Bien Phu. GCMA Commando Groups "Grapefruit," "Banana," and "Areca," already operating in the area, would provide a forward screen for the column. Colonel Then, who commanded the four battalions, now baptized the Northern Groupe Mobile, hoped to draw Vietminh regulars away from Dien Bien Phu, contain them by the hit-and-run tactics of his commandos, and swing south of Limestone Pass toward Muong Nha. There, after being reinforced by four more battalions, he would strike out for "Isabelle."

Even this plan was overambitious. Only two parachute battalions were available, and they were from the Vietnamese National Army. Their reputation had not been enhanced by Langlais's refusal to accept them for service at Dien Bien Phu. The Laotian chasseur battalions of the Northern Groupe Mobile were also of doubtful quality. Although some Laotians had fought well in their own territory, their languid life-style and pleasure-loving culture did not lend itself to the hard requirements of sustained combat. Colonel Then's plans for airlifted infantry reinforcements were optimistic in view of the limited landing strips available, their condition, and their short length. Other obstacles to success included a shortage of coolies and mules to carry the column's supplies and Dien Bien Phu's first call on air support, both supply and tactical.

The terrain to be covered on foot posed a major problem. The jungled mountains and deep valleys were hostile barriers calling for a superhuman effort. The monsoon rains, which could often cancel any help from the air, could also turn a steep trail into a mud slide in minutes and swell small streams into rushing, impassable torrents. A sudden downpour could be followed by a merciless sun that sucked moisture from the limestone soil, turned mud to dust, and required huge amounts of potable water to keep troops from dehydrating. Progress often depended on the slow progress of machete-wielding trailblazers, a tortuous process that led to heat exhaustion.

Now, instead of a broken enemy licking his wounds following a defeat at Dien Bien Phu, the "Crèvecoeur Column" would be facing regular Vietminh battalions and regional units largely unaffected by the bloodletting in the Muong Thanh Valley and buoyed by news of Vietminh successes there. Tribal irregulars working for the Vietminh were tracking the French and reporting on their strength, direction, and speed. From April 21, elements of the column were in intermittent contact with the enemy. Giap's headquarters was monitoring the evolution of Operation "Condor" with particular care and preparing to block the column's access to Dien Bien Phu.

While the Vietminh infantrymen, sappers, and gunners continued the nightly pressure on the French strongpoints, some of Giap's political cadre were fully occupied with a continual campaign of psychological warfare. Undermining enemy morale had long been recognized as an integral part of the revolutionary struggle. Now, with the shrinking of the defense perimeter and the proximity of the opposing forces, the effort was increased. Loudspeakers were installed close to the French wire to broadcast propaganda messages targeted at specific units and ethnic groups. Vietnamese "puppet" troops and T'ai tribesmen were urged to leave their French "masters" and join their compatriots in the liberation struggle. Legionnaires, Moroccans, and Algerians who had deserted or been captured addressed their former comrades in German and Arabic in an attempt to encourage defections. At one point the slow cadence of the "Chant des Partisans" could be heard playing from a Vietminh loudspeaker. This song of the French Resistance, with its mention of a population rising to overthrow an oppressor, was undoubtedly meant to teach a political lesson. However, a number of the officers and men at Dien Bien Phu had fought the Germans as members of the Resistance or during the liberation of France. For many of them, the tune served more as a reminder of difficult times in the past and as an inspiration rather than a depressant.

The French psychological warriors were also busy. Thousands of air-dropped leaflets fluttered down onto Vietminh positions and supply routes. Much of their content centered on China's role in the conflict and its use of the Vietminh as cannon fodder to advance its own form of imperialism in the region. The French emphasized China's traditional role as an enemy of Vietnam and reminded the Vietminh that Vietnam's ancient military heroes were revered for the past defeats that they had inflicted on the Chinese. Such propaganda was based on historical fact, but it hardly applied to the current tactical situation. The peasant *bo doï* might not have had a deep appreciation of history, but he could see that the Chinese were there to help and that many of them were sharing the risks of battle with their Vietnamese comrades. He also knew that the weapons that he was using, the supplies that sustained him, and the trucks that transported them had come from China. Thus, whatever the lessons of history or his personal feeling, the enemy of his enemy was his friend.

The Vietminh political cadre was also concerned about troop morale. Although General Giap—unlike the French—had the luxury of rotating units in and out of the line, some Vietminh units were obviously better than others. This fact meant that the better units were repeatedly asked to perform the impossible. The resultant heavy losses produced what the Communists called "rightist tendencies," a political shorthand for lack of commitment, doubt, and combat fatigue. The full panoply of agitprop procedures was brought to bear on these waverers: political lectures, self-criticism sessions, talks by respected senior officers and heroes of the Vietnamese Revolution. Propaganda banderoles, loudspeaker messages, and group singing, combined with rest periods, decorations, and adequate food, were all part of the treatment. A strong morale was essential for the final phase of the campaign since so many of the replacements were raw recruits facing their first test in battle. Giap therefore made sure that the replacements had a cadre of stolid veterans who would act as their mentors.

The French were also fighting a battle for the hearts and minds of the tribal peoples. The abandonment of Lai Chau had been a blow to the long-standing French links with the T'ai tribes. The Vietminh were making a special effort to obtain the support of the T'ai, Meo, Lolo, and Yao. Nevertheless, the French officers and noncoms of the GCMA (GMI) who continued to lead the tribal irregulars against the Vietminh provided an anchor of solidarity in the region. Like the Chinese at Dien Bien Phu, their physical presence provided a guarantee of outside support. Unfortunately for the mountain tribes, it would prove to be a guarantee without substance.

On April 26, 1954, the diplomats were preparing for the Geneva Conference, which would decide the fate of Vietnam. Two days earlier, the foreign ministers of France and Great Britain had met with the U.S. secretary of state in Paris. Georges Bidault, Sir Anthony Eden, and John Foster Dulles reviewed for the last time the possibility of an allied intervention in Indochina. By now it had become a Catch-22 proposition. Dulles made it clear that the U.S. could not move without congressional approval, and that would be possible only with a guarantee of British participation. In fact, Congress was insisting on a great deal more. In addition to British involvement, the legislators had asked for support from the "free nations of Southeast Asia," as well as the Philippines and the British Commonwealth. The Americans were also demanding that the

French push ahead with real independence for the Associated States of Indochina and pledge to keep fighting the war. The French, determined to save what they could in the circumstances, did not take kindly to such demands. Pham Van Dong, representing the Vietminh, knew that a French defeat at Dien Bien Phu could provide him with an obvious diplomatic advantage. He was, however, wary of Chinese and Soviet objectives and did not intend to be pressured by his more powerful allies. Although the lives of thousands were at stake, the conference was not to begin till May 8. Hampered by protocol and distrust, it would proceed in an atmosphere of smoke and mirrors. Secret meetings, half-truths, and diplomatic rebuffs were to be the order of the day as each participant jockeyed for position and pushed his own particular agenda. Previously, on April 27, Prime Minister Churchill had informed the House of Commons that Great Britain was opposed to any joint military action in Indochina. Two days later, President Eisenhower, speaking at a press conference, had stated that the U.S. would not take unilateral action in Indochina. The fate of the Dien Bien Phu garrison was now up to the generals.

The pilots of the French navy had done an excellent job of air support during the failed attempt to retake "Huguette" 1. They, as well as the American CAT pilots flying the C-119s, had earned the continued respect of the Dien Bien Phu garrison for their willingness to take risks. Watching the darting attacks of the fighter-bombers had become a welcome diversion. Infantrymen who risked their lives on a daily basis were astounded by the daredevil courage of the pilots. When the fighters roared in low at the enemy gun positions, guns blazing, the besieged troops shook their heads in admiration, agreeing that these pilots "must be crazy!"

First Sergeant Bleyer of the Legion had watched the fight for "Huguette" 1 from his position on "Eliane" 2. He had been wounded by grenade fragments while escorting a water detail to the "Huguettes" a few days earlier. It was his second wound. Now, he saw a navy "Hellcat" zooming in through heavy antiaircraft fire for a dive-bombing run. Bleyer and his fellow Legionnaires held their breath as the tubby fighter suddenly began to belch smoke. Notwithstanding the hits that it had received, the "Hellcat" succeeded in loosing two 500-pound bombs on its target. The pilot, Lt. Bernard Klotz, realizing that his aircraft was finished, pushed back the canopy and parachuted over the battlefield. "He came down in no-man's-land between us and the Viets," Bleyer recalled. "Gniewek, Quinard, Frocchi, Dufour and I formed a small Commando and, under the nose of the Viets, we succeeded in bringing Lieutenant Klotz to safety." The risk involved in Bleyer's action was revealed by the understated comment "I harvested a bullet in the arm during this affair." Despite some painful torn ligaments, Lieutenant Klotz then joined the air force officers at Dien Bien Phu in supervising air-ground liaison.

Each day the enemy artillery kept up its sporadic harassing fire, the shells whistling in to pound the defenses. With what had become a reflex action, the defenders threw themselves into the nearest trench or dugout and crouched under the doubtful protection of their steel helmets. Not all the casualties from shellfire were fighting men. Caporal Chef Robert Blondeau, the GCMA commando who was now assigned to the Eighth "Shock" Battalion, recalls: "The female dancers of Deo Van Long's Royal T'ai Ballet were quartered in a blockhouse on 'Claudine.' One of them was hit by an artillery shell. We gathered her up with a shovel and broom. Only a hunk of hair remained."

While radio intercepts by French intelligence confirmed the arrival at Dien Bien Phu of 25,000 *bo doï* fresh from Vietminh training camps, the Legionnaires prepared for the celebration of Camerone. This famous battle of April 30, 1863, found a detachment of sixty-two Legionnaires facing a force of 2,000 Mexican regulars at the Mexican pueblo of Camerone. After a long day of combat, the five surviving Legionnaires died fighting, skewered by Mexican bayonets. Since that day, to "do Camerone" has meant to fight to the end against heavy odds. The special significance of Camerone was not lost on the hard-pressed Legionnaires at Dien Bien Phu. On April 30, the senior Legion officer present read the official account of the battle over a field radio link. Each Legion dugout and position at Dien Bien Phu celebrated Camerone in its own way. Normally, the celebration is marked by a special meal and abundant drink. At Dien Bien Phu the mess kits held combat rations, and the toasts were drunk with vinogel. While the Legion remembered its past, the Vietminh were burrowing their way toward "Huguette" 5 and 4, and the airdrops continued. Over a period of four nights, 300 volunteers had jumped into the valley, but the strength of the opposing forces was now ten to one in Giap's favor.

Throughout the night of April 30, French listening posts reported an increase in enemy activity. On May 1 the Vietminh celebrated the Labor Day of International Socialism with a show of red flags and military marches blasting from their loudspeakers. Infantry units could be seen moving into position. Forward observers reported enemy gun crews openly moving their pieces to new positions as if aware that the French gunners had received orders to hoard what remained of their meager munitions.

At 1700 hours the Vietminh artillery barrage began. Howitzers, heavy mortars, and recoilless rifles joined in a storm of relentless fire that poured tons of high explosives into Dien Bien Phu. Bunkers and soggy trenches collapsed or simply disappeared. Many of their occupants were killed and mutilated. The deafened survivors clung to the shaking earth, fighting to catch their breath through the stench of cordite and thick smoke. Two of Giap's divisions, the 312th and the 316th, were preparing to attack the eastern hill positions of "Dominique" 3 and "Eliane" 1 while the 308th was targeted on "Huguette" 5. Their assault units could have asked for no better morale boost than the sight of the damage being done by their guns. After three hours of steady pounding, the firing slackened, and the *bo doï* poured out of their trenches.

An entire Vietminh assault regiment threw itself at the eighty-man company from Bréchignac's battalion holding "Eliane" 1. French artillery fire cut down many attackers, but it was too spaced and intermittent to break the assault. By midnight, with less than a dozen men holding the position and their commanding officer suffering from a skull wound that had exposed his brain, Bréchignac sent in his last available company. Its commander was killed shortly thereafter, but the paras continued to resist, mounting counterattacks in small groups against overwhelming odds. By 0200 hours "Eliane" 1 had fallen. Caporal Chef Claude Sibille of the First Chasseurs Parachute Battalion describes that night as his worst at Dien Bien Phu. He remembers the wounded from "Eliane" 1 falling back on his position. "They arrived all night, a mix of French and Vietnamese, completely shell-shocked. The Vietminh 105-millimeter shells were coming in: air bursts, contact fuses, and delayed-action fuses that buried themselves in the mud to explode later. We lived with the presence of death. It was part of our life."

The attack on "Dominique" 3 was just as intense. The position was held by a mixed force of Algerian riflemen and T'ai. Considering the past behavior of these units, Dien Bien Phu headquarters had no illusions about holding the position. There was so little confidence in the Algerians and T'ai tribesmen that a reduced company from Bigeard's Sixth Battalion had been sent to bolster them. But the gods of battle are both fickle and unpredictable. Under attack from two Vietminh regiments, the Algerians and the diminutive T'ai dug in their heels and fought with unexpected fury. Without hope of reinforcement and lacking artillery support, the riflemen and tribesmen defended their positions with automatic weapons, grenades, and bayonets, making the enemy pay dearly for every yard of trench taken. After midnight the small force was running short of ammunition and suffering heavy losses. At 0400 on May 2, after six hours of constant combat, Maj. Maurice Chenel, the strongpoint commander, informed Dien Bien Phu that no one on "Dominique" 3 remained in a fit state to fight. He then cut his last link with the outside by destroying his radio.

To the west, the Vietminh 308th Division had attacked "Huguette" 4 and "Lily," a supplementary strongpoint created after the loss of "Huguette" 1. But the Legion paras on "Huguette" 4 had counterattacked successfully, and the Moroccans on "Lily" had held. A major assault was then launched on "Huguette" 5. Two full Vietminh regiments hit the strongpoint from the north and west while a third remained in reserve. Lieutenant de Stabenrath, wounded on April 17, commanded "Huguette" 5. He, Lieutenant Junior Grade Boisbouvier—who had already been wounded three times—and three noncoms were holding the position with twenty-five Legion paras. With thousands of *bo doï* participating in the attack, an objective observer could have been excused for thinking that the action would be over in minutes. Instead, the Legionnaires held for an hour and a half. Ninety-one years later, Lieutenant de Stabenrath and his men had fought their own Camerone.

It was now clear to all at Dien Bien Phu that they were witnessing a major enemy effort to crush the fortress and bring the battle to an end. The nighttime attacks had cost the garrison the strength of an entire battalion. Desperate for reinforcements to make up at least that number, Dien Bien Phu awaited the scheduled drop of the First Colonial Parachute Battalion, the last of Cogny's airborne reserves. The night of May 3 saw the arrival of only one of the battalion's companies.

"Huguette" 4 was attacked shortly after midnight on May 4 by an entire enemy regiment and four additional battalions. The determined resistance was led by Captain Jean Lucciani of the First BEP and his mixed force of paras and Moroccan riflemen. Once again the Vietminh dead were piled high on the barbed wire. Lucciani, who received a serious head wound during the fighting, describes the drama of that night with the simple statement "There were 3,000 of them against eighty of us." At 0335, de Castries and his staff were aural witnesses to the fall of "Huguette" 4. A sputtering radio message from one of the few surviving officers informed the central CP that only a handful of men were still on their feet. His auditors then heard him die, shot down at the radio as the Vietminh fought their way into his trench.

At 0900 hours on May 4, Brigadier General de Castries sent a secret telegram to Major General Cogny informing him of the loss of "Huguette" 4 and of the heavy casualties suffered by the enemy. He also explained that his own losses had been acute and pointed out that, despite his repeated requests, the remainder of the First Colonial Parachute Battalion had not been dropped. He insisted that the drop take place that night. The remainder of the message, a detailed analysis of the situation, deserves to be quoted in its entirety.

OUR PROVISIONS OF ALL KINDS ARE AT THEIR LOWEST—FOR FIFTEEN DAYS THEY HAVE BEEN REDUCED LITTLE BY LITTLE—WE DON'T HAVE ENOUGH AMMUNITION TO STOP ENEMY ATTACKS OR FOR HARASSING FIRE THAT MUST CONTINUE WITHOUT PAUSE—IT APPEARS THAT NO EFFORT IS BEING MADE TO REMEDY THIS SITUATION—I'M TOLD OF THE RISK RUN BY AIR CREWS WHEN EVERY MAN HERE RUNS INFINITELY GREATER RISKS.—THERE CANNOT BE TWO WEIGHTS AND MEASURES—THE NIGHT DROPS MUST BEGIN AT 20 HRS INSTEAD OF 23 HRS—THE MORNING HOURS ARE LOST BECAUSE OF FOG AND THE PLANNING FOR NIGHT DROPS, WITH THE INEVITABLE LONG INTERVALS BETWEEN AIRCRAFT [THAT] PERMIT ONLY RIDICULOUS RESULTS.—I ABSOLUTELY NEED PROVISIONS IN MASSIVE QUANTITIES—THE VERY SMALL STATE OF THE CENTER OF RESISTANCE, THE FACT THAT OUR ELEMENTS ON ITS EDGE CAN'T LEAVE THEIR SHELTERS WITHOUT COMING UNDER FIRE FROM SNIPERS AND RECOILLESS RIFLES MEANS THAT MORE AND MORE OF THE CASES DROPPED ARE NO LONGER RETRIEVABLE—THE LACK OF VEHICLES, THE LACK OF COOLIES, OBLIGE ME TO USE EXTREMELY EXHAUSTED UNITS FOR RECOVERY PURPOSES—THE RESULT IS DETESTABLE. IT ALSO CAUSES LOSS-ES—I CAN'T EVEN COUNT ON RETRIEVING HALF OF WHAT IS DROPPED. BUT, THE QUANTITIES THAT HAVE BEEN SENT TO ME REPRESENT ONLY A VERY SMALL PORTION OF WHAT I'VE REQUESTED. THIS SITUATION CANNOT GO ON—I INSIST, ONCE MORE, ON THE BROAD AUTHORITY THAT I'VE REQUESTED IN THE MATTER OF CITATIONS—I HAVE NOTHING TO SUSTAIN THE MORALE OF MY MEN WHO ARE BEING ASKED TO ACCOMPLISH SUPERHUMAN EFFORTS. I NO LONGER DARE TO GO SEE THEM WITH EMPTY HANDS—END—

This plea reached Hanoi a few days after the aircraft carrier *Belleau Wood* had arrived in the Gulf of Tonkin. The carrier, loaned to the French by the U.S. Navy and manned by a French crew, carried the American-built "Corsair" fighter-bombers of Squadron 14-F. These swept-wing aircraft had proved themselves in close ground-support missions with the U.S. Marine Corps during World War II and in Korea. Although the French pilots were still getting the feel of the "Corsairs," Cogny's headquarters was expecting them to bolster the air effort at Dien Bien Phu and supplement the already effective action of the naval participation. This was not to be. The "Hellcats" of Squadron 11-F from the aircraft carrier *Arromanches* had borne the brunt of the naval action over Dien Bien Phu. The squadron was now suffering from battle fatigue. Six of its twenty pilots had been shot down, and the rest had either crash-landed their aircraft or brought them back damaged by antiaircraft fire. Recognizing the strain on both pilots and aircraft, the naval command grounded the squadron. Understandable as this order was, it could not have come at a worse time.

On May 3, the senior officers of Major General Cogny's staff were asked to prepare a top secret plan for a breakout attempt by the

Dien Bien Phu garrison. The sensitivity of such a risky move, and the potentially disastrous effect that any premature leak might create, called for a special security effort. The plan, with the unfortunate code name of Operation "Albatross," was simple enough. The able-bodied survivors were to break through the enemy lines in a south-easterly direction at dusk under cover of artillery fire, air support, and small-arms fire from the walking wounded. They, the seriously wounded, and the hospital staff would be left behind. Each man would carry only his personal weapons and four days' rations. The escapees would push through the jungle to a rendezvous with the Operation "Condor" force close to Muong Nha on or about May 20. Commando Groups "Grapefruit," "Banana," and "Mollat" would assist in the operation. The plan warned the GCMA (GMI) commandos not to direct the withdrawing garrison toward zones occupied by other maquis in the northwestern region since such an action would reveal their location to the enemy. Provision was also made for the establishment of small supply dumps along the route of withdrawal, containing food, medicine, and radio batteries. The dumps were to be protected by commandos and tribal irregulars who could act as guides.

The timing of the breakout was left to the discretion of Brigadier General de Castries. There was little doubt that the commander of Dien Bien Phu would be the best man to judge the appropriate moment for the attempt. But such responsibility at this point in the battle was indeed an "Albatross." Already instructed to resist to the last minute "without thought of falling back," de Castries was now faced with the problem of preparing for the tentative breakout without shattering the morale of his men.

Colonel de Crèvecoeur had already been informed by General Navarre that bad weather and the needs of Dien Bien Phu had killed the chances of the Operation "Condor" column receiving its promised airborne reinforcements before eight days. Navarre had then left the next move up to Colonel de Crèvecoeur. In such an uncertain situation, the relief column halted and took up a defensive position on the north bank of the Nam Ou River.

On May 5, Colonel Lalande at "Isabelle" was informed of the breakout plan. The garrison of "Isabelle" had been engaged in the continued bitter struggle for strongpoint "Wieme" until the process of repeated counterattacks had become too costly. The Vietminh artillery was now concentrating on knocking out "Isabelle"'s artillery, piece by piece. Lalande noted that the Operation "Albatross" breakout required "Isabelle"'s garrison to hold long enough to protect the withdrawal and then form a rearguard for the retreating column. The weight of the final decision as to timing would rest largely on Lalande's shoulders.

The staff officers who had drafted the breakout plan in the high-ceilinged, drab offices of the Citadel were not all in agreement on its worth. In an atmosphere of clacking typewriters, ringing phones, and rushing messengers, they looked out the rain-streaked windows at the evening traffic of Hanoi and pondered the fate of Dien Bien Phu. They knew only too well what their comrades were enduring. Most of them were also painfully aware of the wide gap between what was happening on the ground and the orderly paragraphs that they had just committed to paper. The misgivings of Colonel Bastiani, Cogny's chief of staff, who had opposed Operation "Castor" in November 1953, were made clear in an official note dated May 3.

> Colonel Bastiani, Chief of Staff, Ground Forces, North Vietnam stated that it involves the lives of 8,000 men and the honor of the Expeditionary Corps, Far East.
>
> The real problem that has not been faced is the sortie from the basin of Dien Bien Phu. This sortie can be conceived either in force, or by the infiltration of small groups.
>
> However, considering the exhaustion of the garrison, the nature of the terrain, the disposition and forces available to the enemy, he believes that this sortie, in any case, will be transformed into a ghastly flight, into a rout, and that only a few individuals will escape.
>
> Up to now, the defenders of Dien Bien Phu have covered themselves with glory, they have earned the admiration of the Free World. We do not have the right to tarnish that glory.
>
> Accordingly, he declares himself resolutely opposed to the execution of such a project.

Bastiani was not alone in opposing Operation "Albatross." But, Bastiani's opposition notwithstanding, Operation "Albatross" appeared to be the garrison's last hope.

Major Grauwin's hospital had now become an earthly replica of Dante's Inferno. Artillery fire directed at the hospital dugouts and bunkers often made it impossible to clear the fetid shelters of human waste. Paras, Legionnaires, Algerians, Moroccans, Senegalese, Vietnamese, and Vietminh wounded shared the cramped quarters, their legs overlapping. Some lay on litters outside, under the rain, waiting for death to clear a space. The calf-high, sticky mud of the hospital floor impeded the movement of medics and doctors. The pits dug outside for the amputated limbs and bits of flesh removed by the surgeons filled quickly. The putrifying jumble of dismembered arms, legs, and feet under a snowy mantle of quicklime resembled the work of some mad, surrealist sculpture. Since the start of the monsoon rains had increased the prevailing dampness, Grauwin and his staff had been fighting an epidemic of gangrene. He would later record a new phenomenon. Unwounded men involved in manhandling supplies and ammunition to the strongpoints were collapsing and dying with no symptoms other than exhaustion—a situation that made the phrase "dead tired" a macabre reality. At one point Grauwin, describing the state of his wounded and the impossible conditions of his overcrowded hospital, pleaded with Bigeard to stop "this massacre." Bigeard, however, told Grauwin to get on with his work while he and his men continued with theirs, adding that they all might still "get out of this."

The surviving American quad-.50 mounts were still doing their deadly work, the deep rhythm of their firing a reassuring symbol of Dien Bien Phu's continued resistance. Their heavy firepower had often been the deciding factor in breaking enemy assaults and providing cover to hard-pressed French units. Each mount was surrounded by a veritable dune of spent .50-caliber casings. Some of the French fighting men were now wearing American-supplied flak jackets that had been parachuted to the garrison. Heavy and awkward, the jackets provided more psychological assurance than physical protection. One can only guess how many had been supplied to the Vietminh thanks to misdropped cargoes.

Captain de Bazin de Bezon, the commander of the First Colonial Parachute Battalion, jumped into Dien Bien Phu with his headquarters group and a reduced company on May 5. Champing at the bit after being delayed in Hanoi by the weather and upset that his battalion was being fed into the battle in droplets, he was in a dark mood. Bigeard described de Bazin's arrival at Langlais's CP in his book *Pour une parcelle de gloire.*

> He [de Bazin] said to us, "What the hell did they send us to do here? All is lost and my men are tired." I responded—"Shut up!" Langlais jumped up and bawled him out—"We aren't asking for your opinion, but for you to get clobbered with the rest of us." That same morning [de] Bazin had his thigh smashed by a shell. It's better to be an optimist!

On May 5, de Bazin's men took over the shattered, corpse-strewn defenses of "Eliane" 2 from the weary Legionnaires of the First Battalion of the Thirteenth demi-Brigade. The paras thus inherited a particularly worrisome problem. For many days the Vietminh had been digging a shaft under "Eliane" 2. The work had been too consistent to be anything other than the work of sappers intent on placing a mine under the position. The Legionnaires, who had listened to the daily thuds and scrapings, had been well aware that a sudden silence could mean that the mine was about to blow. They had not been sorry to turn over the premises to their successors. Now the paras became uneasy listeners while trying in vain to find the sap's entry.

The details of Operation "Albatross" were being discussed in de Castries's CP. The brigadier general had decided to remain at Dien Bien Phu with the wounded. Langlais, Bigeard, and the other combat commanders were to break through the Vietminh lines and head for Laos, with the paras leading the way. Fifty kilometers to the southeast, the "Crèvecoeur Column" was still in its static position. It was a nerve-racking wait. The screening commando groups were reporting increased enemy contact and rumors of large-scale Vietminh troop movements in their direction. To confuse enemy radio eavesdroppers, the operation had been rebaptized Operation "Ariège." Operation "Condor" had passed into history.

While de Castries's staff was preparing for the breakout attempt, Cogny received a four-page top secret report from Lieutenant Colonel Levain, his chief intelligence officer. The report predicted the enemy's reaction to a breakout attempt and analyzed his probable countermeasures.

Levain pointed out that the destruction of cannons, mortars, and tanks prior to a breakout attempt would alert the heavy concentration of Vietminh forces ringing Dien Bien Phu. He stated that such a demolition would also leave the garrison without the means to defend itself if the breakout failed. In that case, the Vietminh would profit from a superiority in firepower, in addition to knowledge of terrain, physical condition, and morale. Levain cautioned that if the withdrawal was not well controlled once the men passed through the barbed wire, it could quickly turn into a rout. In that case, he predicted, the Vietminh would soon make propaganda capital of it, using captured, disgruntled troops to dramatize the event. If, Levain warned, some high-ranking officers happened to be among the escapees, the Vietminh would claim that the officers had abandoned their men and would "be believed by their side as well as ours." He also emphasized that the French press would be informed in detail of what had taken place and would "tell the story without particular goodwill." The lieutenant colonel recalled the heroism shown by the garrison "up to now" and concluded, "It would be heartbreaking to see so much military glory tarnished by such a sad end." But Levain's frank analysis had come too late. Major General Cogny had already reconfirmed that de Castries would have to make the final decision on Operation "Albatross." The same message to Dien Bien Phu then clouded the issue by mentioning that the value of "prolonged resistance on the spot" remained de Castries's "glorious mission."

General Giap wrote:

> Certain indications led us to believe the enemy wanted to break out of
> the encirclement and open a retreat route at any price. . . . We fol-
> lowed the projects and preparations of the enemy closely and
> assigned the units occupying our lines to the west the task of tightly
> controlling all the routes and trails linking Dien Bien Phu with the
> Laos-Vietnam frontier.

By May 6 the approximately 3,000 men still fighting were sleep-
walking their way through combat. They were numb from exhaustion and lack of proper food. They had developed what American
veterans of the Pacific campaigns in World War II had called "the
500-yard stare," a bloodshot, vacant look, focused on the enemy
lines. At Dien Bien Phu the same stare had been reduced to thirty or
fifty feet. They washed down Maxiton "uppers" with smelly water
from the polluted river and fought against sleep with heavy, aching
heads. Despite their poor physical condition and continued hard-
ships, they were fighting with a doggedness born of desperation.
They were not speaking of a "glorious mission" but had formed their
own band of brothers, a tight-knit group that fought as a team and
seemed to have rejected the heavy odds against it. At dawn they had
watched silently as ninety-one men from the First Colonial
Parachute Battalion drifted earthward over their positions. These
paras would be the last reinforcements to reach Dien Bien Phu.

May 6 would also see the death of a legend. James B. "Earthquake
McGoon" McGovern was one of the CAT pilots flying supply drops
over Dien Bien Phu in his C-119. This huge, bearded man was
known throughout the Far East for his flying exploits, his prowess at
eating and drinking, and his first-name acquaintance with comely
bar hostesses from Taiwan to Saigon. Prior to Dien Bien Phu, he
could often be found holding court at the check-clothed tables of a
Hong Kong restaurant, surrounded by CAT crewmen, CIA operatives, and assorted characters in a real-life *Terry and the Pirates* environment. Since flying the resupply missions under fire, he had railed
at the hesitancy and ineffectiveness of some French pilots in attacking Vietminh antiaircraft batteries. During a mission his candid,
unprintable comments burned through the ether. At one point, he
and his fellow pilots, reminding the French that they were on a civilian contract, refused to fly unless they could be guaranteed an effective fire-suppression effort.

The sky over Dien Bien Phu was clear and crowded with aircraft
the morning of May 6. Fighters, bombers, and transports were taking
advantage of the good weather to pound the Vietminh and deliver
their parachuted cargoes. McGovern was flying with a full load of

ammunition. As he entered his drop run, his C-119 shuddered from the impact of a thirty-seven-millimeter antiaircraft shell that knocked out one of its two engines. A second hit threw the heavy transport into a spin. The C-119 plummeted to earth behind Vietminh lines, its six tons of ammunition exploding in a gigantic black cloud. On May 7, a priority telegram from the U.S. Consulate in Hanoi informed the State Department that the French delegation general had just informed them that "A C–119 WAS SHOT DOWN YESTERDAY BY ACK ACK FIRE SOUTH OF DIEN BIEN PHU. ENTIRE CREW, COMPOSED OF TWO CAT AMERICAN PILOTS (NAMES UNKNOWN) AND TWO FRENCH CREW MEMBERS, REPORTED LOST." McGovern and Wallace Buford, his copilot, would be the only Americans to die at Dien Bien Phu.

11

No White Flags

". . . I don't think the free world ought to write off Indochina."
President Dwight D. Eisenhower

The sudden sound was high-pitched and nerve-shattering. The fast-approaching banshee wail was like nothing heard before. The shriek died when the explosions began. Within seconds the din became continual as one devastating salvo after another plowed into Dien Bien Phu's defenses. In the late afternoon of May 6, the Vietminh had unveiled their "Stalin Organs." These twelve-tubed "Katyusha" rocket launchers were the same impressive weapons that the Soviets had used so effectively against the Germans in World War II, the "death givers" that Wehrmacht veterans of the eastern front remember in their nightmares.

"My worst experience at Dien Bien Phu," Caporal Chef Blondeau recalls, "was the first salvo from the 'Stalin Organs.' It was like a passing train. The rockets landed on the CP." These explosive-laden missiles screamed through the air in a rushing blur, creating more casualties, pulverizing the sodden earthworks, exploding munitions stores, and disorienting the remaining defenders. Not to be outdone by the newly arrived rocket batteries, the Vietminh's conventional artillery joined in the massive barrage. The curtain had gone up on Giap's "Third Phase": the occupation of the last eastern strongpoint and newly established positions, a reduction of the enemy's perimeter and air space, heavy pressure on the central redoubt, a general attack on and the complete annihilation of the enemy.

Earlier that morning, the men in the garrison of Dien Bien Phu had realized that their time was running out. The artillery in the

159

main position was so short of ammunition that the seven remaining 105-millimeter howitzers had less than 1,000 rounds between them and these had to be allotted in small quantities. The strongpoint commanders had already been warned that there were no reinforcements available to repel new assaults and the men in the trenches were short of ammunition and grenades. It had appeared that things could not become worse. Now, trying to seek shelter from the sudden storm of steel, the defenders knew that they had been mistaken.

After two hours of bombardment, the Vietminh launched their assault. The *bo doï* came forward in massed groups to shouts of *"Tien liên!"* and *"Mau lên!"* from their officers and cadre. First they attacked the key position of "Eliane" 2. There Capt. Jean Pouget called in enough artillery to halt the assault and add 200 enemy dead to those already scattered around the strongpoint. Then it was the turn of "Claudine" 5. A counterattack by bearded Foreign Legion sappers momentarily stemmed the relentless enemy tide. The defenders of "Eliane" 2 reported an ominous cessation of digging under their position. The attack had now become general. A small group of Vietnamese survivors from the Fifth Bawouan were holding off a regiment of *bo doï* on "Eliane" 4, and the remnants of Bigeard's battalion were under heavy pressure on "Eliane" 10. Langlais and Bigeard were doing their best to meet new threats by shuffling their remaining manpower, but they were opposing an enemy "steamroller." Reduced companies and platoons were decimated trying to reach the hard-pressed strongpoints. Only one serviceable artillery piece remained in action on "Isabelle."

At 2300 the two tons of explosives buried under "Eliane" 2 were detonated. The mine shook the ground with a muffled tremor, and the earth opened to vomit its crust into the sky. With it went weapons, equipment, body parts, rocks, and hunks of dirt. An entire company from the First Colonial Parachute Battalion seemed to have disappeared in the explosion. Miraculously, five survivors, rallied by a sergeant, continued to resist, directing automatic-weapons fire on the advancing enemy. Expecting some promised reinforcements, Captain Pouget counterattacked with his remaining force to push the enemy back to the brink of the crater created by the mine. Just prior to dawn, with only thirty men left on "Eliane" 2, Pouget tried to make radio contact to find out what had happened to his reinforcements and to seek immediate permission to fall back on "Eliane" 3. He finally reached Legion Major Michel Vadot in de Castries's CP and learned that the reinforcements that he needed so desperately had been redirected to another position. Vadot denied Pouget's request to withdraw. "After all," Pouget was told, "as a para you must fight to the death . . . or at least until morning."

"Understood," Pouget replied. After informing Vadot that he was going to destroy his radio, Pouget received a radio message from a Vietminh operator who had been eavesdropping on his conversation. A nasal voice speaking in French suggested that he delay the destruction to hear a rendition of the "Chant des Partisans" offered on the part of "President Ho Chi Minh." Pouget fired into his set to end the unwanted concert. Later, after throwing his last grenade, he was knocked unconscious by a concussion blast and captured. Two sergeants firing a heavy machine gun from the hulk of an abandoned French tank on "Eliane" 2 were to fight on until their last belt was exhausted.

Similar dramas were occuring throughout the stricken fortress. A secret résumé of intelligence reports compiled by Cogny's headquarters tells part of the story.

DIEN BIEN PHU—Night of May 6–7

22.15 hours

- Violent bombardment calibers 105 and 75 [mm] and mortars on the entire position, particularly on Eliane, Artillery Zone and CP.
- Intense harassing fire on Isabelle (3 guns out of action).
- Vietminh are in contact on entire east face of D.B.P.

24.00 hours

- Munition about to be exhausted, 500 rounds of 120 [mm] remaining.
- Eliane 2 situation confused.
- Eliane 4 contacts on the position.
- Claudine 5 attacked.
- Junon attacked.
- Artillery—Dien Bien Phu: 7 pieces of 105 [mm] still in action.
               Isabelle: 1 piece   "   "   "   "   "   "

02:00 hours

- Munitions: difficult ammunition situation for 120mm mortars.
- Some elements still holding Eliane 2 and part of Eliane 10.
- Claudine 5 has had to be evacuated—a blocking force is holding the trenches near the barbed wire.
- Neutralization by artillery of Isabelle and Dien Bien Phu.
- Attempt to close gap underway on Eliane 10.

04:00 hours

- Unchanged
- Hand-to-hand fighting inside Eliane 2 and 10.
- Harassment of Dien Bien Phu and Isabelle.
- Indications of renewed V.M. attacks on East face of D.B.P.

06:00 hours

- Eliane 2 fell at 04:00 hours. Our last elements couldn't be supplied with ammunition.
- Preparing friendly counterattack on Eliane.

Resume of the situation at daybreak

- Eliane 2, Claudine 5 have fallen.
- Fighting continues on Eliane 10.
- The V.M. have been chased from Eliane 4 where they had established themselves.
- Counterattack underway to retake Eliane 2.

Both sides knew that the "Elianes" were the key to Dien Bien Phu. This understanding was not exclusive to staff officers or field commanders. It was shared by paras and Legionnaires, as well as the *bo doï*. The Vietminh troops had been thoroughly prepared for the final offensive by their political cadre and had gone into battle determined to win. The French troops, despite being short of men and ammunition and aware that they could not depend on outside help, were just as determined to fight on. This clash of wills, cultures, and ideologies was a deadly mix. The last forty-eight hours of combat were to be the most fierce at Dien Bien Phu. Gen. Tran Do's description of the night of May 6 reflects the bitter quality of the fighting.

> Every section of the communications trenches leading to the enemy positions were [*sic*] drenched with the blood of our fighters. In his agony the enemy offered his fiercest resistance, concentrating his fire at the junction of our communications trenches. He launched every Platoon, every group he could reorganize against our assault. But our men and officers at Dien Bien Phu were imbued with the determination of President Ho Chi Minh, of the Party, of the Government and of the General High Command.

Elements of two Vietminh regiments attacked "Eliane" 10 and 4. Captain Botella and the remnants of his Fifth Bawouan took the full force of the first assaults. As always, the Vietminh were seeking a soft spot in the French defenses, and they had chosen to attack their countrymen, the paras of the Vietnamese National Army, the "puppet troops" that they so despised. But Capt. Pham Van Phu and his company fought like no "puppets" that the enemy had ever encountered. Only when the mass of oncoming infantry threatened to overwhelm the outnumbered paras did Botella order them to give ground.

The whole landscape was now a gigantic, lethal son et lumière display. The intermittent, ghostly glow of parachute flares pushed back the darkness and then fizzed out. The night was rent by the flash of exploding grenades, bursting shells, the curving paths of tracer fire, and the abrupt vertical leap of their ricochets. The "Katyusha" rockets screamed in like packets of fiery meteors to blast craters in the mud and drop more defenders at their posts. The cacophony of sound was so intense that even those with undamaged eardrums thought that they were deaf. Troops fighting to hold the approaches to the Bailey bridge over the Nam Yum River could see that the river was filled with corpses. They floated in clumps, without much movement, like a blocked logjam.

Dawn on May 7 found the antagonists preparing for another round. But if the French defenders resembled a brave but badly battered boxer, the Vietminh generals were in the enviable position of managers able to send a fresh substitute into the ring. New Vietminh units, moved forward under cover of darkness, were now ready to continue the attacks.

Lieutenant Colonel Bigeard recorded his feelings of that morning with a certain awe.

> It's hallucinating! After 56 days of combat one doesn't sleep, one eats very little, we've lost weight, shelters have collapsed into the mud, the dead are everywhere . . . the wounded lie in the trenches begging to be carried to the aid station. The survivors live in a dream. Nevertheless, the night of May 6th–7th is fantastic. We're still holding, we're still hoping (evidently not everyone). We're staggering but we're avoiding the knockout blow.

The air force made a special effort on May 7, but the weather was bad, and the opponents were so closely engaged that it was hard to find a proper target. "Waves of planes coming from Hanoi and Upper Laos hurriedly dropped bombs and strafed," Gen. Tran Do recalled, "but our anti-aircraft was very active. Those planes flying with no coordination with the infantry below looked like yellow leaves at the mercy of a gust of wind."

The central CP was still in radio contact with the surviving out-posts. "Eliane" 4 had become a cachement area for paras from vari-ous battalions under Bréchignac's command. It was also packed with wounded who were being treated by a surgical team and the doctors and personnel from three battalion aid stations. By 0930 "Eliane" 4 was being overrun and "Eliane" 10 was under heavy attack. Bigeard would later write of receiving Bréchignac's last mes-sage.

"Bréche to Bruno: —they're arriving en masse. I'm destroying my radio sets. *Adieu*, Bruno." Then Botella was speaking. "Dédé to Bruno: This time, it's finished. *Adieu*, Bruno. Tell *le gars Pierre* [Langlais] I liked him a lot." —*"Au revoir*, Dédé." Bigeard wiped the tears from his cheeks. "No," he said to himself, "it's not possible." At about the same time the remaining members of Bigeard's battal-ion on "Eliane" 10 were being submerged by waves of shouting attackers.

At the GMI bunker near the hospital, cameraman Pierre Schoendoerffer noted that the Meo intelligence operatives who, up to now, had been fighting with cool detachment had silently slipped away into the jungle. As participants in the no-quarter "shadow war" of intelligence, they had no illusions about their chances of survival after capture by their blood enemies. Some of the remaining T'ai were also leaving their posts, donning the ragged trousers and jack-ets that they hoped would identify them as hapless tribesmen after they had left Dien Bien Phu. Some Moroccan riflemen were already signaling their readiness to surrender to the enemy. In readying the breakout force for Operation "Albatross," Langlais had withdrawn some Legionnaires from the eastern defenses. This fact had not gone unnoticed by the Moroccans and T'ai.

On the morning of May 7, Brigadier General de Castries was in direct radio contact with Major General Cogny. De Castries's trou-bled voice related the disastrous situation at Dien Bien Phu and went into considerable detail on troop shifts, unit strengths, and his intention to hold on "claw, tooth, and nail." Throughout the sorry litany Cogny responded to each item with a short, noncommittal *"Oui"* and a few expressions of agreement. When de Castries hesi-tantly broached the subject of Operation "Albatross" and explained his plans for its nighttime execution, Cogny gave his approval. The conversation closed with de Castries outlining his plan to remain with the wounded, those units not included in the breakout force, and the "Rats of the Nam Yum," the slackers whose ranks had swollen since the intensification of the fighting. Shortly thereafter, Cogny sent a telegram to Colonel Lalande on "Isabelle" reiterating that any decision to participate in Operation "Albatross" was to be taken on the colonel's initiative.

By noon the activation of Operation "Albatross" was under discussion in Langlais's CP. The plan now called for two columns, one of paras, the other of Legionnaires, to break through the enemy lines and head for Laos. But events were moving fast, and intelligence reports showed new Vietminh trenches appearing along the western perimeter. It was obvious that a column heading toward the southwest to link up with the Operation "Condor" column—the escape route suspected by the Vietminh—would stand less chance than one moving directly west into the jungle. With a questionable choice of words, Bigeard code-named the breakout attempt Operation "Bloodletting" and was speaking of the probability of 80 percent casualties. But the detailed planning turned out to be time wasted. By 1300 hours Operation "Albatross" had become inoperable. The commanders of the units chosen to participate had informed Bigeard that their men were too exhausted to undertake a fighting breakout, much less a jungle trek of any distance. At 1600 hours Dien Bien Phu acknowledged the fall of "Eliane" 3 and reported hand-to-hand fighting around "Eliane" 11 and 12 and "massive V.M. infiltration over the entire western front of the central position."

The wounded were arriving at the hospital covered by a sticky mantle of blood-streaked mud. The fly-covered dead had become so numerous that Major Grauwin had ordered the new corpses piled on the hospital roof, one on top of the other. Grauwin wrote:

> In the trenches that lead to the CP, throughout the central position, the wounded are crowded in a long, unending column, some sitting, some standing, and the line ends where the contact with the Viet begins. Some of them are dead, they are sinking into the mud. Those coming in from the strongpoints walk on them and they sink a bit more. No more litters, no tent canvas, nothing.

One group of wounded from "Eliane" 4 staggered into the crowded shelter more dead than alive with a message for Grauwin. Their Vietminh captors had sent them on ahead to tell the doctor that they would soon be arriving at the hospital.

The last radio contact with Hanoi took place shortly before 1700 hours on May 7. There are various versions of the actual conversation, but there is no doubt that Cogny insisted in his message to de Castries that Dien Bien Phu was not to capitulate. After a cease-fire at 1700 hours, de Castries was to allow the battle to flicker and die. Cogny emphasized the magnificent performance of the garrison and insisted that it not be spoiled by a formal surrender. Above all, Cogny insisted, *"There can be no hoisting of the white flag."* This stipulation was emphasized by repetition. General de Castries informed Cogny that he had ordered the destruction of all ammunition, weapons, and matériel. As he spoke, the CP was already reverberating to the blasting of demolition teams and the chain explosion of the remaining ammunition dumps. African gunners of the Colonial Artillery were heaving the heavy breechblocks of their guns into the Nam Yum River. Phosphorus grenades were burning out the barrels and breeches of the howitzers, and gun and mortar crews were smashing their sights. Individual troopers were destroying their small arms. It was time for Dien Bien Phu to say good-bye. According to most sources, de Castries signed off with a simple *"Au revoir,"* and Cogny responded with an equally uninspired "Well, then, *au revoir, mon vieux."* The May 7 intelligence roundup produced by the Citadel in Hanoi sums up the situation with the laconic notation "17:30 hours—no radio contact with Dien Bien Phu."

The main position was now occupied by a milling, uncertain mob. Sporadic bursts of fire and the thump of grenades could be heard in the distance, but the noise faded and died. Although some combatants remained in their trenches awaiting further developments or orders, others had ventured into the open. Encouraged by the sudden calm, they stood above ground for the first time in days to stare at the destruction around them and the thick columns of black smoke rising from the destroyed dumps. Blinking at the last rays of the setting sun, they reveled at the silence. Some helped the wounded; others scavenged for food. The "Rats of the Nam Yum" had emerged hesitantly from their holes and shelters along the riverbank, uncertain of the reaction of their former comrades-in-arms.

The first *bo doï* appeared, advancing cautiously in small, tight groups, arms at the ready. Then more broke cover, trotting forward in sections and companies toward the French dugouts. Suddenly the battered defenses were crawling with Vietminh troops who probed the trenches and shelters, shouting to the defenders to come out. Some grizzled French veterans were astounded by the youth and apparent nervousness of the advancing *bo doï.* Earlier, fearing that Bigeard would suffer some form of reprisal for past actions and the role that he had played at Dien Bien Phu, de Castries had urged him to escape on his own while there was still time. But Bigeard had made the decision to remain. By the time the Vietminh had begun to form their prisoners in columns, de Castries had prepared himself for the enemy's arrival. When Capt. Ta Quang Luat led his men into the damp-walled CP demanding the whereabouts of the general, de Castries was waiting. The tall cavalryman was wearing the red *calot* of his spahi regiment and a clean uniform. The decoration ribbons on his chest were a bright bar of color in the semidarkness. After a brief exchange relative to the cease-fire, de Castries and his staff were herded out of the CP. Major Grauwin caught a brief glimpse of his "frightfully pale" commander being led away.

Whether a white flag or flags ever flew over the French positions at Dien Bien Phu remains a subject of dispute. In his account of the battle, published in 1963, Gen. Tran Do mentions the appearance of white flags more than once. Describing the fall of the central position, he states, "Golden starred red [Vietminh] flags sprang up everywhere. The golden rays of the sinking sun intensified their hue while blurring the white of the defeated enemy's flags." The military writer Erwin Bergot, himself a veteran of Dien Bien Phu, recalls that a large, white cargo parachute draped over the limbless tree trunk near de Castries's CP may have been a source of the white-flag rumor. Bernard Fall's meticulous research makes the point that not one of the survivors that he interviewed mentioned a white flag and "not once did even Communist propaganda invent one." He also states that when the Vietminh restaged the fall of the fortress days later for the Soviet cameraman Roman Lazarevich Karmen, the Vietminh setting the stage for the filming omitted any show of white flags.

Some battle-weary individuals or the noncombatants clustered along the Nam Yum River may have signaled their readiness to surrender, but my own interviews with Dien Bien Phu veterans produced no affirmation of the presence of white flags on May 7. Bigeard later wrote of his reaction to the "no white flags" order in a tone reflecting his dissatisfaction with Hanoi's handling of the battle. "[De] Castries pointed out that Hanoi had decided to stop the fighting at 1700 hours, to scuttle everything, but not to surrender; no white flags . . . delicate intention of our big bosses . . . one doesn't surrender but one fights no more . . . it's necessary to wait for the Viets, arms hanging at our side." In the end, the courage of Dien Bien Phu's defenders makes any argument over white flags a sterile exercise. One thing was certain. The flag now flying over de Castries's CP was red. It bore a gold star and the gold embroidered slogan "Determined to Fight and Win."

The wait in Langlais's CP was brief but anguished. The paras and their commanders doubted that their treatment by the victors would adhere to the rules laid down in the Geneva Convention. Since the beginning of the Indochina War, they had been the enemy's bête noire, foiling Vietminh plans, defeating enemy units in battle, and inflicting innumerable casualties. Now, in a valley filled with enemy dead, the paras were not optimistic about their fate. Word had been passed to destroy their red berets to avoid identification as paras. The cadaverous Langlais had burned his and replaced it with a floppy, broad-brimmed campaign hat. The gaunt, frowning Bigeard was reflecting on the loss of his proud battalion. He had retained his beret. He was determined to wear it in defiance of the Viet and as a symbol of respect for his men.

Pierre Schoendoerffer remembers waiting for the Vietminh in Langlais's CP. He recalls:

I felt rage and bitterness at being abandoned. I had the feeling of not being commanded, but I hadn't had time to think about it during the battle. Then there were shouts in Vietnamese just outside the CP. A para noncom said, "Here they are." Bigeard announced, "I'm not raising my hands!" None of us did. There were no white flags. I said to myself, Observe everything, don't miss a thing.

The para commanders joined a column of prisoners slogging their way through the mud and beyond the perimeter. Schoendoerffer relates:

We left the putrification of the battlefield, and suddenly we saw grass, trees, and inhaled a good odor. There was a clear sunset, and high in the sky the last "Dakota" was dropping a cargo of medicine. The Vietminh were tense and very young. Despite their heavy losses, there was no brutality. We climbed a hill, and, reaching the crest, we could see an entire valley filled with Vietminh troops ready to attack. They watched us intently as we passed.

Later, when the column paused, Schoendoerffer had his first personal encounter with the enemy. He recalls:

A Vietminh soldier approached me. He began to shout directly into my face in Vietnamese. His face was angry, and I expected trouble. Then he thrust out his arm. His hand held a half-finished cigarette. He nodded, indicating I should smoke. When I did, he laughed loudly, and all the others joined in.

Caporal Chef Claude Sibille, a survivor from Bréchignac's battalion, recalls leaving his dugout following the cease-fire clad in shorts, helmet, and bulletproof vest and carrying his carbine. "A Viet took my carbine and bulletproof vest. I thought I was going to be shot. We hadn't eaten much for eight days, no cigarettes, and we were out of rations. As we were herded away, I heard a bird singing. That was my best day at Dien Bien Phu."

After being flushed from his hospital, Major Grauwin had told Lt. Geneviève de Galard-Terraube to remain close to him in the column of prisoners. They crossed the Bailey bridge and struck out in the direction of the "Five Hills." He noted that *bo doï* were everywhere, as far as the eye could see, and that hundreds of bodies covered the fortifications of "Eliane" 2. Then a Vietnamese officer stopped the column, and Grauwin's despair was suddenly replaced by hope. He described the moment in his book.

> A voice, in French: "Are you Major Grauwin?"
> "Yes."
> "You must return to your hospital and continue to care for your wounded. It's an order from the High Command of our Army."

Colonel Lalande at "Isabelle" had been powerless to help Dien Bien Phu. His strongpoint had been neutralized by a constant artillery barrage. Unable to raise Dien Bien Phu on the radio and unable to obtain instructions from Hanoi through a circling C-47, he decided to attempt a breakout to the southwest. At 2100 hours on May 7, "Isabelle"'s garrison, a two-battalion mixed force of Legionnaires, Algerians, T'ai, tankers, and artillerymen, slipped through the barbed wire in a desperate bid to reach the distant mountains. The attempt was a disaster. The Vietminh were waiting, and what had begun as a planned withdrawal soon became chaos. In the confusion, Vietminh troops were mixed in with Lalande's columns. Firefights broke out to their front, flank, and rear. By midnight it was all over. Both Lalande and the tenacious Lieutenant Wieme, who had commanded his T'ai on the strongpoint bearing his name, were prisoners. Only about one hundred men were to escape and make their way through 200 kilometers of hostile jungle to safety in Laos. The battle for Dien Bien Phu had ended.

Approximately 8,000 Vietminh troops had died for their victory, and over 2,000 soldiers of the French Union forces had payed for the defeat with their lives. Of the 6,452 French Union troops wounded in the campaign, 1,500 were surviving in Major Grauwin's hospital and the battalion aid stations. The spartan Vietminh jungle medical installations, where orderlies were trying to perform a doctor's work, were filled with an estimated 15,000 wounded. None of these figures include the unrecorded deaths on both sides: the French escapees who died in the jungle; the small, isolated GCMA patrols that were ambushed; the PIM killed by artillery fire; the coolies bombed and strafed while working on Provincial Route 41; and the Vietminh political cadre and patrols killed by tribesmen loyal to the French. The tribal populations of the northwest paid a heavy price for living in the vicinity of Dien Bien Phu. Bombing, strafing, and artillery fire took their toll of civilians. Fate and international politics had forced many villages to take sides in the contest, and, for some, the choice was to mean destruction and death. On May 8, a coded message informed the commanders of the Operation "Ariège" ("Condor") relief column that Dien Bien Phu had fallen. Shortly thereafter, the column was ordered to fall back into Laos. It turned into a fighting withdrawal during which one of the Laotian battalions suffered heavy losses.

Halfway around the world on the same day, the diplomats were gathering at a conference table in Geneva to decide Indochina's future. At Dien Bien Phu, the Vietminh were sorting out their prisoners, dividing them into sections of fifty, and starting them on the long march to the jungle prison camps beyond the Black River and in Thanh-Hoa Province. The Vietminh had taken some 10,000 prisoners and were in a hurry to move them out of the reach of any French rescue attempt. Most of the prisoners were still trying to cope with the fact that the battle had ended, that they were still alive, and that they had survived the first hours of captivity. They had learned to exist on a day-to-day basis, and few were concentrating on the future. It was just as well. Ahead of them lay a jungle march of 500 miles and the "Camps of Green Hell." Some had already decided to escape at the first opportunity. Bigeard had stuffed a silk map of Tonkin into his boot, and Bréchignac was ready to join him in an escape attempt.

Ironically, May 8 also marked a high point of success for the GCMA (GMI) tribal commandos operating on their own under the command of the unorthodox Lt. Col. Roger Trinquier. With the main Vietminh effort concentrating on Dien Bien Phu and the problems of supply and reinforcement, thousands of French-led guerrilla fighters emerged from the jungle to liberate their abandoned villages from small enemy caretaker forces. To its astonishment, the French High Command received confirmation that Lao Cai, a key town on the Chinese border, had been taken by Meo and T'ai tribal commandos of the "Cardamom Force." Even more miraculous was the recapture of the T'ai capital of Lai Chau, north of Dien Bien Phu, abandoned by the French in December. Far to the northwest, a guerrilla force from the Meo and Man tribes was laying siege to Caobang, another border town and entry point for Chinese supplies. The advance guard of the "Cardamom Force" had been moving south from Lai Chau toward Dien Bien Phu when the fortress fell. Now all they could hope to do was retrieve stragglers and shadow the prisoner-of-war columns in the hope of recovering any escapees.

The successes of these jungle-wise guerrillas proved that Colonel Trinquier and many other commando and para officers had been right in pushing for a more widespread use of nonconventional forces in Indochina. Instead, the French High Command, blinded by military conservatism and locked into its traditions, had seen fit to use tribal troops in a set-piece battle—and then complain when they did not behave like experienced line regulars. Unfortunately, any lesson that could have been learned from the successful tribal offensive in the mountains was no longer applicable. With the cease-fire, some commandos succeeded in making their way to Laos, but many more died, hunted down by Vietminh regulars. Months after the signing of the Geneva Accords, isolated bands of guerrillas under French officers and noncoms were still surviving and fighting in the jungle. The last recorded radio message, a plea for parachuted munition, was picked up *two years* after the fall of Dien Bien Phu.

As the columns of prisoners moved through the jungle toward the camps, it was soon apparent that the poor physical condition of the garrison at the beginning of the trek would have grave consequences. The daily ration of 800 grams of rice, supplemented by the rare peanuts or an occasional banana, provided a minimum of nourishment, and the prisoner's energy and body fat were quickly burned up by the effort of the march. The survivors shed what little weight they had maintained during the siege. With it went the ability to fight infection and disease. Malaria, dysentery, beriberi, and open sores that failed to heal were commonplace. The period of time that a prisoner could help carry a bamboo litter bearing a sick comrade became shorter and shorter.

The Vietminh *can bo*, or political officers, had separated officers and noncoms, noncoms and men. They had also formed sections of the columns according to ethnic divisions and political vulnerability. These exhausted, defeated prisoners were a propaganda windfall for the *can bo*, and the Vietminh psychological-warfare campaign was constant and intense. Few days ended without lectures and self-criticism sessions. The prisoners were repeatedly told that they were "war criminals" and could redeem themselves only by admitting the error of their ways and by seeking the clemency of "Oncle Ho." An insidious campaign to turn the prisoners one against the other was based on racial differences and talks on the evils of imperialism. The paras were watched closely. Their previous refusal to participate in the cinematic restaging of the battle had marked them as potential troublemakers.

Robert Mallet, a noncom from the Second BEP, penned a concise description of his experiences during the march along Provincial Route 41 in the direction of Tuan Giao.

With Coalan, Maioli, and two other noncoms of the Second BEP, we attempted to escape three times. The last time we were captured by villagers armed with coup-coups who were preparing to give us a very bad time. We were saved at the last moment by a shot fired in the air by a Viet regular whose detachment was passing not far away. We were then locked for thirty-six hours in a sort of bamboo cage, fed and watered like animals, and handed over, tied up, to the guards from one of the last columns of prisoners from Dien Bien Phu. We resumed our march in company with our new companions. It was a distressing spectacle to see them wrapped in bandages, marching under the sun and the rain.

Mallet arrived at Camp No. 73 in Thanh-Hoa Province after a four-week march. The French, Germans, Vietnamese, and T'ai were separated from other nationalities. Mallet and his group were quartered in an abandoned pagoda. Suffering from a hernia, he was declared unfit for labor by a Legion medic who was acting as supervisor of the dispensary. Mallet's subsequent encounters with the camp's political officer border on the comic and reveal a certain political naiveté on the part of the Vietminh.

That heartless bastard could find nothing better to do, after handing me a bamboo swatter, than to assign me to exterminate the flies in my corner of the pagoda. The dead flies had to be presented to him each evening, perfectly aligned on the floor, in order that he could count and verify my daily cadence and my contribution to the edification of Socialist society.

The courses of political education were astoundingly naive, and the subjects chosen raised protests from those attending. Coalan and Van Enoo were the most virulent [protesters]. Spotted by the political officers, they were to be among the last prisoners liberated. Old [French] Communist newspapers were our source of political information. We particularly appreciated l'Humanité for the quality of its paper, with which we rolled cigarettes from the butts we'd found. As to reading, I don't recall having read one line of that rag that celebrated the victory of our enemies.

There were frequent political assemblies, including the local villagers, organized to celebrate "something or the glory of someone." The prisoners were ordered to join in the festivities by singing in national groups. The contribution of Mallet's group was a "failure" since they bellowed scatological French army "guardhouse" songs, angering the presiding political officer.

Caporal Chef Robert Blondeau remembers the day in his camp when all prisoners were assembled to view a Soviet propaganda film, titled *Meeting on the Elbe*, that re-created the linkup of U.S.-Soviet forces in 1945. "An American officer was depicted walking toward the Soviets with a whiskey bottle protruding from his pocket," Blondeau recalls. "Then, pointing to the binoculars hanging on a Soviet officer's chest, the American asked, 'What are those?' Our laughter made the V.M. political cadre very angry."

But the daily ordeals of the camp were no laughing matter. Mallet describes a "trial" of his companion Maier and a group of Hungarians, Poles, Czechs, and Swiss Legionnaires for allegedly killing and eating a dog. Attached to poles in the center of the camp, the Legionnaires were subjected to public accusation and a long harangue from the dog's owner, followed by a speech from the political officer on the vices of colonialism. Mallet expected the worst. But, he explains, "It was only a cruel game, as they were granted clemency by Oncle Ho." All around him, prisoners were dying of malaria and dysentery. Those admitted to the makeshift infirmary died a few days later from lack of medicine. "I believe," Mallet noted, "that about 50 percent of our group died from illness in a period of three months."

Bigeard, Bréchignac, and two other officers attempted an escape but were recaptured by regionals, beaten, and brought before a "People's Tribunal." As the ringleader, Bigeard was condemned to death, but the sentence was never carried out. Schoendoerffer and Péraud decided to try their luck while being transported to the camp in a truck convoy. They had carefully noted that their "Molotova" truck was in darkness for several seconds when it rounded a curve and was beyond the reach of the following vehicle's headlights. After much straining and wriggling, Péraud fished a penknife from Schoendoerffer's pocket. They cut their bonds, waited for the brief darkness, leaped to the ground, and sprinted for the jungle. They then became separated. Schoendoerffer hid in a swampy depression among some fallen tree branches. He could hear the shouts of the pursuing guards and see the flash of their lights. When a *bo doï* approached, he ducked underwater. The guard stepped on his submerged head. His reflex action in resisting the sudden pressure gave him away. Beaten and threatened with death, he was thrown back on the truck. Péraud, who had survived a Nazi death camp during World War II, was never seen or heard of again.

If some prisoners resisted the enemy's propaganda and risked execution through their defiance, others went with the tide. It was primarily a question of survival. A subtle but effective system of punishments and rewards was in operation. Those who cooperated received slight additions to their daily rice ration or an added bit of buffalo meat or a dried piece of pork. Those who did not had their rations cut. Many of the defeated and depressed troops, sick and far from home, felt that they had been abandoned by their army and nation. They provided a fertile ground for the seeds of doubt, dissension, and division planted by the busy *can bo*. Group punishment, whereby many men would suffer from the nonconformity of one of their number, was a favorite tool of the political cadre. The refusal of an "unrepentant colonialist" to toe the line could mean a seriously ill comrade might go without medicine.

Nor was the psychological conditioning of the prisoners limited to their part in the Indochina conflict. North African and African troops were asked simple questions about why they had come to fight in Vietnam when their own lands were still under colonial rule. Long-captured French Union troops, trained by the Vietminh and the Chinese in Communist propaganda techniques, were seeded among the prisoners to live with them as trustees and informers. These turncoats, talking in the captives' own language, supplemented the *can bo*'s arguments and advised their countrymen of the liberation struggle at home. The smoldering Algerian revolt against French rule would burst into flame on November 1, 1954. This bloody conflict would find some French and Algerian survivors of Dien Bien Phu fighting on opposite sides in another war that would signal the final collapse of the French Empire and divide the French nation. With variations, the same techniques were used on Legionnaires from East Germany and Eastern Europe with mixed results. The "progressives" among them were promised transport by Soviet aircraft to their homelands.

Although all prisoners, including the French, were submitted to the Vietminh's brainwashing techniques and suffered extensively in the camps, surprisingly few cases of gratuitous brutality were recorded. Most beatings and ill treatment were the result of escape attempts or unwillingness to bend to the Vietminh's iron discipline. Some old scores were doubtless settled among intelligence operatives and special units, but the files that contain such reports are not yet accessible. Some survivors admit that their captors sometimes did not have much more to eat than the prisoners. But the Vietminh were hardened by long experience in the jungle and short rations. They had also been conditioned by their own propaganda. Their prisoners were the hated "mercenaries and colonialists" that they had heard so much about. The Vietminh did not have the Bushido creed of the Japanese that classed prisoners as disgraced warriors better dead than alive. But the rules of the Geneva Convention on prisoners were unknown to the average *bo doï*, and the survival of his captives was not a major preoccupation.

The most severe treatment was reserved for the Vietnamese "pup-pet" troops captured fighting in the ranks of the colonial and Foreign Legion paras or as members of the Fifth Bawouan. Officially scheduled for intensive "reeducation" by their captors, lit-tle is known of their fate. Some Vietnamese escapees did make their way to safety. A few remained in the French army, while others joined the ranks of the Vietnamese National Army when the French withdrew from Vietnam.

Tortuous negotiations and Vietminh propaganda ploys delayed the evacuation of the French wounded from Dien Bien Phu. A major sticking point was the question of including Vietnamese National Army wounded in the evacuation operation. The Vietminh consid-ered them as "puppet traitors" to be dealt with separately. The ques-tion was under discussion at the conference table in Geneva. On May 18, the French foreign minister, Georges Bidault, stated that such an arrangement violated the principle of nondiscrimination and offered air evacuation for equal numbers of Vietminh wounded to any point designated by the Vietminh command. A secret telegram to Washington from the U.S. delegation at Geneva under-lines the subtle language of propaganda in the Vietminh delegation's reply to Bidault's statement.

DRV [DEMOCRACTIC REPUBLIC OF VIETNAM] DELEGATE REITERATED ACCEP-TANCE PRINCIPLE NON–DISCRIMINATION BUT STATED NUMBER VIETNAMESE WOUNDED VERY LOW BECAUSE "FRENCH COMMAND CONCENTRATED AT DIEN BIEN PHU BEST TROOPS OF [FRENCH] EXPEDITIONARY CORPS," ADDING THAT ORIGINAL GARRISON HAD CONSISTED OF ONLY ONE–EIGHTH VIETNAMESE AND MANY OF THESE SURRENDERED WHOLESALE ABANDONING FRENCH DURING FIGHT.

After more negotiations, which also included the French Red Cross and the French High Command in Vietnam, the Vietminh agreed to allow the Vietnamese wounded to join the evacuation process. One of the prices that the French paid for this concession was a promise not to attack Provincial Route 41 from Dien Bien Phu until the evacuation was completed. With this stumbling block removed, the last seriously wounded were to leave Dien Bien Phu in early June 1954.

This period of grace allowed the Vietminh to speed the redeploy-ment of their divisions toward the delta. A secret "Weekly Situation Report" from the army attaché at the American Embassy in Saigon covering the period May 23 through May 29 led with the comment that the Vietminh 304th, 308th, 312th, 316th, and 351st Divisions were "ADVANCING MUCH MORE RAPIDLY THAN THE FRENCH HAD ANTICIPAT-

ED IN THEIR MOVE TOWARD THE DELTA" and went on to say, "THE FRENCH NOW ESTIMATE THAT THESE DIVISIONS CAN BE READY TO ATTACK THE DELTA BY 15–20 JUNE."

Although the numbers game is ethereal and difficult to apply when speaking of individuals, it is estimated that of approximately 11,000 French Union troops—both ablebodied and wounded—captured at Dien Bien Phu, approximately 3,300 were to be returned in September 1954 under the terms of the Geneva Accords.

As the delegations at the Geneva Conference split more hairs, traded concessions, and moved toward an agreement in July that would impose a cease-fire, "temporarily" divide Vietnam at the seventeenth parallel, withdraw French forces from the north and Vietminh forces from the south, and schedule elections in two years' time, the U.S. was moving toward full involvement in Indochina.

At a press conference four days after the fall of Dien Bien Phu, President Eisenhower had been asked whether Indochina should be allowed to join the Southeast Asian Defense Alliance proposed by Secretary of State Dulles and whether it was "still indispensable to the defense of Southeast Asia." The president had responded in the foggy phraseology for which he was famous.

> Well, of course, . . . I talked about the cork and bottle—well, it is very important, and the great idea of setting up an organism is so as to defeat the domino result. When each, standing alone, one falls, it has the effect on the next, and finally the whole row is down. You are trying, through a unifying influence, to build that row of dominoes so they can stand the fall of one, if necessary. Now, as far as I'm concerned, I don't think the free world ought to write off Indochina. I think we ought to all look at this thing with some optimism and some determination. I repeat that long faces and defeatism doesn't—don't win battles.

With a bit of study, the meaning was clear enough. Eisenhower had identified Indochina as a tottering domino whose fall to the Communists would threaten the other nations of Southeast Asia, and had indicated that the U.S. was not prepared to "write it off."

On May 14, Secretary of State John Foster Dulles sent a secret NIACT telegram to the U.S. delegation in Geneva. Excerpts from the message indicate Dulles's willingness to take on a "kingmaker" role in Vietnam.

DETERIORATING POLITICAL AND MILITARY SITUATION VIETNAM REFLECTED IN SUCH TELEGRAMS AS SAIGON'S 2372 INDICATES NEED FOR URGENT CONSIDERATION OF POSSIBLE COUNTER MEASURES. APPEARS FROM HERE THAT

FIRST STEP THIS CONNECTION IS TO URGE [EMPEROR] BAO DAI TO RETURN AT
ONCE TO VIETNAM. IF BAO DAI PROVES UNRESPONSIVE TO [AMBASSADOR]
HEATH'S APPROACH YOU SHOULD DISCUSS WITH BIDAULT RE POSSIBLE FUR-
THER STEPS TO BE TAKEN. . . . IF BAO DAI DOES NOT RESPOND AFFIRMATIVE-
LY TO FIRST SUGGESTION, MIGHT BE PUT UP TO BAO DAI THAT UNLESS HE IS
WILLING ACCEPT OUR RECOMMENDATION, FRENCH AND U.S. POLICY WITH
REGARD TO HIM AND HIS REGIME WILL HAVE TO BE REEXAMINED.

Six days later, a secret National Intelligence Estimate by the CIA
on "The Probable Military and Political Developments in Indochina
over the Next 30 Days" warned, "Political stability in Vietnam will
probably deteriorate during this period. In the absence of Bao Dai
. . . factionalism has become extreme, and the Vietnamese central
government is virtually paralyzed. It is possible that the Vietnam
central government will disintegrate during the next 30 days." On
June 26, Ngo Dinh Diem arrived in Saigon to take up his duties as
prime minister. Under increased pressure from the Americans, Bao
Dai had reluctantly appointed the chubby Catholic to bring order
out of chaos in South Vietnam. The CIA's Col. Edward Lansdale
and his team were waiting to help him in this task. With Diem, the
United States finally had its own man in Saigon.

The nights at Dien Bien Phu had become quiet once more. The
dan cong and coolies who had worked all day clearing the debris of
war, burying the approximately 10,000 French and Vietminh dead,
and repairing bridges and roads gathered by flickering cooking fires
under the stars. Most of the nylon parachutes had been salvaged, but
a few still gleamed in the darkness like shrouds. The T'ai tribesmen
who had fled for the mountains had begun to drift back, astounded
by the pitted, treeless landscape that had been their valley and mar-
veling at the fact that any human beings could have survived such
destruction. The twisted barbed wire glistened in the moonlight. The
sagging strongpoints and battered trenches were empty and silent,
but they still smelled of death.

EPILOGUE

Following the Indochina War, as I pursued a diplomatic career with various overseas assignments, I continued to encounter echoes of Dien Bien Phu. In 1961 I learned of Brigadier General Gilles's death from a heart attack not long after his son had been killed in action in Algeria. I encountered a former officer of the Fifth Bawouan in a Marseille waterfront restaurant as he prepared to depart for Algiers and a new assignment. A few years later I had lunch in a Paris bistro with former Lieutenant Colonel Fourcade, who had retired as a general. At about the same time I caught a fleeting glimpse of a stooped, civilian-suited Major General Cogny in the Paris Métro. When I was assigned to Vietnam again in 1964, I met an ARVN officer who had served as a noncom in the colonial paras and a Corsican pilot who had flown supply flights to Dien Bien Phu and had since engaged in a more shadowy type of delivery.

In 1974, while serving as U.S. consul general in Marseille, I attended a reception for General Marcel Bigeard, then state secretary in the Ministry of Defense, later to become a member of the National Assembly. I was not sure that he would recognize me, but I was looking forward to meeting him again. As he prepared to address the gathering of government officials, high-ranking military officers and members of the consular corps, Bigeard spotted me in the crowd. "As soon as I finish my brief talk," he announced, "I am going to greet a consul among you who was with us when we were gritting our teeth at Dien Bien Phu." Although the general was exaggerating the risks that I had taken in that far-off valley, his words, under the circumstances, were the equivalent of a decoration.

In 1991, when I returned to Vietnam as a journalist, I observed some of the shooting of Pierre Schoendoerffer's film *Dien Bien Phu*, in which Donald Pleasance plays a cigar-puffing "Howard Simpson." I watched the French tricolor hoisted again over the rococo Hanoi Opera House for the purposes of the film and spoke with some of the active-duty French parachutists temporarily detached from their units to reenact the jump scenes for the cameras. In Ho Chi Minh City, I sat in an air-conditioned reception room of Reunification Hall, the former Freedom Palace, while a relaxed General Giap answered my questions and explained a victor's view of the battle. That meeting, those with other participants, and my own experiences convinced me that the lessons of Dien Bien

179

Phu—do not underestimate a guerrilla foe; beware an overdependence on air power; expect guerrilla forces to be flexible and adapt-
able; consider the debilitating factors of a hostile environment; avoid
the pitfalls of a latter-day colonial attitude; and ensure that any overseas military involvement will have government and public support—are as important today as they were in the past.

In early February 1993, President François Mitterrand paid an
official visit to Vietnam, the first by a French leader since France's
departure from Indochina. Pierre Schoendoerffer, whose film had
been released in France during 1992, was invited to accompany the
presidential entourage. He joined Mitterrand when the president visited the battlefield of Dien Bien Phu to pay homage to his nation's
dead. The two men stood together at sunset at "Dominique" 2 while
Schoendoerffer pointed out features of the now-peaceful terrain that
had once been furrowed by shellfire.

Daniel Camus, Robert Blondeau, and five other Dien Bien Phu
veterans returned to Vietnam during the same period. With the
cooperation of Vietnamese officials, they visited Dien Bien Phu,
Hoa-Binh, Caobang, and Lang Son. They traveled the route that they
had marched as prisoners and found that the jungle had reclaimed
the infamous camps that had all but disappeared. In February 1993,
General Bigeard stated that, for him, such visits were premature.
But he also plans a return to Dien Bien Phu. When he dies, he
intends to be cremated and have his ashes dropped over the valley,
thus rejoining his comrades-in-arms.

On May 7 each year, at 1815 hours, a group of veterans gathers
on the dusty paving stones in front of the church of Saint-Louis des
Invalides in Paris for a religious service dedicated to the dead and
missing of the French Expeditionary Corps in Indochina from 1945
to 1954. Most of the gray-haired veterans are survivors of Dien Bien
Phu. They wear their medals on civilian suits and red para berets or
colored *calots* indicating their old regiments. Some carry the flags of
their units, and there are many family groups and unaccompanied
widows.

The white marble interior of the church glistens with shafts of
bright evening sun that reflects from the gold of the altar. Large tricolor flags are draped behind the altar, and the mass is celebrated to
music from a booming organ and the singing of an excellent choir.
The sermon, delivered by a chaplain, himself a veteran, concentrates
on what the men endured, those who died or were wounded in
action, and the many who died in captivity. He takes pains to point
out that all cannot be blamed on the Viet and mentions that those

involved at the time had felt deserted by both Paris *and* Hanoi head-quarters.

To most of the younger civilian and military officials attending the service, Dien Bien Phu is a distant symbol, a glorious defeat, and a ceremony that appears annually on their appointment calendars. To the veterans, it is a brief moment for memories of hardship and death, comradeship and the rough battlefield humor that others will never understand. Following the mass and a brief military ceremony in the courtyard, those who fought at "Gabrielle," "Béatrice," "Anne-Marie," "Huguette," "Dominique," "Claudine," "Eliane," and "Isabelle" drift off to celebratory dinners. Depending on the advice of their doctors, or in spite of it, many glasses will be raised to the fallen and to the not-so-distant time when they stood alone at Dien Bien Phu.

Index